Essex Conversations

Essex Conversations

Visions for Lifespan Religious Education

COLLECTED BY

**The Essex Conversations
Coordinating Committee**

Skinner House Books
Boston

Printed in Canada.

Cover design by Suzanne Morgan
Cover illustration by Patricia Frevert

ISBN 1-55896-414-2

Library of Congress Cataloging-in-Publication Data

Essex conversations : visions for lifespan religious eduction / collected by the Essex Conversations Coordinating Committee.
    p. cm.
Includes bibliographic references.
ISBN 1-55896-414-2 (alk. paper)
    1. Unitarian Universalist churches—Education.   2. Religious education.   I. Unitarian Universalist Association. Essex Conversations Coordinating Committee.

BX9817.E77 2001
268'.891—dc21

                                                    00-048246

10 9 8 7 6 5 4
06 05 04

We gratefully acknowledge use of the following material:

Lanterns: A Memoir of Mentors by Marian Wright Edelman. Copyright © 1999 by Marian Wright Edelman. Reprinted by permission of Beacon Press, Boston.

Songs from the Center of the Well by Swami Chetananda (Rudra Press, 1985). Reprinted by permission.

The Ministry of the Child by Dennis Benson and Stan Stewart. Reprinted by permission of the authors.

"Separate Truths" reprinted by permission of Penny Hackett-Evans.

Ode to the Dodo by Christopher Logue. Reprinted by permission of the author and David Godwin Associates.

We also gratefully acknowledge Jean McKenney, who provided invaluable assistance to the Essex Conversations project since its inception. Jean is the assistant to the director in the Religious Education Department at the Unitarian Universalist Association.

Note: On page 2 and 130, references are made to the "merger" of the American Unitarian Association and the Universalist Church of America. Though the word *merger* is occasionally used, informally, in fact the two predecessor organizations were legally consolidated rather than merged.

Contents

Introduction

Twenty-five years ago, Unitarian Universalist religious educators and other leaders gathered at the Stonehouse Club in Rhode Island to answer the question: "What is our vision for lifespan liberal religious education?" Their reflections, published as *The Stonehouse Conversations*, were part of an Association-wide process to determine our needs for new religious education curricula and other resources. This process, which sought perspectives from a broad cross-section of the UU community, included the creation of the Religious Education Futures Committee and Religious Education Advisory Committee and the reorganization of the UUA Department of Religious Education. The *Stonehouse Conversations* served to inform and inspire discussions of religious education issues for many years.

As we enter the third millennium, we again face the challenges and opportunities of evaluating our religious education programs and developing new approaches and resources. The time is right to bring new visions as well as new tools to expand our understanding of religious education. The essays collected here contain vision, prophetic spirit, and theological reflection. They are value-based and contain seasoned wisdom. Some are speculative, idealistic, intuitive, and imaginative; others are practical. While they express diverse viewpoints, they all speak to how vital religious education is to our faith. All urge hopefulness in a new era.

You will find among the authors some of our most celebrated and influential leaders. Perhaps you will also discover someone new. The papers here are presented as they were prepared for Essex, without substantive editing, so that the voice and thoughts of each contributor remain clear. It is a rich banquet, a feast to devour.

I found a symmetry to the papers: relatedness, connection, interdependence, co-creation, cooperation, relationship, inclusivity, partnership, and interaction. It was exciting to find such common themes. This reaffirms for me how important and central a new and enlarged vision of religious education is to our movement. The visions that these papers have delineated present us with many possibilities that point to the end of the marginalization of religious education within our congregations.

For me, religious education activity is a mindful focus to the mystery of life, a promotion of relationship and empowerment. In bringing together two aspects of life—religion and education—religious education includes all the intellectual, moral, and spiritual understandings that nurture the practice of a religious way of life. It is central to all that we do in our religious communities. By examining its meaning and understanding its real value, we can provide a clear direction to our religious education programming.

Background

In the spring of 1998, a coordinating committee composed of Rev. Makanah E. Morriss, Rev. Patricia Hoertdoerfer, Rev. Dr. Susan Harlow, and Rev. Frances Manly began to organize a convocation of UU religious leaders to bring together the threads of the past and present in order to provide a vision for the future of Unitarian Universalist religious education. This planning group represented the UUA Religious Education Department, the Liberal Religious Educators Association (LREDA), and the Sophia Fahs Center at Meadville/Lombard Theological School. In the fall of 1998 I replaced Makanah Morriss on the Coordinating Committee. The group formulated the following mission statement for this new gathering of religious educators: "To imagine and articulate the core of Unitarian Universalist religious education by key leaders from various perspectives at the dawn of the twenty-first century."

Funding was received from the Panel on Theological Education; the Fund for Unitarian Universalism; the Unitarian Sunday School Society; LREDA; Meadville/Lombard Theological School; and the UUA departments of Religious Education and Congregational, District, and Extension Services. The coordinating committee selected religious leaders from different geographical areas of the continent, representing academia; large, midsize, and small societies; the UUA Religious Education Department; religious education field staff; ministers of religious education; directors of religious education; parish ministers; theological students; youth; and the Journey Toward Wholeness Committee. Scholarship, experience, and competence were the qualities we sought in the thirty-two participants who accepted our invitation. In addition, letters requesting input into the process were sent to twenty-two affiliated UU organizations.

The Process

Participants were invited to one of the two conversations; the first was held in April 1999 and the second in April 2000. Participants were asked to submit papers in response to three questions:

- As we enter the twenty-first century, what is the core of our evolving Unitarian Universalist faith?

- What is your vision of the goals for our lifespan religious education?

- What are the vital components for Unitarian Universalist curricula?

The papers were shared within each group and read before the gathering. Each group was self-contained, with the papers and conversations shared only within that group until both gatherings had been completed. At each meeting, participants were given twenty minutes to present the main ideas of their papers. This was followed by twenty minutes of small-group conversation, then fifteen minutes of large-group discussion. The focus of the papers included social, economic, and cultural issues; the congregational context; children and youth in the twenty-first century; adult religious education; the role of teachers, parents, and religious educators; and the underlying philosophy of liberal religious education. The presentations were audiotaped. Each gathering opened with a worship time in which participants shared symbols of their ministry in religious education, recognized our UU legacy, and honored our UU mentors. There were also opportunities to share pivotal moments and transformative events in the participants' religious education journeys. After the individual presentations, a final day was devoted to assimilating what we had learned into three areas:

- Ways to Sustain Reflection

- Ways to Continue the Conversation

- Ways to Create new Structures

Hopes and Expectations

The religious education of children, youth, and adults has been a concern of our liberal religious movement from its beginnings in America. Today we know that a unified view of religious education is essential to our Unitarian Universalist faith. We must energize religious education. We must imagine and articulate a religious education that supports our shared Unitarian Universalist values and reflects the diversity of our community. We sought during the Essex Conversations to articulate a renewed sense of educational purpose, a clear expression of liberal religious faith, and a revitalized commitment to Unitarian Universalist religious education.

All religious educators have a lifelong challenge of excellence in their work that demands reflection as well as action. As seekers who share the search for truth and meaning, our commitment demands that we look at religious education holistically and philosophically. Religious education requires from us preparation, study, discipline, and the strong intention to create positive results for ourselves, each other, and our world.

The coordinating committee hoped that the Essex Conversations would provide guidance to the UUA Department of Religious Education and would help Unitarian Universalists renew our collective sense of mission, revitalize our commitment, and clarify our vision for UU religious education. The Essex Conversations, and the many conversations they are inspiring, come at a good time for our Association as the Religious Education Department prepares to develop a new comprehensive lifespan curriculum for the twenty-first century. These conversations are just one way that we welcome broad participation in the curriculum-visioning process.

Our hope is also that the papers presented here will help your congregation articulate and clarify its vision for liberal religious education within your faith community. Each congregation determines what best fits its own needs in religious education. These papers can be guides for your search.

Ways to Use this Book

The *Essex Conversations* are a tool to help you and your congregation clarify your understanding of Unitarian Universalist religious education and set goals for your religious education programming. Each congregation has the freedom to design a religious education program that uniquely articulates the faith and mission of its members. You can use this book as part of a process that reflects the uniqueness of your religious community and enhances its vision as a learning community. A renewed sense of purpose and commitment to lifespan religious education for children, youth, and adults in your congregation can be realized.

Some suggestions for using this book to inspire your own conversations are:

- Create adult education opportunities in order to facilitate reflection on any or all of the essays or the issues they raise.

- Initiate focus groups to consider specific themes and their relationships to the participants in that group (for example, youth, young adults, parents, parish ministers, and so on).

- Read the book in preparation for your own experience of the Essex Conversations process, using the three key focus questions (page xv).

- Set up a series of discussions. Select a group of papers that seem particularly relevant to your congregation and discuss those papers in depth.

- Have smaller groups choose one paper to discuss and then share their conversations with a larger religious education visioning group.

- Deliver—or encourage others to deliver—a sermon on this topic from the pulpit.

- Use these papers to engage your entire congregation in a conversation about how religious education can be a centerpiece of congregational programming.

- Participate in a Renaissance Philosophy Module, created for professional religious educators, in which this book is used as the reader.

- Organize youth or young adult groups to discuss the Essex Conversations.

- Hold a visioning retreat for your religious education committee using material from the Essex Conversations.

- Include some part of the Essex papers or process in your teacher training.

- Have your congregational board meet for three hours to discuss the Essex Conversations and try to articulate a philosophy of religious education for your congregation.

- Make a discussion of the Essex Conversations the focus of LREDA chapter meetings, district or cluster religious education Committee meetings, and UUMA chapter meetings.

- Visit the UUA website at http://www.uua.org/re/essex for summaries of the papers and audio excerpts of the taped conversations.

The Essex Conversations have already inspired those who participated, but the true value of the process comes from the conversations that continue at the congregational level. Our hope is that you will use this book to help stimulate a conversation and a vision for religious education in your spiritual community.

REV. LENA BREEN
Director of Religious Education
Unitarian Universalist Association

As we enter the 21st century, what is the core of our evolving Unitarian Universalist faith?

What is our vision of the goals for lifespan religious education?

What are the vital components for Unitarian Universalist curricula?

Educating for Faith

Rev. Dr. Barry M. Andrews

Unitarian Universalists are not accustomed to using the word *faith*, perhaps because it smacks too much of credulity. On this score, we tend to side with Archie Bunker who once remarked, "Faith is believing what any damn fool knows ain't so." Our reluctance to use the term is part and parcel, I think, of our aversion to traditional religious language in general. Often we shy away from words such as *faith, God, prayer,* and *soul* because their meaning is different for us than for other religious groups and we fear being misunderstood. Another reason, I suppose, is that such terms lack intellectual currency in the rational, secular culture that Unitarian Universalism has traditionally inhabited and drawn from.

Nevertheless, I think it is important to consider the meaning and place of faith in the context of Unitarian Universalism, especially where religious education is concerned. For one thing, the situation is changing. Unitarian Universalism has always been a fluid faith (if I may use the term), more like a river than a rock, to cite the metaphors Diana Eck used in *Encountering God.* In spite of efforts to keep it within the confines of Christianity during the nineteenth century or of Humanism in the twentieth century, Unitarian Universalism has always remained open and responsive to the spiritual needs of those who have sought us out and chosen to stay.

It stands to reason, then, that Unitarian Universalism will continue to evolve. Indeed, I think we have seen important changes during the twenty years of my ministry to Unitarian Universalist congregations. A major development has been an increasing sense of ourselves as a religious denomination. In an address entitled "Unitarian Universalism in the Second Millennium," Carl Scovel indicates several characteristics of this growing denominationalism in our movement, including the fact that we now have a symbol, the flaming chalice; a credo; the seven Principles; a prayerbook; a hymnal; and a name, Unitarian Universalism. These, among other indicators Scovel points to, have all developed in the years since the merger of the Unitarians and the Universalists in 1961. I could name several more. However we feel about this development (which the early Unitarians would have decried as sectarianism), I think it is increasingly well established.

More recently, we have seen steady growth in our congregations. Families account for a significant percentage of the number of new members. Typically, parents say that they are looking for a religious education program that fosters religious identity and a sense of belonging, nurtures spirituality, provides an ethical framework, and helps them and their children answer the difficult questions of religion and life. As adults, they are seeking something for themselves as well; namely, to find a sense of meaning and purpose in life, to discover answers to life's fundamental questions, and to belong to a community for mutual support, sharing faith and pursuing common interests with others.

My own experience of Unitarian Universalist congregations is borne out in a survey conducted by Dr. Wade Clark Roof, author of *A Generation of Seekers: The Spiritual Journeys of the Baby Boom Generation*. Roof observes that after falling away from religion in their youth, increasing numbers of Americans are returning to the fold as adults. By far the most common reason given for their return is "for the sake of the children." Says Roof: "The presence of young, school-age children and feelings of parental responsibility for them drives [sic] boomers back to church to enroll their children in religious education classes." The research indicates that only 14 percent of single young adults have become reconnected with congregations, and the number only goes up to 16 percent for married couples without children. But 52 percent of the returnees are married couples with children. Clearly, having children is the single greatest factor in the influx of new adult members in our congregations.

It has often been remarked that many of the adults joining our congregations today—singles and empty-nesters, as well as parents—did not have a traditional religious upbringing. For large numbers of new members, "church" is a novel experience. Because they were not raised in a church, relatively few come to Unitarian Universalist congregations with the sense of religious rebelliousness that brought so many to our congregations in years past. Newcomers today are curious, open-minded, and intelligent. They are liberal in their theological outlook, eclectic in their spiritual tastes, and strongly committed to the principle of personal choice in religious matters.

Because so many were not raised in churches they tend to share the ambivalent feelings of the unchurched in our society toward religious institutions. Moreover, they tend to be less religiously "literate" than those who, a generation earlier, had gone to Sunday schools in large numbers, even if they had a strong negative reaction later on. Still, they are motivated by a strong, if inarticulate, desire to address a religious void in their lives. Most visitors I talk with say that they are looking for "a spiritual experience" and for a community that cares about them and shares their values. New Unitarian Universalists tend to be more comfortable with religious language and ritual than the "come-outers" of previous years. In fact, they find it puzzling and ironic that there is so little mention of God, prayer, soul, and the like in our worship services and Sunday schools.

It is somewhat paradoxical that people without a strong sense of religious identification and who are ambivalent about religious institutions nevertheless seem to want to know that they are joining not just a church, but a denomination. Moreover, they expect that we will use rather traditional religious language, symbols, and rituals, even if we understand them in a uniquely Unitarian Universalist way. (I would add that many long-time members of our congregations insist that they want this, too.) In short, I would say that many if not most Unitarian Universalists today want to believe that Unitarian Universalism is a bona fide faith, on a par with other faith traditions, and not just a philosophy of religion.

Faith is a term that gets used in a number of different ways. Some people equate faith with belief. Many Unitarian Universalists have faith in this respect. For example, Theodore Parker was wont to believe that the arc of the moral universe is long, but that it bends toward justice. Other people use the word to mean a religious tradition, as I did in the previous paragraph. They speak of the Christian or Jewish or Buddhist faith.

Wilfred Cantwell Smith, author of *Faith and Belief*, prefers to view faith as something apart from either belief or religion. Belief is the holding of certain ideas. One does not have faith in a concept, he insists; one has faith in the reality about which propositions are fashioned. Nor is faith religion. For Smith, religion represents a cumulative tradition, including scriptures, myths, symbols, ethical teachings, creeds, rituals, and so forth. Faith, as he understands it, is deeper and more personal than religion. While it may be engendered by a religious tradition, "it is a quality of the person and not the system. It is an orientation of the personality, to oneself, to one's neighbor, to the universe; a total response; a way of seeing whatever one sees and of handling whatever one handles; a capacity to live at more than a mundane level; to see, to feel, to act in terms of, a transcendent dimension."

I feel that an understanding of the meaning and importance of faith is essential to our work as religious educators and to the future of Unitarian Universalism. I agree with Smith that faith is more fundamental than belief or religion in the quest for meaning in life. My own understanding of faith, however, owes more to Emerson and James than it does to Smith.

Ralph Waldo Emerson made a distinction between Reason and the Understanding, meaning by these terms something different from what they signify for us today. For him Reason was an intuitive faculty; Understanding a rational, intellectual process. He described them in the following way in one of his letters: "Reason is the highest faculty of the soul, what we mean by the soul itself; it never reasons, never proves; it simply perceives, it is vision. The Understanding toils all the time, compares, contrives, adds, argues; near-sighted, dwelling in the present, the expedient, the customary." Theodore Parker, incidentally, made the same distinction; and for both Parker and Emerson it was the basis on which they distinguished religious consciousness from the forms of religion. Today we might say that this is the difference between religion and spirituality. Both of them felt that Unitarianism placed too much emphasis on religion, or the forms of religion, and not enough on spirituality.

William James, although he was by no means a Transcendentalist, draws a similar distinction between what he terms *percepts* and *concepts*. For him, ideas, thoughts, and intellection are synonymous with concepts, while percepts are likened to sensations, feelings, and intuition. For James, as for the Transcendentalists, these two mental functions are or should be complementary.

In James's view, we are presented with—immersed in—a world of immediate experience, which he describes as a stream of consciousness. This "perceptual flux" consists not only of sensations, emotions, and intuitions, but also of feelings of depth, awe, connection, mystery, and the like. It can never be superceded. Only here are the deeper aspects of reality to be found. We cannot lift ourselves out of it.

This world of pure experience is the source of knowledge. Our perceptions are vague, but they are full of significance. We struggle to make sense out of them. The process of conceptualization represents an effort to articulate the meaning and significance of our perceptions. From these perceptions we elaborate theories, structures, and philosophies and derive values, arts, and languages. Still, James insists upon the primacy of perceptual experience and maintains that conceptual knowledge is forever inadequate to the fullness of reality as immediately revealed.

Nevertheless, his final word is that percepts and concepts are complementary and require each other in the same way that we must have two legs in order to walk or that scissors need two blades to cut. As James puts it in *Some Problems of Philosophy,* "The two mental functions thus play into each other's hands. Perception prompts our thought, and thought in turn enriches our perception. The more we see, the more we think; while the more we think, the more we see on our immediate experiences, and the greater grows the detail and the more significant the articulateness of our perception." In this process our understanding of the perceptual world increases. As experienced relations are articulated and accumulated, this world becomes more coherent. Neither percepts nor concepts taken alone know reality in its completeness; both are a necessary part of the process.

Analogously, I would say that faith is comprised of both spirituality and religious identity, and that these are interdependent.

Spirituality, as I understand it, is largely personal and perceptual. It is made up of those values, beliefs, and religious experiences that relate to our own individual experience. It has to do with our own innermost thoughts and feelings about life and death and the nature of things—our own answers to the questions, Who am I? Why am I here? What is expected of me? What happens when I die?

Religious identity, on the other hand, is communal and conceptual. It represents those values, beliefs, and rituals that a group of people hold in common. It has to do with preserving values and offering encouragement and support to people in putting them into practice in their everyday lives. It is a community's attempt to answer the big questions. It is largely conveyed through concepts, stories, symbols, and rituals.

In my view, spirituality and religious identity are reciprocal. On the one hand, our spirituality needs to be shaped by a heritage of wisdom that is preserved in our religious community and conveyed to us by our elders and spiritual mentors. On the other hand, religious identity is shallow and ineffectual without a depth of personal feeling and individual commitment. A rich spiritual life is the nourishing ground of any religious tradition. It is through faith, the congruence of spirituality and religious identity, that religion comes to life and finds expression.

This understanding of faith may help us to assess the sufficiency of our current approach to religious education and guide us in the direction we need to go at this point in our history. I am not the first to note that the term *religious education* itself causes problems for us. It has been suggested, for example, that "religious growth and learning" might be a preferable phrase. It has also been said that our pedagogy should take account of different learning styles and teaching methods. Nevertheless, it has been difficult for us to "break out of the box" when it comes to religious education. We still tend to assume that religion is a subject of study; and so we learn *about* God, other religions, and our Unitarian Universalist history and heritage. Being very intellectual to begin with, it is easier for us to approach the task of religious education in a highly conceptual, cognitive way. Unfortunately, we end up teaching religion, not faith.

One of the manifestations of denominationalism in religious education has been the emphasis on religious identity and our statement of principles in the curricula that are currently available. This represents a welcome improvement over the previous generation of Unitarian Universalist religious education materials—the so-called multimedia kits—which made no mention of our religious history or heritage. Many of the new programs are well written, but there are several major deficiencies. One of these has to do with the fact that they were written by different people at different times for different reasons. Taken together they lack an overall scope and sequence. There is no continuity or progression from one level to another.

An equally serious problem is that the current generation of curricula cannot be said to develop faith as I have described it. There is more to faith than religious identity, no matter how strong. Moreover, learning *about* religion—one's own or that of others—is not the same as being religious. William Ellery Channing once observed that "the great end in religious instruction is not to stamp *our* minds on the young, but to stir up their own; . . . not to form an outward regularity, but to touch inward springs." In a similar vein, Emerson insisted that religion is neither belief nor ritual; it is life. "It is not something else *to be got*, to be *added*; but is a new life of those faculties you have."

Along with fostering religious identity, there needs to be an equal emphasis on nurturing spirituality in our church school programs. In addition to teaching our principles, we should seek to acquaint children, youth, and adults at first hand with the sources of our religious tradition, especially those direct experiences of transcending mystery and wonder that lead to a renewal of the spirit. This is not only in keeping with the nature of faith as I see it; it is also consistent with what parents, teachers, ministers, and religious educators have been asking for in recent years. There are many ways of nurturing spirituality in our programs, including worship; but spirituality must be fully integrated with religious identity in our curricula as well.

I believe it is time for us to give serious consideration to the need for a new generation of religious education curricula, suited to the needs of a new century. We cannot go into the future continuing to teach the lessons of the past. We cannot continue to cobble together the semblance of a curriculum out of existing materials. Our denomination (and I use the word advisedly) is in need of a core curriculum in Unitarian Universalist faith development. In light of my comments here, it should be developmental in two ways. First, it should aim to encourage faith development and character formation based on what we know about these matters from personal knowledge and the available literature. Second, it needs to be developmental in the sense that each piece of the curriculum builds from one level to the next.

It is unclear at this point what a core curriculum in Unitarian Universalist faith development might look like. Spirituality, like faith itself, is hard to define. But, as Emerson might say, the Understanding will always have difficulty comprehending the intuitions of Reason. Nevertheless, a spiritual life of richness and depth, developed from a young age, is the necessary foundation of our Unitarian Universalist faith. It is not enough to educate children, youth, and adults in our religious history and heritage. Even when we are successful in this, the identification is more conceptual than emotional. Rather, we must seek to develop faith for the reason that faith represents the integration of both spirituality and identity in the fullness of the religious life.

I would also expect a certain amount of resistance to the notion of introducing spirituality, including the use of religious language and spiritual practices, in our religious education programs. But I think our church schools are more progressive on this issue than our congregations as a whole. In my experience, parents and teachers are very receptive to the idea of a curriculum emphasizing spiritual growth, faith development, and character formation. I suspect, too, that there will be differences of opinion on what a core curriculum might consist of, although I do believe there is more agreement on the need for one now than there was twenty years ago.

In spite of these difficulties, and others I could name, it is crucial that we set our sights on producing such a curriculum. We are at a critical juncture in our history. If we are to continue to attract new families to our churches; to prevent children, youth, and adults from drifting away; and to increase our effectiveness as a denomination in the world and among our congregations, we will need to help individuals of all ages to grow in faith by more fully integrating their spiritual life with their sense of identity as Unitarian Universalists.

∾

Rev. Dr. Barry M. Andrews is the minister of religious education at the Unitarian Universalist Congregation at Shelter Rock in Manhasset, New York.

Outside the Box

REV. SUSAN DAVISON ARCHER

When the classroom wing of our church burned down in 1986, many things were lost. But in the post-fire days, of all that was shoveled out into the dumpster, what I felt as the greatest loss was our button collection. I remember one of the members unearthing the metal canister from a charred cabinet. In it the buttons remained, albeit covered with a thick coat of soot—the interestingly gnarled metal lumps, the beads, the carved wood, the big and little designs of every color and shape—buttons contributed over many years from many sources. I saw images of children and teachers coming to get the button can, for craft projects or just for play, to make designs or pictures, all the remnants to be recombined back into the box for another day. I saw images of adults coming to contribute their buttons, sometimes with stories of where they had come from.

When we found the button can, for a moment I had been hopeful. Maybe we could save them! In reality I was probably somewhat delusional after working for several days in the roofless building, already soaked from hoses, now redrenched from the heavens. There was no way to wash the thick soot from all those wondrous pieces.

I did have to wonder why I was so touched by the loss of those buttons. It had something to do with meaning across ages, across generations, continuity, and a never-ending collection because it was continuously replenished. How many hands had been laid on them, the wise hands of grandmothers mending clothing of long ago, and the small hands of little ones, some of whom are by now grown up? The buttons contributed to this collection were never bought, always brought; were never too many, but always enough. The meaning of these buttons for me had something to do with stability, solidity, memories, and hope. It was hard to let them go.

It was a few days later, Sunday morning, when we, the adults and children of the congregation, gathered in the sanctuary, smoke damaged, without electricity or heat, to mourn our loss. But more than mourning, we also celebrated what could not be taken from us. As we sang "May Nothing Evil Cross This Door," it was clear that the building was gone, but the religious community remained. We had something that could not be taken from us. We would sustain one another. Our collective faith could not be destroyed. We still had our roots. We would always be able to count on them.

So, as I write this paper I ask myself, what is it that we need to take with us into the next century? I think back to the buttons and to the religious community gathered after the fire. I think about the need for belonging, the need for a community of shared values and dreams, the need for sustaining relationships, for comrades with whom to join hands on behalf of a common good.

In the culture evolving out of the last decades of this millenium, these needs are very often not met, or they are met in such insufficient ways that there remains a deep longing for something to count on. Everyone is working. Work hours are longer than they have been for a long time. Children and parents are separated each day for more hours than many were in the past. Extended families living near one another are becoming more rare. Many places of work have felt less satisfying because there is no loyalty on the part of employer or employee. Life may be lived in segments, sometimes with people who seem more like interchangeable functionaries than partners in a worthy or constructive endeavor. I do not need to go on. I suspect these kinds of changes will be noted in one way or another by many of us. Much of what I found valuable as represented in the button can seems to be slipping away.

Because of this shift in our culture, as I look toward the next century I see some very particular ways in which religious education might help congregations provide what so much of the rest of the culture cannot or will not.

For the purposes of these conversations I have selected three areas that to me seem especially critical for religious education efforts: intergenerational community and our ministry to families, living in partnership with the world, and the special needs of adolescents. In each of these areas there are both programmatic and structural components of our ministry for growth and learning. I will discuss these components for each area. However, before that, I will attempt to ground them in an understanding of our Unitarian Universalist faith.

The nature of the "center" of our faith is certainly an ongoing discussion. In these days of shifting cultural values and norms our theological self-understanding sometimes seems to be built upon shifting sand. However, ours has always been a faith that has resisted an immutable foundation. More often, we have seen the foundation of our faith in the courage to be open to fluidity, new eyes, new data, new experience, new people.

When Earl Morse Wilbur began his historical tracing of the roots of Unitarianism he began with three identifying characteristics: freedom, reason, and tolerance. Throughout our best moments these elements have been wrapped in an adventurous spirit of search. A commitment to those three principles has provided us with a very rich heritage indeed. It has led us to a polity in which we have a healthy respect for that tension between individual and community out of which we are called to seek for the best of both our individual and collective hearts and minds. Add to that the powerful loving embrace of all of humankind that has been handed down from our Universalist forbears and, in many ways, I believe that we UUs have an especially valuable theology, a truly relevant faith to offer the twenty-first century. We are living in a world that wants control and predictability, but is likely to find none. I believe that ours is a faith that is ready to engage what appear to be challenging new patterns and paradigms as well as reemerging tasks from previous eras.

The Intergenerational Community and Our Ministry to Families

Seventy-hour work weeks for adults, extended child care, and school, soccer practice, music lessons, and "recreation programs" in clearly delineated time slots for our young ones have made the possibilities for spontaneous family "happenings" more rare. Job mobility has dimmed the concept of "extended family" for many parents and their children. Our congregations have an opportunity to nurture what is often not found elsewhere. St. Exupery's exhortation to "bring up our children" with connection from generation to generation applies here. But, in order to do that, it is important that as religious communities we plan with intention for needs different from those of midcentury religious education programs. It is important that the structure of religious education not just add one more time slot to complicate weeks already over-scheduled with planned experiences. Rather, it is important to build a community to carry the lessons, values, and sense of continuity that once were primary in the extended family structure.

As I visit congregations I notice that basic religious education structure, gratefully sometimes with creative appendages, seems in large part still to be modeled on the post-World War II Protestant model. There are classes for children on Sunday mornings; adults and children are sent in separate directions as they enter the door. A coffee/fellowship period—sometimes for everyone, sometimes age segregated—provides the climax of the morning. This model has served us well in the past. But how does this experience support families with children? I remember once trying to work with parents whose four-year-old simply would not adjust to her religious education classroom, who would scream every Sunday morning when her parents left. In frustration one parent blurted out, "I don't know what the problem could be. She is perfectly fine for nine hours a day of child care during the week, and in her ballet and music classes on Saturday." It seemed clear to me that Sunday morning and one more separation and one more formal time slot were simply the last straws for this child. She needed to be with her family; she needed time to breathe.

Am I advocating that we do away with children's religious education classes altogether? Absolutely not! What I am advocating is putting out a variety of structural models of learning and growing and encouraging congregations to assess their needs and to think "outside of the box" in response to those needs. Many structural possibilities exist that might serve. For instance, what if there were intergenerational opportunities for religious education that happened before or after Sunday morning worship? Each religious education class could be designed for families to attend together, with more age-segregated and informal activities available for children while the adults are at worship. (Children could attend the first part of that worship or attend their own children's worship first.)

Or, what if religious education took place on Wednesday night following an intergenerational potluck (perhaps ordered, rather than "brought" food for tired families), after which there might be a fun (not labor-intensive) intergenerational activity followed by more traditional religious education classes? (This might be combined with a "centers" model of congregational committee/ministries meetings; children might even be invited/nominated to be part of some of the committees.)

My point here is not the "what" of the structure. It is rather that we find ways/permission to free ourselves from structures that were designed for and worked well for families in earlier times. We are a creative people. Let us lift up possibilities, engage in "what if" thinking, that might provide for families who don't often have the opportunity to be together, whose time is so strictly regulated, who don't often have extended families with grandparents, cousins, etc. Let us think about scheduling that might better fit the needs of family patterns as they exist in particular congregations. The one-size-fits-all era seems to be over.

Even more diversity in choices of materials might accompany such an effort. I can see "manuals" on how to run simple meal gatherings with outlines of simple fun intergenerational activities to follow—with an emphasis on playing together (e.g., paper bag skits, singing, art a family can do together, etc). I can see curricula written with roles for children and adults together. I can see guides for building an intergenerational social action committee—or simply social action efforts with input and leadership possibilities for all ages. How about intergenerational long-range planning, building, and grounds committees?

Program possibilities that support families might also include more parenting help—but perhaps in a variety of structural formats. When could parent study or support groups meet? Do the meetings all need to be face-to-face? What about intermittent face-to-face meetings with Internet bulletin boards, or chats within congregations? The range of possible formats is wide.

Another program focus could include adult religious education experiences/curricula that are designed to be built into committee meeting formats. This approach might be reenergizing to the "work" as well as providing for adult growth experiences. I recently heard Robert Kegan say, "Burnout is not from too much to do, but rather from going too long without a personal growth opportunity." In frustration over lack of participation in more traditionally scheduled adult religious education opportunities (evening series, forums, etc), some colleagues have begun to consider the idea of using a part of committee meetings to engage in adult religious education experiences, well integrated into the larger mission of the particular committee. The efforts of many congregations in revisioning their mission and shifting to "shared ministry" models might especially lend themselves to this kind of "thinking outside the box."

At this time in my district work I see a few congregations taking modest steps toward new visions of religious education that respond to these changing needs and life patterns. I am grateful for the recent efforts in the UUA Department of Religious Education in the area of ministry to families. We are heading in a helpful direction; now let's support one another as we move forward into "who knows what" ideas for the future.

Living in Partnership with the World

Lately I have become intrigued by the work of Daloz, Keen, Keen, and Parks, *Common Fire: Leading Lives of Commitment in a Complex World*. How is it that some folks, in the midst of giant complexity in their own daily life management, also are able to live out their lives as active citizens of the larger work, to care about what happens "out there," and to act in response to that caring?

The research reported in *Common Fire* points to the ways that support people, grow people who put living lives of commitment at the center of their being. The researchers used particular criteria as they looked for these kinds of people. One criterion was evidence that they see their work as serving the well-being of society. Another was evidence of perseverance and resilience—doing work for a minimum of seven years without burning out and having some sense of how to work without burning out. The researchers looked to see if there seemed to be an ethical congruence between life and work. And they looked at each person studied for a level of engagement with diversity and complexity—awareness of what they were doing within the context of the global community.

For most of the study participants, the roots of commitment went back to childhood. The research further helped to uncover what particular common elements in growing up were present in those people who live their lives with a strong commitment to the larger welfare.

Many of the shared elements were ones that had already been acknowledged by our liberal religious education tradition, based on our concern for what we know of developmental patterns and needs. Trust, a sense of personal competence and agency, critical-thinking skills, and engagement with "otherness" were some of the powerful elements in childhood, with ongoing reinforcements in adulthood, that seemed to make a difference in how people live their lives. I would hope that in the twenty-first century we would continue to be very intentional with our programming for people of all ages, to reinforce these inner experiences of growing.

I would also hope that we would give professional and lay leadership opportunities to examine the notion of partnership, of how people can live and work together as creative partners. I think, on a global scale, that will be required for livable outcomes in a crowded world. On a more personal and local scale, I believe that our congregations can be strengthened and can learn more about partnership by practicing it, modeling it for one another, both among children and adults. Leaders and planners might engage in dialogue about what this might mean, might look like, by reading such works as *The Power Equity Group* by Carol Pierce,

Leadership and the New Science by Margaret Wheatley, and similar writings. In the UU District of Metropolitan New York, my colleague Howell Lind and I intentionally use these and other materials to challenge teams of religious professionals in congregations to look at their own relationships, to experiment with partnerships that encourage creative interchange and require trust. We try to model that in our behavior with one another and hope that they will be models as well. We are beginning to expand our more intentional partnership to other district lay leadership and we encourage parish-based professionals to do likewise with their leadership. The shared ministry model is "catching on" in several congregations. All of these intentional structural changes are at the heart of how we can educate ourselves and our young ones about living in a world built on partnership.

The Special Needs of Our Adolescents

Although my observations here are brief, I think this area deserves a very large part of our attention. As we know, adolescence—the time of reweaving the earlier strands of developmental stages into a strong identity to serve us and society in the years thereafter—is an especially difficult time in our growing. It is important to the well-being of our culture that this stage happen "well." It is even more important that we not leave these young people without our support and care. This is a long-standing attitude among UUs. Our religious education professionals, ministers, and advisors often have done enormous work in this area and deserve our deep thanks. However, taking seriously that very important adolescent need for adults—other than parents—with whom to journey through the teenage years, and juxtaposing that need with the overstressed lives of adults who might once have been available to our young people, I become concerned. Not that we don't have some excellent folks who do serve well as advisers and mentors. However, in my district work I am aware that in many congregations volunteer positions in youth work are often the hardest to fill and are often filled in a piecemeal way that does not provide the stability and continuity that teens need. I recognize that a committee of the UUA is currently investigating issues around advisers and I am very much looking forward to receiving their report. But I want to weigh in my opinion now.

It has been many years since we as religious educators began to advocate that paid positions, at least in medium and larger congregations, needed to be established. It is my hope that, as we enter the twenty-first century, we can begin to strategize how to shift norms toward more paid youth advisers (perhaps even shared youth advisers?) who have adequate training and will commit adequate time to our teenagers. Our teens seem to have fewer and fewer adult guides to model that one can live a worthy and meaningful life, and who will know and care deeply about each one of them. I believe we need to acknowledge the required depth of this work and begin to expect a more "professional" status in relation to it. The quality of volunteer youth work in small congregations will be enhanced by this, just as volunteer religious educators have been helped by the growth of a tier of professional religious educators.

So, my vision for religious education in the next century has to do with making sure we continue to provide those very special qualities I associated with the button box: sharing meaning across generations, a dependability in the religious community, and continuity through loss of the old and through engagement with the new; a community that values each separately and still provides safety for the whole to do the work within and the work in the world. Such a vision seems possible, growing out of a covenantal polity that is pliable enough to acknowledge tension and to allow for joy at new creation and possibility. The ways we shall preserve and renew our communities of growth and learning and support are many, some probably as yet unknown to us. The central truth of who we are carries on. I close with an affirmation of these words from "Reinventing the Church" by Beverly and David Bumbaugh:

> The church exists to proclaim the gospel that each human being is infinitely precious, that the meaning of our lives lies hidden in our interactions with each other. The challenge we confront is to be a church which does not bury that great truth beneath all our business, but which enables us to encounter each other with wonder and

appreciation and expectation, to call out of each other strengths and wisdom and compassion we never knew we had.

As a faith tradition we have a substantial contribution to make to the next century. In times of long work hours for adults, high degrees of scheduled time for children, and rarer experience of extended family, there are many who long for a deep sense of belonging, stability, tradition, and hope. Throughout our Unitarian and Universalist histories, commitment to freedom, reason, and tolerance has given us a lively engagement with new possibilities while a sense of love for all humanity has encouraged our compassion and commitment to a worldview larger than our individual need. Ours seems to be a faith ready to engage in what appear to be challenging new patterns and paradigms as well as reemerging tasks from previous eras.

Given the particularities of needs of people in this time, our commitment to religious education needs to focus on many areas. The three that I have highlighted are the intergenerational community and our ministry to families, living in partnership with the world, and the special needs of adolescents.

In response to the need for intergenerational community and our ministry to families, I suggest commitment to "thinking outside of the box" as we envision structures for religious education that may not be based on the old Sunday morning models that separate families and ages. It would be helpful to have more program materials to help congregations "do" religious education sometimes as parents and children together, to outline ways to do fun/play nights, to find ways to include religious education in committee meeting times, to suggest models for inclusion of all ages in the work of some committees.

In response to the need for increased focus on living in partnership with the world, we need to continue to lift up the relationship between inner growth and outer action; and we need to continue to acknowledge the role of basic developmental growth in the ability to participate in a commitment to the common good. The notion of partnership is particularly critical on our shrinking planet, and intentionally putting partnership into practice at the congregational level may have consequences well beyond its walls.

The needs of adolescence are of special concern to me. We know that the presence of worthy adults in their lives are critical to their "becoming." We know that it is becoming more difficult to find adults willing to spend the amount of time necessary to provide consistent relationships. Is it time to advocate making the position of youth adviser a professional one?

~

Rev. Susan Davison Archer is a minister of religious education currently serving as religious education consultant for the Unitarian Universalist District of Metropolitan New York.

Toward Wholeness
and Liberation

Rev. Marjorie Bowens-Wheatley

*The purpose of religion is to allow us to unmask all the false
faces of the world. The purpose of education is salvation.*

—Rebecca Parker, *"Congregation as Theological School"*

As a parish minister of color with working-class roots and consciousness serving in a mostly white middle-class movement, I am
painfully aware of our difficulty in confronting one of the most
pervasive "false faces of the world" of which Rebecca Parker
speaks. Rhetorically, we sing that wonderful hymn: "Where is our
holy church where race and class unite?" In this new century, now
that significant groundwork has been laid, it is time to move
beyond the rhetoric. This requires a critical examination of our
past and present. With such an examination of our chosen faith,
coupled with a commitment to a more comprehensive religious
education program, I am confident that, institutionally, we will be
more solidly on the road to spiritual wholeness. Indeed, this road
may be our salvation.

There are many compelling reasons we need a more comprehensive approach to religious education. First, it will help us to
move toward communities of spiritual wholeness and liberation
and to be intentional in developing or embracing a theology of the
church, a theology of ministry, and a theology of culture. Second,
comprehensive religious education acknowledges that congregations teach by an explicit as well as an implicit or "hidden" curriculum. Third, it will help us to embrace religious education as

part of the total work of the church. If a congregation's curriculum represents the learning experiences in the immediate environment and beyond, then, as Maria Harris suggests in *Fashion Me a People*, the church does not *have* religious education; rather, the whole church *is* religious education.

Paul Tillich urged us to question everything of human construction. The question I seek to address in this essay is: Do our historic and most fundamental norms, values, and assumptions (which remain part of the dominant culture of Unitarian Universalism) stand in the way of our becoming a faith community that is liberating for all people? In addition, I will briefly highlight two issues that demand dialogue if we are to become a more open and diverse religious movement: claiming our institutional identity more fully and moving from liberalism to liberation.

Identity

Identity involves formation and change. To what does an individual who joins a Unitarian Universalist congregation assent? What history and traditions, what assumptions and practices does that person inherit? How will becoming a Unitarian Universalist shape or change that person's self-identity? How will those who are already part of a congregation (or the Unitarian Universalist movement) be changed? What resources are available to individuals and congregations that support members as they move through the internal psychological, behavioral, structural, and perhaps theological change that frequently occurs?

Paul Rasor argues in "The Self in Contemporary Liberal Religion" that there is a twin crisis in Unitarian Universalism: an identity crisis and a prophetic or justice crisis. These, he suggests, are intertwined with our preference for individualism over community: "The notion of moral identity can help address the identity crisis in liberal religion. This crisis is partly the result of the liberal tendency to see identification with a community as leading to loss of individuality. The liberal myth is that moral stands are arrived at through unencumbered and disembodied reason."

Further, Rasor identifies how these countervailing points of view inhibit social justice work and can become stumbling blocks when there is no common theological grounding or understanding of our religious history and tradition:

> much liberal religious justice work seems to come from individual convictions arrived at independently of the religious tradition. These are important, of course, but they don't help generate a *religious* or *theological* grounding for *praxis*. And since they don't emerge from a sense of shared identity, these actions are difficult to sustain over the long term. This tendency is reinforced by our traditionally individualistic self-understanding: Social involvement is something each of us can choose to do or not do. Liberal burn-out is often the result.

Our Unitarian Universalist identity—including inherited history, heritage, and culture—is an important aspect of our implicit or hidden curriculum. When powerful identity and cultural forces collide with this hidden curriculum, they can be impediments to moving toward spiritual wholeness and more fully embracing the task of liberation from oppression. Such opposing forces include:

- Our historic *institutional identity* and cultural ethos. The Commission on Appraisal's 1997 report, *Interdependence: Renewing Congregational Polity*, cites sociological characteristics associated with what James Luther Adams called "the religion of the successful." The report states, "In addition to our ethos, our *mythos*—the often unconscious ideas, feelings, and cultural expressions that many Unitarian Universalists in the United States hold—may also be important to understanding our collective identity." The tendency is to claim our history selectively, lifting up what makes us proud while diminishing (if not dismissing) that of which we are ashamed;

- Our *liberal* religious past on the one hand, and a selective approach to human *liberation* on the other;

- Our unwillingness to move toward *sustained engagement* and dialogic action with oppressed communities based on a sociocultural and theological analysis, the former being a prerequisite of the latter.

These dynamics suggest multiple opportunities for ministry within our congregations: (1) support for the spiritual growth of individuals and the religious community as a whole; (2) empowering people to transform dehumanizing social structures; and (3) pastoral support for individuals who are actively engaged in the process of social transformation.

Pastoral support and care is a neglected dimension of anti-oppression education. In seeking to "do the right thing," individual Unitarian Universalists sometimes find themselves deconstructing old myths of history and tradition, sorting out the deepest meaning of their personal commitment to social justice. New levels of awareness—which are inherent in change processes—often result in confusion or what Robert McAfee Brown calls "creative dislocation." This introspective process can lead to questions such as: Who am I in relation to what I am working for? What am I willing to risk in order to bring about social change? While this process can ultimately move the work forward, it sometimes leads to a crisis of faith or confidence for individuals engaged in the process of social change. Many liberal activists have found that, in spite of a high level of formal education, the complexity of social issues requires further learning and deep engagement in the world. Spiritual counseling is sometimes necessary in this process of re-assessment, re-learning, re-affirmation, and renewal.

One way we express our identity is through stories. In her book *The Name of War*, Jill Lepore discusses some of the stories of identity formation among the Puritan colonists—our historic ancestors. Of the stories that shaped our history and identity, which will we choose to tell, and how will we tell the story? Will we acknowledge that, owing (at least in part) to our birth in the Enlightenment Movement—with individualism as a primary value—we are often inclined to choose the needs and interests of individuals over the interests of the community at large? Will we tell *the whole story,* including our tendency to be uncritical of the benefits and privileges deeply embedded in the shadow side of our Puritan heritage? Will we acknowledge the paradox of our history: that ours is a religion rooted in New England Puritanism, remembering both the promise and the privilege this implies? On the one hand, for decades, we embraced the promise of a prophetic covenantal faith *for Europeans* based on freedom of religious choice. On the other hand, we ignored or rationalized the consequences of our complicity in dehumanizing non-Europeans (i.e., "removal" and genocide of First Nations peoples in New England, and collaboration with the enslavement of Africans during the formative years of Unitarian Universalism and what was to become the United States of America). How will our transmission of the Unitarian Universalist story and identity affect those who are contemplating becoming "one of us"?

Liberalism vs. Liberation

Like many UUs of color, over the years I have been "betwixt and between," an "insider-outsider," sometimes loving our faith deeply, at other times throwing up my hands in despair, wondering if we will ever be an institutional catalyst for social *transformation*. While marginalized groups within the Unitarian Universalist movement may experience this kind of cognitive dissonance more often or with greater intensity than those in the UU mainstream, other factors may be more significant influences in the process of transformation.

In *Black Pioneers in a White Denomination*, Mark Morrison-Reed articulates two competing paradigms of freedom. Most people of European heritage, he says, think first of freedom of conscience, the right of free speech or a free press (liberalism), while the primary concern of most African Americans is freedom from bondage and oppression (liberation). These competing paradigms vie for our attention, sometimes confusing—if not stifling—our approach to anti-oppression and other social justice work. A number of people have already investigated this subject, including James Luther Adams, Jack Mendelsohn, Paul Rasor, Frederic Muir, and Cornel West. In lieu of a comprehensive review of their writings, suffice it to say that the goals and strategies of liberals and liberationists differ in significant ways. My primary interest in highlighting these differences is to explore how religious education can be enriched by liberation theology to strengthen our justice making and education work toward the goal of social transformation.

The classical liberal vision seeks "to make free," to provide opportunities for individuals to realize freedom, but stops short of confronting systems that stand in the way of freedom. By contrast, the liberationist vision sees structures of oppression as inhibitors of freedom and seeks new relationships that lead to freedom from oppression. Liberationists believe that good works by the middle class (including some reformist social programs) are not enough to overcome structural oppression; Paul Rasor suggests that what is needed is "a radical realignment of the social and economic order." The liberationists' goal, therefore, is to call society to account for social injustice and to transform oppressive social structures. Liberation theology seeks to restore right relationships. It is not a one-time event, but recognizes the need for an ongoing process of struggle to preserve and uphold freedom, justice, and equality.

In spite of a liberationist theory-in-use (justice), the liberal theory-in-practice centers on (1) an uncritical focus on freedom *for individuals* (as compared to the liberationists focus on freedom *from systemic oppression*), (2) an accommodation to the status quo (including dominant cultural norms), and (3) support for modest social reforms that ultimately benefit the middle class more than the working class and the oppressed. Jack Mendelsohn states the problem of this paradox clearly in *Being Liberal in an Illiberal Age:*

> The trouble with too many liberals, according to radicalized blacks, women, youth, gays, and peace activists, is their complacent spirit. Yes, they have a decent concern for social change. But where is their passion? Where is the sense of their own oppression? Buried in middle class standards. That's where it is. Tucked into the benefits that infuriating unjust social structures have bestowed upon them. Yes, they would like to share these benefits with the less fortunate, those who have been locked out and denied access, but at little or no cost to themselves and their children.

What liberalism and liberation have in common is that each is engaged in a project to extend human freedom, but liberalism's approach is inadequate, in part, because of its tendency to view freedom in the abstract—without exploring a critical question: *freedom for whom to do what?* Thus, it is not surprising that liberal programs are often disappointing to those who seek methods and resources that lead to freedom from oppression.

Education as Justice

In *Pedagogy of the Oppressed,* the late Brazilian educator Paulo Freire wrote,

> Because love is an act of courage—not fear—love is a commitment to other people. No matter where the oppressed are found, the act of love is a commitment to their cause—the cause of liberation. And this commitment, because it is loving, is dialogical. . . . Only by abolishing the situation of oppression is it possible to restore the love which that situation made impossible. If I do not love the world, if I do not love life, if I do not love people, I cannot enter the dialogue.

In the last half of the twentieth century, Unitarian Universalist curriculum and training were our primary approaches to social justice education—a liberal approach—and we have done good work in this area. We have provided spiritual resources and achieved greater equality for women within our ranks. We have done important work around gay, lesbian, bisexual, and transgender issues—most recently hate violence, gay marriage, and the Boy Scouts. Our nationally recognized sexuality education work has led to heightened consciousness around issues of gender equality, abuse, and choice for women. This work has saved lives. Many of us are involved in environmental protection work and are active in trying to save social programs that protect the poor. Our social justice resolution study resources for congregations have been important educational and consciousness-raising tools. Study circles have proven useful in raising awareness and promoting dialogue on issues of racism. Anti-bias and antiracism training have been important in increasing both individual and institutional commitment to reducing oppression. So, we must ask: How can we use these resources to move people from awareness and liberal social action to strategies that will ultimately lead to freedom from systemic oppression?

Freire's ideas, which informed my practice for several decades, were brought into a fresh focus at the 1999 Meadville/Lombard Winter Institute by two of our most esteemed scholars and theologians, Rebecca Parker and Bill Murry. In their presentation, the two advanced the idea that our congregations can become theological centers where people begin to "unlearn" the things that diminish the human spirit and oppress rather than enhance life.

Education "for critical consciousness" and "as the practice of freedom," pioneered by Paulo Freire and described in *Pedagogy of the Oppressed* and *Education for Critical Consciousness*, has been applied in several poor countries and urban areas in the United States by people like bell hooks and Ira Shor, and may prove useful for Unitarian Universalists as well. The Freire method seeks to move people from naïve awareness to critical consciousness and then to action. He calls this *conscienizaçâ*: "learning to perceive social, political, and economic contradictions, and to take action against the oppressive elements."

Paul Rasor writes that, as a process of theological reflection, praxis is "always striving to link religious beliefs and symbols to action in the world." It provides a venue and a context for deepening understanding of values and theological claims. "By stressing the centrality of *praxis*," he says, "liberation theology affirms that its goal is not just conceptual clarity or advocacy of a particular form of social organization, but rather a transformed and liberating way of life." Liberation theology is also inherently relational. It assumes that we encounter the holy in relationships with others. It is through relationships that we are transformed, opening up the possibility of the creation of communities of love and justice. In contrast to liberal theology, liberation theology is inherently humanist in that it draws its program from the concrete experiences of the people rather than from abstract universalized principles or values. Liberal programs, as a solution to human freedom, have meaning only within the cultural, linguistic, and religious framework in which they are embedded.

I would add that our congregations could also serve as centers for people to move from compassion in silence to compassion in action for social transformation. But Freire's praxis method holds another key for us. For Freire, praxis—rooted in love—must be dialogic. It brings people who seek reconciliation into relationship. He writes, "The *raison d'être* of liberation education . . . lies in its drive toward reconciliation." Because it is rooted in the doctrine of love and reconciliation, I believe that the Freire method holds a key for religious liberals as we claim our commitment to human liberation and freedom. I am not proposing that we limit our method to the Freire model, but that we consider all methods that lead to liberation. There are other useful approaches to healing and reconciliation (e.g., Gandhian nonviolence, etc.).

Applied in a faith community, the Freire method might be focused around

- teaching critical thinking skills and systemic analysis using resources and direct experiences that focus on the dynamic relationships and interconnected web of oppression.

- praxis groups that offer structured opportunities for critical dialogue, theological reflection, and transformative action; are committed to a process of problem posing; and are directly engaged with oppressed communities.

Until we have gained a clearer understanding of our hidden curriculum—the paradox of liberalism and liberation in relation to our Unitarian Universalist identity—we will continue the approach–avoidance syndrome in confronting the twin evils of racism and classism. Diversity will continue to be an uphill battle.

We have only just begun to explore what a liberationist approach to Unitarian Universalist religious education might look like. It may be that in our project of freedom, white middle-class Unitarian Universalists are unable to enter into "relationships of sustained engagement" with oppressed communities, as we are called to do by the Business Resolution adopted at the 1997 General Assembly, "Toward an Anti-racist UUA." If we are to move forward in our project of human liberation, perhaps it is time to heed James Baldwin's call to reexamine everything—our history, heritage, traditions, assumptions, and practices. In "The Price of the Ticket," Baldwin writes,

> In the church I come from . . . we were counseled, from time to time, to do our first works over. . . . To do your first works over means to reexamine everything. Go back to where you started, as far back as you can, examine all of it, travel your road again, and tell the truth about it. Sing or shout or testify or keep it to yourself: but know whence you came.

If we are to move from dialogue to authentic social transformation, I believe that religious liberals need to learn a pedagogy of liberation—engagement in praxis: action for justice that stands on more solid ground through ever-deepening theological reflection.

Unless we begin to unravel all the layers of our hidden curriculum—our institutional identity, individualism, social isolation, disconnection, and the shadow side of our liberalism—we are likely to repeat our most ineffective work. In Romans 12, the writer offers a perspective that might serve us well: "And be not conformed to this world, but be ye transformed by the renewing of your mind." Unless we witness to and actively participate in the process of transforming our own faith community and society at large, we are a people who choose to be conformers (liberals) rather than transformers (liberationists) of this world.

It is our task to continue this critical conversation with a goal to being more effective in depth and breadth of our antioppression work and movement toward spiritual wholeness. It is my hope that critically exploring these issues will help us to see more clearly the impediments to our spiritual wholeness and liberation.

∾

Rev. Marjorie Bowens-Wheatley is the adult programs director in the Religious Education Department at the Unitarian Universalist Association.

For the Generations
to Come

REV. SUSAN SUCHOCKI BROWN

One of my favorite stories from the Jewish tradition is about the old man who was observed planting fig trees. The observer asked, "Old man why do you plant these trees? Truly, you a man of great age and wisdom, do not expect to live long enough to reap a harvest; it will take many years for them to bear fruit." The old man answered, "I am not planting them for me but for the generations to come."

What is our vision for the goals of religious education as we enter the twenty-first century? What are the components of this vision?

My vision is to create and nourish a genuine religious community that honors the worth and dignity of every person, recognizes the glory of being gathered with others in community, and prepares each person, exposed to the ideas and ideals of Unitarian Universalism, with all that is necessary to bring peace, harmony, love, joy, and justice into the larger world. The components of my vision involve finding a way to integrate a religious community's inherited norms, culture, and learned and beloved experiences, while honoring, recognizing, and encouraging the exploration of possibilities for new visions. I want us to accomplish this in a manner that encourages the ministers, the teachers, and the members of the congregation to discover ways to speak to our deepest human needs, hopes, and fears through the use of symbols, rituals, ceremonies, and celebrations.

Unitarian Universalists have long held a recognition of an indivisible oneness with all existence and the value of a personal search for meaningful interpretation of life and the universe through individual experiences and interactions. We have also recognized that one's sociocultural status, sexual orientation, gender, personal knowing, genetic predispositions, and inherited and acquired skills have an effect on our perceptions of reality. We are individual beings and we are social beings.

A tension has emerged as we struggle to correct the tilt toward extreme individuality, which has often been taught and honored at the expense of communal experiences. This tension is not just unique to our UU religion. It is being reevaluated and discussed by many theologians, scholars, social scientists, and ethicists as we come out of the Enlightenment into the age of postmodernism.

I believe that at the core of our UU faith is the desire to be included in and a vital part of a community of hope. Yet this community struggles with how to be a place that allows, supports, and encourages the seemingly competing notions of continuity and change. In his perennial book, *The Religions of Man*, Huston Smith writes, "Religion has sometimes been prophetic; it has always been conservative." He explains that this is one of six aspects of religion. He says that this helps the future generations avoid trial and error experiences, and that it connects humans in a chain of culture that is crucial to the continuity of the institution. This tendency, Smith explains, although it serves humans well, "providing freedom for enormous innovations and advance," can be bad or good depending in each case on the values it is conserving. Churches as organizations can be rigidly structured, stable, and resistant to change. One of the tasks of UU religious education is to find how to balance these two themes: innovation and continuity.

We are living in an increasingly diverse world. Multiculturalism, anti-oppression, and antiracism efforts are not just concepts we in UU churches wrestle with but those with which the entire world is struggling. Our children are living in a world that is very different from the world they see in the sanctuary on Sunday mornings. The discrepancies between their lived realities and the Sunday experience needs to be addressed by developing programs, curricula, worship, reading, and musical resources.

Teachers, ministers, and congregations need to be made aware of the exciting possibility of religious education as a transformative experience. Our youth know that social justice, racial justice, peace efforts, ecological and animal rights, anti-oppression, and multiculturalism are part of their daily lives. Yet when they walk into a congregation they see limited resources set aside for these important issues; they see committees that meet more than work; they see political maneuvering to keep social justice programs afloat or stagnant. With incredible clarity they see the structures that oppress rather than free. However, even though our children have a lot more exposure to people of color and have many multicultural experiences, this will not necessarily make them anti-racist, anti-oppressive change agents. They may have quality relationships with others, which is an admirable goal of religious education, but if they have not been given the tools do to social analysis and organization, they will end up helping perpetuate racism and oppression. Our own UU theologian and critic, Dr. Bill Jones, reminds us that racism will mutate, and without the proper diagnostic tools and approach to transformation, we will end up being part of the problem rather than part of the solution.

Our young people have a sense that what they are doing, while trying to learn to live in an increasingly diverse world, and what the congregation is doing are not compatible, not in alignment. They wonder, as many others do, why it is a great mystery that churches should be involved in the larger community doing social justice and transforming society. The religious education that I envision for the twenty-first century has a commitment to anti-oppression, antiracism, and multiculturalism and prepares learners through education, personal awareness, exercises, analysis, and organizational skill development. This, I believe, would lead us to become whole/holy justice-seeking spiritual institutions of relevance to our youth and the world.

One of our tasks for the twenty-first century is to bring and bind the individual's sense of incompleteness into a state of spiritual wholeness. It is all right to teach, model, and explain that we are incomplete by ourselves, for this can lead to experiencing a sense of discontinuity, separateness, and incompleteness, which in turn can motivate us to move toward a sense of wholeness, holiness, and right relationship with ourselves and others. Religious education should help us have encounters, experiences, or exchanges that remind us and make us aware of the inherent worth and dignity of every person. This, after all, is the first of our defining Principles and Purposes. Yet it is not enough by itself.

Religious education should allow for, encourage, and be structured to allow a breaking down of personal and/or social barriers. It should not deny or minimize personal guilt and/or personal shortcoming. It should acknowledge that lack of experience or education may be inhibiting us from fully grasping the final defining Principle of Unitarian Universalism, which reminds us of respect for the interdependent web of all existence of which we are a part. I think this can be a cornerstone of a transformative religious education that can move us to work toward the goal of world community with peace, liberty, justice, and equity for all. This will also require seeking cross-cultural, multilingual translations, interpretations, and experiences.

Walter Rauschenbusch, the great social gospel leader of the early 1900s, taught and wrote that we must not neglect the young, that we must find ways to break out of personal pietism (read individual spiritual practices) to bridge the gap between church and social concern. Our youth do this almost intuitively, yet I wonder if we have really tapped into their incredible passion, energy, and idealism, and if we have discovered how to ground this theo/alogically and religiously for them.

It is time to rethink some of the ways that curricula get developed; to explore new horizons and new sources of writers and contributors; and to discover and examine ways to make the connection between personal religion and social concern. It is time to rethink how we train and prepare ministers of religious education or directors of religious education. How do we identify, support, and encourage the development of people of color into this crucial ministry?

A major portion of my vision for the goals for our liberal religious education lies in the recognition that religious education demands a total congregational ministry that includes spiritual, economic, and social support for DREs/MREs, and all teachers, child-care providers, and the religious education committee members.

The Reverend William Bascom was the minister of the First Congregational Society of Leominster Unitarian in Leominster, Massachusetts, from 1815 to 1820. He was married to Catherine Gannet, the sister of Ezra Styles Gannet. Their ministry was the first to introduce religious education to the youth of the congregation. In the last year of Bascom's stormy pastorate, Catherine taught a class of children at their home on Saturdays. This was the beginning of "the great controversy" over religious instruction in Leominster. Bascom's ministry did not survive that controversy. A history of the congregation written in 1993 states, "Mr. Bascom tried to establish a Sunday school but it was overwhelmingly opposed by the people." The Reverend Bascom's ministry ended with a negotiated settlement. Among the many issues leading to his leaving was his desire for religious education of the young.

Dr. Rufus Stebbins, who in 1862 became president of the American Unitarian Association and who was the first president of Meadville Theological School in 1844, was minister of First Church from 1837 to 1844. When talking about religious education, he wrote that its chief aim was to, "Awaken the hearts of the pupils' religious sensibilities and impart to their mind religious principles." Obviously, the congregation had grown beyond its earlier reluctance, and religious education was now considered vital. This didn't happen without education, dialogue, and exposure of the congregants to the value of religious education.

I have a vision of religious education assisting in the maintenance of community throughout all generations with enough continuity to sustain itself. At the same time, religious education should ensure freedom and novelty so that teachers can engage, understand, and meet students where they are. This is needed so that students can learn how to become committed, dedicated, and interested teachers and so that students will want to become parish, community, or religious education ministers someday in the future.

How are these visions and goals grounded in, and how do they affect, the core of our evolving Unitarian Universalist faith?

In a pamphlet published by the American Unitarian Association in the late 1800s, Charles Everett wrote,

> It is the soul in its pressure toward the full realization and consciousness of itself and of its divine relationships, that has made the world. To the Unitarian [sic] the divine force is a constant element of history. It is a force to blossom into the beauty of the flower, unnoticed in the seed. When human life began—this strange and varied life of humans with its loves and its longing—this divine force was still present, guiding, uplifting. The divine life was responding even though unconscious. The dignity of human nature consists in the grandeur of its possibilities. Amidst eternity flowers, blossoms, seed give back to the soil and give to others.

The vital components of our UU religion are to awaken the seed of potential within others; to provide pathways to full realization of the gift of self; to awaken through ritual, word, song, and movement the mystery of living, the reverence for and awe of life; and to model believing, feeling, willing, thinking, acting, and witnessing our statements of faith.

On April 5, 1992, at 7:00 P.M., I was ordained by the Unitarian Universalist congregation of Winchendon, Massachusetts. My family, my friends, and those who are now colleagues in the ministry stood around me and with me, as I stated, "It is with a sense of awe and joy, a healthy fear and trembling, and a deep sense of obligation and opportunity that I accept and would take up the ministry to which I am being ordained." And, though that was a moment in my life, a moment I would not forget, the moment was just that, it was just a slice, just the coming together of years of education and experiences with religious learning and religious training. I am not speaking only of my theological education from Andover Newton but the education at the feet, knees, and blackboards of those many teachers who indeed believed that what they taught me could help to change the world. These teachers were for me what our teachers are for our children: models and mirrors through which they can see the world as adults do.

Education of our youth is a two-way street. We are, each one of us, the mentors and the mirrors of the world for these children. It is indeed up to us to model behaviors that will teach our youth how to bring and find meaning, harmony, peace, joy, and justice in the world.

There are core values that are crucial, that need to be taught, in order to make our world livable, sustainable, and lovable. They are the simple things learned at the knee of my grandmother and grampy Fay, such as kindness to others, respect for others' property, and respect for the universe and the creatures in it. There are the more scholarly things I learned from my third-grade teacher about reading, writing, and reciting poetry. I have a notebook from my high school freshman year world history class. It is written in my very best penmanship and if you have ever seen my hand-writing you would be surprised I could write so neatly. It is ordered, neat, and one of my treasured possessions. Through the teacher of that class I learned an appreciation for other cultures, other histories, and how we are all part of the interconnected web of existence.

From my religious education teachers I learned not to fear the one called God. The God who my friends told me lived on a cloud, knew all that I was thinking, especially my naughty thoughts, and was waiting until I died so I could be properly punished. From these religious educators, the teachers in my senior-year class, the minister, the minister's spouse, visiting ministers, and the members of the congregation, I learned to question, to listen to my doubts, to search for verification, and to know that life is good and has meaning in spite of turmoil, pain, and struggle. I learned the difference between right and wrong. I learned the value of community, the pride of selfhood, and the pain of being out of right relationship with others. All this I saw mirrored through the lives of the adults who were my teachers. I developed my identity as a person of the female gender, a heterosexual, white, and thus privileged, middle-class Unitarian Universalist.

One of my visions for UU religious education for the twenty-first century is to find ways to aid and assist the many young persons now in our religious education programs in the development of their racial and cultural identity. This is crucial to the next century, especially as the Fulfilling the Promise survey revealed that about 8.5 to 10 percent of our children and youth are bi- or multiracial. I ask, do we as educators know the vital ingredients that will help these children develop a healthy racial identity? What do our ministers, religious educators, or theological schools need to develop these skills?

Teaching is a two-way street. We learn through the wonder and awe of the child who is exploring and defining his or her self-hood. We learn through the adolescent who is struggling with being part of, but not yet accepted by, the adult world. Adolescence is that boundary state that is so hard to watch, harder still to parent, and amazingly beautiful as the child emerges from wounded and wounding adolescence with enthusiasm and idealism to early adulthood as co-friend, co-creator, and carrier of wisdom. The adult teacher is mentor and mirror to the children in the religious education program, and the children are models and mirrors for each of us. Being mentors and mirrors, models and ministers is the enduring core of our evolving Unitarian Universalist faith.

Mary Elizabeth Moore wrote in *Education for Continuity and Change,*

> Education has to do with the maintenance of community through generations. This maintenance must assure enough continuity of vision, value, and perception so that the community sustains its self identity. At the same time such maintenance must assure enough freedom and novelty so that the community can survive in and be pertinent to new circumstances. . . .

If God had acted only in the past, then tradition would simply involve preserving the past. But if God has acted in the past, is acting now, will act in the future, then tradition involves living in a stream of history, keeping alive the memory of participating in God's present action and hoping for God's future.

We are at a point in our UU history when we should begin to evaluate what aspects of our tradition should remain, what new aspects should be introduced, and what a new vision of community will look like. Religious education should be stimulating and engaging, innovative and creative, and it should have stability and variety. It should elicit feelings and ideas, should encourage exploration and excitement, and bring enlightenment. It should occur by modeling, explanation, dialogue, and the maintenance of good order and discipline.

Some questions still remain that require dialogue and more discussion. These are vital questions as we approach a new century of religious education. These are questions we, our congregations, our UU leaders, our theological schools, and our young people must wrestle with: What are the vital ingredients in helping children develop a healthy racial identity? What do our ministers, religious educators, or theological schools need to develop these skills? How do we identify, support, and encourage the development of persons of color into this crucial ministry? How does curricula get developed? Who are the writers and developers of and contributors to curricula? How do we make the connection between personal religion and social concern? What is a community of hope? How do we build communities of hope? How do we educate our youth today so they will want to become the teachers and ministers of tomorrow?

∼

Rev. Susan Suchocki Brown is the parish minister of First Church Unitarian Universalist in Leominster, Massachusetts, and chair of the Journey Toward Wholeness Transformation Committee.

Changing Lenses

PAT ELLENWOOD

Some of you may recall that during antiracism work, we are asked to view our actions, programs, and behaviors through an antiracist lens that allows for a clear and coherent view of what antiracism would look like in our organizations and congregations. Similarly, we need a lens for a clear and coherent focus on religious education as integral to the life of a congregation and one of the key elements for vitality, health, and vibrancy in our entire Association.

The executive staff of the UUA has provided a splendid panorama of our Association in their strategic objectives and plan for a capital campaign. Now we need a more finely ground lens to see the important, particular, discrete ideas on religious education that are spread throughout that plan. *Essex Conversations* provides an opportunity to focus on religious education and to look together for additional clear, achievable goals in religious education with almost, but not quite, unreasonable deadlines.

In 1993, I participated in a Star Island workshop entitled "Religious Education in the 21st Century." Trevor Jones, a British Unitarian religious educator, suggested that we imagine our Association as a body with worship at its heart, service its hands and feet, and religious education its lifeblood. This lifeblood circulates through and sustains all parts of our sacred body. I would add a pair of spectacles to that body's head to suggest a clear vision for our future. What impels me now as it has over the past several years is the absolute certainty that religious educators, whether ordained or not, have a crucial ministry within our congregations. It is my hope that these new spectacles will more sharply focus us on specific plans that will establish a real, active, and lasting commitment to religious education. We need to do more than tinker with the current system. We need to work toward a shift in the culture of our congregations.

While talk is important and these conversations are critical, action is equally necessary. We have a responsibility to have honest, thorough conversations and our responsibility also includes action supported by adequate funding. I continue to be haunted by the Commission on Appraisal's 1997 report, *Interdependence*, which identifies religious educators as one of the marginalized groups within our Association. The report noted, " Religious educators have a special identity that is rarely understood or affirmed as a central aspect of congregational life in our movement." If we covenant to affirm and promote the worth and dignity of every person, we must not implicitly add "except for. . . ." Thus, our most serious obligation is to create a firm and fair plan of action that unmistakably affirms religious educators as indispensable to our movement. As a veteran religious educator, I concur with the veteran of the Spanish Civil War who observed, "People who have principles but not programs turn out in the end to have no principles."

Four Strategic Plans for Religious Education

I propose four strategic programs which I believe will lead to a more dynamic, central place for religious education in our congregations and in our wider Association. We cannot insure steady, long-term growth if religious education is not seen as central to Unitarian Universalism.

ENCOURAGE COVENANTAL LEADERSHIP

Carla Kindt in the UUA Department of Development has said, "Religious education is the gateway to our congregations." A gateway alone does not make strong congregations. They need full-service professional and lay leadership working together and providing transformative educational experiences, inspiring worship and lively programs that will attract and retain families and individuals. One important step involves continuing education opportunities for parish ministers and religious educators. Some of these should be joint gatherings with specific strategies to strengthen key relationships and establish ways to work in partnership. The essential goal is to transcend what may be isolated roles and work together to create intentional communities in which preaching, religious education, and pastoral care are all regarded fully as ministry.

In a covenantal model, members of leadership teams must share with each other forthrightly and trustingly the most challenging elements of each role to be able identify ways to collaborate. Schools of theology can offer additional courses of study and field experiences in religious education as a way to more fully appreciate its complexity. Leadership teams of religious educators and parish ministers can openly examine the points of tension that often occur and work toward a healthier relationship by developing the habits of ongoing dialogue. With these kinds of experiences, our religious professionals can better understand how they can covenant with each other and their congregations to create communities where all are partners in ministry.

Parker Palmer, in *To Know as We Are Known*, explains that

> when we examine the image hidden at the root of 'truth' it turns out to be more immediate, grounded, and human than the words we now use to describe the knowledge we prize. The English word 'truth' comes from a Germanic root that also gives rise to our word 'troth,' as in the ancient vow. With this word one person enters a covenant with another, a pledge to engage in a mutually accountable and transforming relationship, a relationship forged of trust and faith in the face of unknowable risks.

That understanding of covenantal language between religious professionals and among members of congregations will provide a new way of being intentional about the kind of community they wish to co-create. Understanding this fuller conception of truth, well beyond truth as mere objective knowledge, is a wonderful example of altering the conventional paradigm so we can see our responsibilities in a wholly new and productive light that will fundamentally change the culture of professional religious leadership across our Association.

The application process for a LREDA grant to improve compensation for religious educators requires a covenant between congregation and religious educator. Congregations have sent unsolicited testimony that in developing a covenant they came to a new appreciation of religious education and realized the importance of making such an enduring sacred promise to each other. These stories need to be told widely and in rich detail to encourage other congregations to refine their thinking about religious education.

DEVELOP A COHERENT CURRICULUM PLAN

A coherent core curriculum with a well-articulated scope and sequence will help bind us as a continental community whose children and youth have a common experience of Unitarian Universalism. No matter what form this core curriculum takes, we need to be mindful of the specific ways in which we are dedicated faith communities. The materials must differ substantially from those in public or private schools. Experiences and explorations that develop our children's spiritual lives must be an integral component of any new curricular initiative. Embedded in the materials should be opportunities for activities and projects to help our children and youth understand the complexity and importance of both individual and social responsibility. The enriching presence of other faith traditions demands that we provide for an understanding of other worldviews. Correspondingly, we must unveil to our young people the proud and important legacy of Unitarian Universalism through stories of the important ideas, courageous leaders, and watershed events throughout history.

High-quality core materials, expeditiously developed, will give religious educators more time and energy for other critical elements of religious education such as continuing education, time for reflection and study, meeting and dialogue with colleagues, preparation for worship, pastoral care, and time with families. Currently, many of us spend an inordinate amount of time searching for appropriate materials to use each year. Many congregations use valuable time and volunteer resources to write their own curricula or to find from among existing curricula enough lessons on a particular theme. I sense considerable eagerness and urgency among my colleagues for well-developed, up-to-date curricular materials. In order to do that, it seems prudent to allocate sufficient operating funds to support the initial curricular vision and planning. It will also require hiring competent curriculum writers and providing sufficient staff to supervise, edit, and publish the new material in a careful, yet timely fashion.

We have limited time to be with our children and youth—in some cases the equivalent of ten school days each year, which means parents are the primary religious educators. Along with a core curriculum, it is imperative that we develop material that parents can use to complement the Sunday morning experiences. It is equally important to develop materials and training sessions that orient volunteers to the curriculum and stress the uniqueness of teaching in a religious community.

We also must be mindful that most of our parents come to us with little or no experience of Unitarian Universalism. They develop their own faith stance as they nurture their children. For that reason, I would encourage the development of curricula specifically designed for parenting through all the stages of faith development. Our congregation developed a highly successful program called *Parenting from a UU Perspective*, which explores our Principles to both learn how to parent our children and to develop coherence between our actions at home and at work.

Initiatives such as Fulfilling the Promise, The Welcoming Congregation, Journey Toward Wholeness, and others in the future need components that include children and youth in the process. Careful conversations among religious educators, parents, and lay leaders can identify what will draw our children into these programs of reflection and transformation.

MODEL FOR INTERGENERATIONAL FAITH COMMUNITIES

In orienting our volunteers, I mention that while we are not the Barbizon School, we need to learn the skills of modeling. Runways and high fashion aside, we must model for our children the kind of adults we wish them to become. Sidney Harris, a Chicago columnist, observed in *Pieces of Eight*,

In some ways, the power of a teacher's personality is even more decisive and permanent than the ideas he inseminates in his pupils. In the fundamental task of living, we learn far more by example than by abstract mental processes. It is the "presentation of self" in a good teacher that makes the lasting impression . . . the indelible memory of the teacher's moral courage, his respect for reason, his desire to share, his eagerness to learn from his pupils as much as he is teaching.

There are wonderful opportunities for that kind of presentation of self. As part of the Coming of Age program, we invite the adult mentors to share the joys and concerns about their responsibilities to our youth. The depth of their emotion is often overwhelming. Some speak at length quite eloquently and others struggle to hold back tears, yet all share the honor they feel at having been chosen to be a companion to a youth during the process. We desperately need all adults of each congregation to take responsibility in this and other ways as our children and youth grow religiously and spiritually.

If we bring a new and broader relational ministry and more consciously model and provide leadership skills, we no doubt will increase well beyond the current 10 percent, the youth raised in our faith who return as adults to be members of Unitarian Universalist congregations. The odds are much greater if youth are engaged by a wide range of openhearted adults and learn by example and experience what it means to lead in all aspects of congregational life, including worship.

As another part of the effort to join the generations, we have to create shared spaces, some of them sacred. We relegate the children to their rooms, the youth to their space, and the adults to the sanctuary. Social rooms are often limited to adults, with the children and youth entering only to search out their parents to ask when they can leave. We must intentionally plan for children and adults to engage in spiritual, service and social, worship, and more practical experiences.

We must pay closer attention to what our children and youth observe in our behavior because they imitate those they love. They are reading us even more than they read the books we recommend. Our lives are available for them one chapter or installment at a time. We can turn the plot at any point. They repeat the talk—the vocabulary, the topics. They say the words and learn the gestures. The imitation may require refinement as in the case of my daughter, who observed her great-grandfather, a Missouri Synod Lutheran, say grace before every meal. Soon after we returned home we had guests for dinner. As I began to serve, she stopped me and asked us all to hold hands. She bowed her head and began to speak in the cadence of her great-grandfather's prayer. "Georgie Porgy, puddin' and pie, kissed the girls and made them cry." There was a substantial difference in theology but otherwise she had paid close attention.

"Talking the talk and walking the walk" is a slogan from the 1960s with roots deep in the heart of rock and roll. The kind of imitation it describes is both playful and valuable, whether a five-year-old imitates her great-grandfather or an early adolescent imitates a trusted adult friend. If we say we value our children and youth, we must encourage congregations to involve them in the real work of our Association. Rev. John Taylor, in *Notes on an Unhurried Journey*, writes, "When adults think of children, there is a simple truth which they ignore; childhood is not a preparation for life; childhood is life. . . . How much heartache we would save ourselves if we would recognize children as partners with adults in the process of living, rather than always viewing them as apprentices. How much we could teach each other. . . . How full both our lives could be."

RECOGNIZE THE CONTRIBUTIONS OF LREDA

I come to this conversation as president of the Board of Trustees of the Liberal Religious Educators' Association and with twenty years experience as a religious educator. Members of the LREDA Board are volunteers that meet three times each year on behalf of our 560 members, supporters, and friends. We have learned the lesson from Ralph Waldo Emerson that one of the most beautiful compensations in life is that no one can sincerely try to help another without helping himself. Our overarching goal is to change the culture within our congregations and the Association so that religious educators, whether ordained or not, are seen as having a crucial ministry. We believe there is an inherent dignity in and fundamental importance of our contributions to the Association. We have carefully chosen three priorities as the foundation of our work for the next five years and are confident that they will contribute to a fuller understanding of religious educators. It is our hope that the administration of the Association will have the generosity of spirit and resources to assist us as we work to bring about this paradigm shift.

Build Alliances. We seek to establish enduring relationships, add our voice to important conversations, and raise the visibility of LREDA within our Association. We are pleased to have begun what we hope will be a continuing dialogue with the administration of the UUA; the leadership of the UUMA; the Religious Education Department; the Congregational, District and Extension Services Department; and field staff. We believe these developing relationships will be mutually enriching. It is our hope that the list of those with whom we are in conversation will continue to grow.

Develop Professional Standards. We have begun a process for identifying what it means to be a professional religious educator. We are working with deliberation to detail the attitudes, skills, qualities, life experiences, and academic study that will be required for one to be designated a LREDA professional.

We expect LREDA's active members to meet the standards we design. At the same time there must be institutional commitment to those religious educators serving the majority of our congregations which are small and have limited resources. We should not reduce the level of services at a time when more women and men are beginning to trust that religious education can be a viable profession.

Educate Congregations about Good Practices. Rapid membership turnover on congregational committees can result in a kind of institutional amnesia. We plan to share with all congregations our understanding of what religious educators need in terms of contracts, job descriptions, covenants, working conditions, continuing education, fair compensation, professional expenses, and benefits in order to perform professionally, efficiently, and effectively. These good practice materials will provide guidelines for hiring and retaining quality professional religious educators. This will contribute to the increase in the tenure of religious educators from the current two to three years, thus contributing to stability in the profession and positioning congregations for growth through a strong program of religious education.

Responsibility for the Future

I believe that we all are responsible for the future. There is no "they" to do the work of shaping a world that embodies the principles we hold dear. It is up to us...each one of us. In an interview in the *UU World*, Toni Morrison helps us understand a compelling call to write her award-winning novel, *Beloved:* "The primary conviction one has when one begins is that it is absolutely necessary. The second certainty is that I alone am the one who can do it." She speaks of what it is to be called to write a novel. We speak of what is to be called to change the culture of our congregations. We must consider the extent to which each of us is responsible, what it is that each of us must do.

As a liberal association I believe we are challenged to avoid an individualistic, hierarchical, competitive, win/lose, limited goods system and achieve one that is cooperative, relational, and dedicated to progress for all. To effect those changes we must lovingly remind each other of what we are called to do.

My passionate hope for the future is that those called to the work of religious education have professional colleagues who mentor them, congregations who are educated in good practices, and institutional support. Let us look to this future through a newly ground lens—a lens that reveals religious education as integral to the health and spiritual growth of Unitarian Universalism. Let our actions embody our Purposes and Principles and Jacques Barzun's simple, sound wisdom, "Ethics have to be seen to be believed."

~

Pat Ellenwood is the director of religious education at the Unitarian Universalist Society of Wellesley Hills, Massachusetts, and president of the Liberal Religious Educators' Association.

Making Sure
There Is a There There

JUDITH A. FREDIANI

There is no there there.

—*Gertrude Stein, describing Oakland, California*

A page of editorial cartoons in the magazine, *The Nation,* caught my eye a few years ago. The collection of images was entitled, "Oxymorons." An *oxymoron* is, of course, an apparent contradiction in terms, such as "jumbo shrimp" or "deafening silence." Not surprisingly, these oxymoronic cartoons betrayed a certain editorial bias: The first sketch depicted "military intelligence"; the second, "political integrity"; the third, "people's government." The fourth was "religious education," and it depicted a young man whose head was open at the top like a trash receptacle. On his outstretched hand stood a cleric pouring garbage—banana peels, apple cores, tin cans—into the young man's skull. I bristled at this image. Surely, I thought, this indictment is directed at orthodox religions with dogmatic religious instruction; surely, our liberal religious education practices are exempt from such a characterization. If anything, we are more often accused of not pouring *anything* into the heads of our children and youth, that is, not giving them specific theological answers or beliefs. Surely, *liberal* religious education is not an oxymoron?

There is an inherent contradiction in religious education. The word *religion* is most likely derived from the Latin *religare,* "to bind tightly" from *ligare,* "to bind." *Education,* on the other hand, is from the Latin *duca,* "to take or to lead." To educate is to take or lead *away.* Thus, the apparent paradox of religious education: simultaneously to bind together and lead out. It poses a pedagogical dilemma for religious educators: how to "teach" Unitarian Universalism without "stamping our minds" on others, particularly defenseless children. This is not a semantic issue, but a philosophic one. What is the nature and purpose of *liberal* religious education as we enter the twenty-first century? In what ways should it bind us together, and in what ways should it lead us out or liberate us?

One image that helps us with this seeming contradiction is the familiar metaphor of roots and wings. In her hauntingly beautiful song, "Spirit of Life," Unitarian Universalist songwriter and activist Carolyn McDade writes, "Roots hold me close; wings set me free." The roots refer to the religious community that binds us gently together, companions and comforts us in our life journeys, and assures us that we are not alone. Psychologist and faith educator Sharon Parks calls this a "holding community." Wings represent the free intellectual inquiry of liberal religion, the freedom to discover and be who we truly are, and the liberation of the human spirit. Liberal religious education is not an oxymoron, but it is a paradox that we continue to trip over and that continues to challenge us to bring our hearts, minds, and spirits to make meaning of life. And meaning making is the essential purpose of religious education.

Of course, to make meaning of our lives in religious community, we have to show up. I am often asked what to tell parents when they ask, "Why should we go to church? We are so busy and our kids are so busy. . . ." The simple answer is, "Because you're so busy!" We should go to church precisely because of soccer practice and violin lessons and hockey and gymnastics; precisely because more of us are working longer hours, traveling more, and commuting farther; precisely because our lives are compartmentalized, structured, task-filled, and goal-focused; because the pressures that drive us and the busyness that fills our days act as a centrifugal force that pulls us away from family, friends, and other human connection, and distracts us from our deep human need to reflect, renew, commit, and make meaning of our lives. The competition for our time is very real, but we are not really too busy. A recent study on how people use their leisure time confirms that people who do more do even more. People who work more also spend more time with their families and have more sex.

Let's accept busyness as a given and, in a paradigm shift see it as a well-disguised gift—an opportunity to identify the essential purpose of the religious community. People have many needs—intellectual, physical, emotional, spiritual—but the faith community must keep uppermost in its mind the religious gifts that are no other institution's primary responsibility or intent. The potential for meaning making is so great, and our time together so short, that we must constantly ask ourselves, What religious needs can we serve that secular schools, challenging careers, loving families, and political and social organizations do not fully satisfy? Helping people develop spiritually and act religiously is our unique responsibility. Facilitating this religious growth and learning is what we as liberal religious educators can uniquely offer. Together, making meaning of life and living a life of meaning constitute the *there* we must make sure is there.

There are many ways to make sure there is a *there* in our congregational life. I will address three which together offer opportunities unique to liberal religious education: lifespan religious growth and learning in an intergenerational community, ethical and spiritual grounding in social justice, and a liberating pedagogy. These visions for the twenty-first century are not new; they are the not-fully-realized visions we have held for a generation or more.

Lifespan Religious Education

"There is a land of the living and a land of the dead and the bridge is love, the only survival, the only meaning," wrote Thornton Wilder in *The Bridge of San Luis Rey*. We call it *lifespan religious education,* a term that evokes an image of a seamless continuum, of a graceful bridge spanning the river of life from shore to shore, from birth to death. And yes, we hope that bridge is love, the beloved community.

Since the Religious Education Futures Committee report of 1981, I and most religious educators have been preaching and teaching the gospel of lifespan religious growth and learning throughout our Association. The rhetoric of "lifespan religious education" permeates our publications, brochures, and mission statements. Yet I am struck with the almost utter failure of the concept to be realized in our denomination. We offer not a solid span that can be safely crossed, but a series of bobbing rafts that allow travelers, if they are sufficiently adventurous or persistent, to leap from one to another. Whoops! Sometimes there is no raft at all for your age group. Welcoming children into the first ten minutes of adult worship, having the youth group clean up after the potluck, and publishing an adult education brochure do not collectively constitute lifespan religious education. Even congregations that have rafts for *each* age group too often are programming for each age group, inadvertently maintaining discrete, segregated communities within the community, missing an opportunity to enjoy the benefits of truly intergenerational life.

What would a congregation engaged in lifespan religious growth and learning look like? It would be the ultimate committee of the whole: a community in which everyone is seen as teacher and learner; in which every age and stage of life is equally valued and equally supported by whatever tangible and intangible resources the community has to offer; in which every age and stage of life is allowed to *contribute* whatever tangible and intangible resources it has to offer; a community in which no decision is made about the life of the community—whether in the areas of worship, physical plant, fundraising, budgeting, social action, the arts, education, or any other—without consideration of its impact on and opportunities for every member of the community.

If this vision seems ambitious, it is no more than a restatement of the goals espoused throughout our ranks. But as a religious organization we are culturally and institutionally resistant to realizing those ideals. Part of our resistance is the persistence of nineteenth-century understandings of what a church is, what worship is, and what education is. To the extent that church is Sunday morning worship-centered, and worship is pulpit-centered, and education is classroom centered, much of the life of the congregation will be characterized by parallel play. If all members were content to play in their traditional spaces—adults in the living room, children in the (basement) playroom—we wouldn't be asking ourselves, Where are the young adults? Why can't we keep a youth group going? Why don't our eleven-year-olds want to come to church? Why do our elders feel isolated?

These questions suggest that we have a strong, institutionalized middle-age bias, and it is therefore not surprising that we best serve that age group. I am often surprised that people are surprised when a child says something profound ("From the mouth of babes!"), or a youth demonstrates skilled leadership ("He'll be running for president one day!"), or an elder does anything ("Seventy-eight and still . . .). Ageism, and the patronizing attitudes it produces, work against lifespan religious growth and learning and the development of the beloved community. When we remember that the gifts of wisdom, love, and service are human capacities found in people of all ages, we will restructure our institutions to change the way we relate to each other religiously. We have examples of the possibilities in our congregations today. Youth and young adults are teaching older adults new ways to worship; participants in *Cakes for the Queen of Heaven* programs are finding that seventeen- and seventy-four-year-old women have much in common and much to teach each other; children, youth, and adults are actively engaged together in social action projects. We can learn from these and many other models. And we can learn from our religious educators who are particularly aware that people of all ages are more alike than different. We can resist our tendencies to compartmentalize people by age and instead nurture the connections among all ages in what may be the last presence of multigenerational life—the religious community.

But genuine respect for all ages and truly intergenerational communities are countercultural prospects that will require institutional transformation to be fully realized. To the extent that *religious education* is synonymous with *kids; religious educator* is associated with *childcare;* and children, youth, and those that serve them are marginalized, we are not achieving the depth and vitality we could as a faith community and a teaching and learning community. Yet creating this lifespan bridge is one of the most valuable gifts a religious community can offer.

Ethical and Spiritual Grounding in Social Justice

On Racial Justice Day at General Assembly in Charlotte, we all broke into small groups to discuss the morning's program. A young woman in my circle was just graduating from high school and about to attend a prestigious university. She was bright and liberal and born and raised Unitarian Universalist. And she was angry. She had been listening to Mark Morrison-Reed and Bill Jones describe their experiences with racism in society and within the UUA. And she was shocked. She said she had been taught that the Civil Rights Movement of the 1960s had basically eliminated racism—that it was ancient history, that we had moved beyond it. She said she was angry because she felt she had been lied to. Why, she asked, didn't my church tell me about the reality of racism?

At the 1984 Unitarian Universalist National Workshop on Social Justice, the Revs. Richard S. Gilbert and Roberta Nelson spoke on the theme, "Religious Education and Social Action: Branches of the Same Tree." The "Compleat" Church, Gilbert wrote, links religious education and social action. "It is a linkage that should not be necessary to make—it seems self-evident." In his address and in many other works, he has described a doctrine of the church as a prophetic, learning, caring, and celebrating community, one that is "insufficient, inadequate, unless all parts are complete and healthy." Gilbert and the First Unitarian Church of Rochester, New York, continue to model this vision.

In her remarks, Roberta Nelson emphasized that social justice is "caught" not "taught." When we model the risks and rewards of justice seeking, and when people of all ages are engaged together in social action, we make meaning of our lives. Nelson quotes Viktor Frankl: "We are doomed to failure if our goal is to find meaning in being happy. Happiness is the side effect of fulfilling the search for meaning." "The work of meaning-making is hard," writes Nelson. "Part of the quest for meaning for me is to put that which I value, prize and cherish into action."

A primary goal of religious education is to build community. Education breaks down the dichotomy between self and others, developing the human capacity to feel identity with and empathy for all other people, increasing our ability to draw from and contribute to ever-widening circles of human communities. As we learn about others, our sense of interdependence, of responsibility to and connectedness with others, grows. When we feel that our welfare is linked to the welfare of the world and that taking care of self is really taking care of community, we are moved to act. Unless and until the world knows perfect justice, education with integrity—religious education that makes meaning—must not only inspire but also equip us to change the world. Rooted in ethical community, we are freed to live ethically.

Unitarian Universalism, including our religious education practices, has a long and strong history of justice seeking. We have used our classrooms and pulpits, our sanctuaries and General Assemblies, our finances and talents, our music and arts, our political and organizing skills, our energies, and our lives to promote a more just world. We should pause to acknowledge our heritage and appreciate our efforts. But we cannot pause too long, because we are increasingly aware of how much could be done. If we can resist our cultural tendency to compartmentalize our religious life into worship, religious education, and social justice boxes; if we can engage all ages in the praxis of reflection and action, we could insure that religious education and social action are indeed two branches of the same tree and that social justice is inseparable from meaning making in our faith. In doing so, we would raise children who are much better equipped than we were to engage in and contribute to their multicultural world. In the process, we ourselves would be transformed into a more diverse multicultural denomination, not because of what we preach, but because of what we do.

A Liberating Pedagogy

In *Fashion Me a People*, Maria Harris wrote, "The very word 'curriculum' conjures up images of boxes piled on top of each other in out-of-the-way places, packed with dull workbooks for children to fill out endlessly in Sunday School." As a person responsible for developing some of those boxes (piled on top of each other in my office), I agree. When we hear the word *curriculum*, our minds do an automatic word association with *classroom*—the classroom of our childhood. Those classrooms grew out of the nineteenth-century pedagogy that sought to prepare a labor force for an emerging industrial society and to "Americanize" an increasingly diverse population. That legacy is so strong in our larger culture that it intrudes on our lifespan religious education programs despite our strong history of progressive educational philosophy and practice; despite the voices of Channing, Fahs, Dewey, Knowles, Freire, hooks, and others we have listened to; and despite the many creative, engaging, and experiential religious education programs throughout our denomination. We need to expand our understanding of *curriculum* beyond the books, boxes, and classrooms in order to fully realize the transforming power available to us as liberal religious communities.

Maria Harris contends that the curriculum is "the entire course of the church's life," the mobilizing of the creative and educative process of the entire religious community. I take that as a warning. All churches teach the same three curricula, Harris continues, referring to Elliot Eisner's model in *The Educational Imagination*. The *explicit* curriculum is what we actually present with conscious intent. The *implicit* curriculum includes the patterns of organization, the procedures, and the attitudes that frame the explicit curriculum. The implicit can reinforce or contradict the explicit curriculum. The *null* curriculum is a paradox; it is what is *not* said and *not* done, but it is *not* neutral. Silence can be deafening, and destructive.

If we explicitly state in our church literature that we value our youth, but have a $200 youth budget, no adults to work with youth, or no willingness to hold a district youth conference in our building, one might conclude from Harris's analysis that the implicit curriculum contradicts and undermines the explicit curriculum. Both "curricula" teach. This view of curriculum is a powerful reminder that we need to pay attention to what the entire community is teaching the entire community. Using this understanding as a new lens would not only help us see our counterproductive practices more clearly, it would necessarily enlist the entire congregation in creating lifespan learning.

If implemented, the-church-is-the-curriculum philosophy would be transforming, but it is not the only useful concept of *curriculum*. When directors of religious education ask me if we have a curriculum to address racism or to explore Buddhism, I can't say,

"Why no, your *church* is the curriculum!" Bigger than a box, but smaller than the entire course of the church (Would you want to be the director of the entire course of the church?) is curriculum as "planned learning opportunities for intentional outcomes"; in other words, creating experiences that give people an opportunity to learn something worth learning. Those experiences need not be bound by a classroom, by age group, or by any form of pedagogy, although they can be. The outcomes, too, need not be limited to traditional cognitive goals and measurable objectives, and hopefully, are not. In fact, we can be proud of our history of eclectic, progressive approaches to education while also recognizing how we are culture-bound in ways that work against our goals.

Curriculum includes intent and process as well as content. "The medium is the message," said Marshall McLuhan. Point taken, but it is not strictly true. The medium is a message; content is a message; action is a message; and silence or inaction is a message. In implementing programs that facilitate lifespan religious growth and learning, we need to attend to each of these components. Because we value the worth of each individual, we strive to treat each other with love and respect. This not only models our religious Principles, but it nurtures a sense of self-respect and self-acceptance that is the basis of love for others. Because we value the use of reason and intellect, we provide factual and conceptual information and encourage critical inquiry. Because our sense of right and wrong is central to the meaning we make of our lives, we act. We articulate our values, we witness them, and we try to live them. And because we don't know everything and can't control everything, we make room for mystery, for awe and wonder, for oneness with a universe greater than the human constellation, for the unknowable and unexplainable. We try to nurture a spiritually meaningful life, that is, a life examined, mysterious, and dedicated—a life examined by the dual standards of reason and morality, a life open to the mystery within and between human spirits, a life dedicated to purposes greater than the interests of the individual. My hope is that we do not lose any dimension of our heritage—spiritual, intellectual, or ethical—because together they define what a liberal religious education offers; together they put a *there* there.

Realizing Our Visions

Abraham Maslow said that "we grow forward when the delights of growth and the anxieties of safety are greater than the anxieties of growth and the delights of safety." To thrive and not merely survive in the twenty-first century, we need to grow forward with our strengths as a liberal religious community, offering lifespan religious growth and learning in an intergenerational community, educating for social action, and providing the freedom to search for truth and meaning. Unitarian Universalism has undergone significant transformation in the past, and we face an opportunity to grow forward again by transforming those aspects of our institutional culture that clip our wings.

We need to expand our concept of religious education, and we need to change our relationship with our religious educators. Too often, directors and ministers of religious education learn the gospel of lifespan religious education only to return to institutions uncommitted to putting the concept into practice. Religious educators educate for social justice in the classroom only to see the implicit church curriculum contradict the explicit—in the ways children, youth, and those who serve them are treated; in the level of institutional resources committed to social action. Religious educators—important facilitators of meaning making in the faith community—are too often excluded from, or severely underrepresented on, the committees, boards, and task forces that make decisions, set priorities, and allocate resources for our religious life. Those engaged in religious education need to be at all the tables, be included in educational opportunities, and be welcomed in partnership with parish ministers if we are to be the beloved communities that offer, in James Luther Adams's words, intimacy (community) and ultimacy (meaning) throughout the life span; if we are to make sure there is a *there* there for all ages.

∾

Judith A. Frediani is the curriculum director in the Religious Education Department at the Unitarian Universalist Association.

Useable Truth

Rev. Dr. Richard S. Gilbert

The nineteenth-century German poet Heinrich Heine was walking with a friend before the cathedral of Amiens in France. "Tell me, Heinrich," said his friend, "why can't people build piles like this anymore?" Answered Heine, "My friend, in those days people had convictions. We moderns have opinions. And it takes more than opinions to build a Gothic cathedral."

Nearly fifty years ago University of Chicago president Robert Hutchins wrote of education as the "last refuge for scoundrels," borrowing from Johnson's similar words on patriotism. Hutchins asked readers to try this test on themselves. If we asked anyone to do something about the social ills of the world and he/she answered that the only solution was education, we could be sure he/she was a scoundrel. Why? Because the person was using education as a high-sounding but meaningless excuse for not doing anything to solve the problem. Hutchins went on to say that if the people who have been effective social reformers had relied solely on education, none of those reforms would have been implemented. In the same vein, Hutchins told students in his farewell address, "The whole doctrine that we must adjust ourselves to our environment, which I take to be the prevailing doctrine of American education, seems to me radically erroneous. Our mission here on earth is to change our environment, not to adjust ourselves to it. If we become maladjusted in the process, so much the worse for the environment."

Far be it from me to demean education as an instrument of justice. It really depends on what kind of education, or religious education, one means. The danger to which Hutchins points is that we confuse education about justice with education as justice making; we muddle justice education as a merely intellectual undertaking with justice education as praxis, the integration of spirituality and social action.

The theme of this paper is "useable truth," based on May Sarton's two-word description of poetry, the story about Heinrich Heine, and Robert Hutchins's insight. They all point in the same direction: "justice, equity, and compassion in human relations," our second Principle. It is my conviction that every Unitarian Universalist, from youngest to oldest, ought to understand that social justice work is as integral to the religious life as spiritual growth. I believe one of our major religious education tasks in the twenty-first century is helping people transform their beliefs and values into effective and meaningful action in the world—a process that has been called *praxis*.

In *Moral Principles in Education,* John Dewey had a simple illustration for this. Told about a swimming school that trained its students in the motions of swimming out of the water, he asked what happened when they plunged in. There was a one-word answer: "Sunk."

Praxis is not simply a trendy buzzword in liberation theology. It is the logical extension of what John Dewey taught many years ago. In *The School and Society* he wrote, "Apart from participation in social life, the school has no end or aim." Knowing and doing cannot be separated. Action is part of the decision-making process. Dewey opposed education as "funded capital," a compendium of facts, the ingestion of which was equated with learning. He was not content to rely on mining capital from the past; he understood the need for teachers and learners to create and recreate cultural capital. In *The School and Society* he made clear that learning took place, not only in the formal structures of the school, but also in the formal and informal structures of the society. Dewey is as current as Paulo Freire, who explicated the concept of praxis learning in *Pedagogy of the Oppressed.*

Hutchins, Dewey, and Freire all sought to help create people who are creatively maladjusted to their culture, people bent on changing the world. They did not wish to create culture consumers, mere digesters of a body of knowledge. All understood "a student is not a vessel to be filled, but a lamp to be lighted." None of them sought to clone contemporary culture, one by one, busily reproducing existing people, conformists to their society.

Clearly, the curriculum for praxis education is not bound up in classrooms and books alone. The religious education curriculum is the totality of experiences, planned and sometimes unplanned, from which we can learn. Forty hours a year, our typical teaching time, is hopelessly inadequate.

Curriculum, as Angus MacLean never tired of reminding us, is composed of subject matter, values, and methodology—or as he expressed it, "SVM." There are necessary facts to learn, knowledge to grasp, but as Alfred North Whitehead put it in *The Aims of Education*, "A merely well-informed man is the most useless bore on God's earth!" And, we might add, "the most impotent change agent."

Values are the religious motivation for action. Too often we prepare for action without adequate attention to the religious values out of which we are acting. Hence, we have acquired the reputation of being "knee-jerk liberals," for whom any *au courant* cause prompts us to action—usually intermittent and ineffective action.

Methodology is crucial, for the way we communicate subject matter inheres in the values themselves. Our methods and our values are inseparable. "The method is the message," as MacLean said, meaning, for example, we cannot teach democracy by authoritarian methods. As the Quaker aphorism has it, "There is no way to peace; peace is the way." We cannot educate for justice without actually doing justice.

In *Christian Religious Education*, Boston College's Thomas Groome speaks of the praxis tradition in these words. "We must stop thinking of putting faith into action and theory into practice," he writes. "Such an understanding implies our values are one thing and our actions another. Instead our religious convictions are an existential whole—in which reflection and action are in continual dialogue. Our decisions are to be lived." It is another way of saying that, "We learn by doing." Religious education and social responsibility are experiential; experience is the medium of exchange between the individual and the world. The Jewish tradition is rich in literature on what is called *tikkun ha' olam*, repair of the world.

This praxis curriculum is both implicit and explicit. While we may carefully design peace and justice programs with social problems as the subject matter, every facet of our church life has educational potential. We may even try to get off the hook of praxis education by tucking in a "social action" course instead of examining the totality of church life in the community as grist for our education mill. Ultimately, the church teaches by what it does. People of all ages understand the real mission of the church by a process of pedagogical osmosis; it is in the atmosphere and action of the total religious community. I find the imagery of "the church without walls" an engaging symbol for the work of the religious community in the world. One of our tasks as educator/activists is to expand the Unitarian Universalist horizon beyond the confines of a religious institution.

Our young people are entering a crisis-ridden world. I do not believe we are equipping them to deal with it. Well-intentioned promotion of our Unitarian Universalist purposes and principles is inadequate. We need to help create experiences where these values bump up against social reality. According to Horace Bushnell, "We live ourselves into religious thinking more than we think our way into religious living."

To address this problem, I suggest that this praxis model of education for justice among Unitarian Universalists has four principles of practice—"the four Es."

First, I believe education for justice begins with one's own existential situation in the world. We do not leap from our typically somewhat self-indulgent lives into action for others by pedagogical tricks. We do not move from the most often comfortable lives of our mostly suburban people to scenes of rural or urban poverty by fiat.

An initial principle for praxis education, then, is to establish linkage between our lives and the problems of the world. It is hard to experience the prosperous middle-classness of most of our congregations and then be catapulted into the world of poverty and oppression that surrounds us locally, nationally, and internationally. Unitarian Universalists have been called "bureaucrats and technicians of the establishment." We have benefited immensely from the status quo in American culture. We are at or near the top of the economic pyramid. The socioeconomic-political system has been good to us. In the words of the prophet Amos, "We have been terribly at ease in Zion."

The question becomes, Can a prophet chair the Board? Can those who have benefited from it effectively analyze, criticize, and change the very system that has been so good to them? Will not our efforts at social reform come a cropper of our own self-interest?

The late Saul Alinsky once wrote in *The Professional Radical,* "The trouble with my liberal friends—and I have lots of them—is that their moral indignation and sense of commitment vary inversely with their distance from the scene of the conflict. Once you're on top you want to stay there. You learn to eat in very good restaurants, to fly first class. The next thing you know these things are essential to you. You're imprisoned by them." A Union Theological School student challenges us with this terse remark: "The liberal in me wants a different world, but the liberal in me also wants the world without changing myself, without any pain."

We might say that the Unitarian Universalist church must become a counterculture to critique and transform the culture. Our task is to make connections between the middle-class lives of most Unitarian Universalists and those who are oppressed by sexism, classism, racism, ableism, ageism, and homophobia—the six horsemen of today's apocalypse.

One of the most effective programs we have developed at First Unitarian Church of Rochester is a series of task forces and classes that involve people of all ages in seeking justice. For eleven years we have partnered with two inner-city schools, tutoring and advocating. When social policy issues affecting the schools emerge, we have a cadre of people with first-hand knowledge of the plight of urban public schools. In another effective program, members of our youth group have been participating in a soup kitchen at a center-city Roman Catholic church. Their subsequent discussions on social problems are informed by their hands-on experience. They become existentially involved.

A second learning principle is education for empathy. Kenneth Clark, witness in the historic *Brown vs. Board of Education* Civil

Rights case of 1954, wrote that our current gods of intelligence, science, and technology are "fickle and treacherous." We have become victims of our own intelligence because we cannot solve problems essentially moral in nature. Preoccupied by objectivity in intellectual pursuits, we have neglected education in empathy—in moral sensitivity. "How does one study a slum objectively?" Clark asks.

Thirty-five years ago, as a youth group adviser at Cleveland's First Unitarian Church, I tried to work on this problem. Each year the church collected good used toys for distribution in a public housing project in the east-side ghetto. There the toys were repaired and repainted by residents, to be sold at low prices at a Christmas fair. That was fine, but I thought more could be made of this effort educationally. So I took members of the youth group down to the housing project to meet with its director and learn something about the problems faced by its residents—education for empathy. She led us through the labyrinthine paths of the welfare system, and we learned how it effectively destroyed families by ruling people ineligible for benefits if the "man" of the household was in residence. This meant either fatherless households, or fathers who secretly lived "in" by night and "out" by day. Here was a real anti-family policy.

Later our group returned to participate in the Christmas Fair, informally meeting some of those who benefited from our charity. There was admittedly something paternalistic in these white, suburban, affluent kids and their young minister rubbing elbows with poor, black, urban people, but it was eye-opening for them and for me—almost forty years later. Incidentally, this action outraged one conservative faction of the church who called me on the carpet for this and similar indiscretions.

Margaret Gorman, a Catholic educator researching the moral development of seventeen-year-olds, found "those children in a segregated wealthy suburb were on significantly lower moral stages than children in a less homogeneous area on the same socioeconomic level." "Ironically," she concludes in "Moral Education, Place, and Social Justice," "the efforts of the parents in the suburbs to keep their children away from inner-city experiences or any other experiences of diversity only keep their children on lower stages, because no disequilibrium occurred. Cognitive dissonance, or the challenge to one's existing cognitive structures regarding right and wrong, are essential to growth in moral maturity."

A third principle of praxis is education for engagement. It is clear we learn better from existential experiences than from abstract ones. While sociological analysis of social problems is an indispensable aid in becoming an effective change agent, it is no substitute for hands-on experience.

In our congregation we have tried to make social responsibility—alongside worship and spiritual growth, the mutual ministry of a caring community, and religious education as a life-span undertaking—an integral part of what we are as a religious community. Each church school class takes on some form of social outreach—from the very young writing cards to our people who are sick or shut in, to our youth group working at the soup kitchen, to an extensive program of task forces for the adult community aimed at systemic change. These ministries are highlighted regularly in our church newsletter and from the pulpit. There is never a question that justice making is part of who we are as Unitarian Universalists.

However, at a board of trustees retreat we sought to find a project that could be truly intergenerational, one that was specific, measurable, achieveable, and consistent with Unitarian Universalist values. After consulting with our mayor and his staff, we received a letter from a kindergarten class at an inner-city school inviting us—urging us—to help them build a playground, both for the school and the neighborhood, as the school is adjacent to a city park. After consulting with the neighbors, having social interactions with the school community, and raising $30,000 with surplus funds, foundation grants, individual contributions, and church school fundraisers, we helped install a new playground. It was an intergenerational community-building project for us as well as a significant contribution to the neighborhood, which was heavily involved in the process. It also had the pedagogical advantage of exposing our heavily suburban population to inner-city residents and vice versa.

Somehow, we need to break through the prophylactic sterility of our suburban experience to make contact, face to face, with those not so "favored." There is nothing like an hour in a ghetto church, a soup kitchen, or a nursing home to raise consciousness. At the same time, research reveals that giving such exposure itself is of little value in moral growth unless it is accompanied by reflection on the experience. Personal experience needs to be integrated with value reflection to be a genuine experience of praxis learning.

T. S. Eliot's "Love Song of J. Alfred Prufrock" introduces us to a fourth principle of praxis education: "Do I dare disturb the universe?" Education for empowerment is a critical and culminating step in effective religious education for justice. It should be our goal as lifespan religious educator/activists to enable programs of peace and justice designed to do no less than change the world.

In *Relating to Our World*, Hugo Hollerorth writes, "To be a human being is to be a dwelling place for power. To move about the world and interact with it is to encounter power. Religion arises, then, out of the effort of human beings to make their way in a world of conflicting powers."

In 1985 my younger son participated in a Unitarian Universalist Service Committee Urban Youth Experience program created by three Denver-area congregations. A group of six UU youth lived with local families and were linked to community social concerns programs from the ACLU to Planned Parenthood, from soup kitchens to shelters. Two weekly reflection periods with a ministerial student provided opportunity for them to analyze their experience in the light of Unitarian Universalist values. It was a powerful personal and social experience for him, one that ought to be replicated.

Education can be the last refuge of the scoundrel if it stops with values clarification and does not provide the means for embodiment. It is unethical to fire the moral imagination of people and leave them without the means to act on their world as change agents. In the words of a soldier in the Spanish Civil War, "Those who have principles but no programs turn out in the end to have no principles."

This is convictional faith. Whole religious people live under an urgency to act out their convictions. The prophets were people who not only discerned their times but acted on them. They were not persons who merely pointed out the injustice of their day as objective bystanders; they were subjective actors in the history of their times.

D. H. Lawrence once wrote, "Whatever the queer little word ("God") means, it means something we can none of us quite get away from, or at; something connected with our deepest explosions." A personal experience graphically demonstrates the point. I was visiting a class of three- and four-year-olds to talk about the flaming chalice as a symbol of our faith. We sang "This Liberal Light of Mine" lustily. I spoke about the flaming chalice, its history and meaning. All very wise, I thought, and I said "Amen." The service over (so I thought), I placed the cover on the sterno can to extinguish the chalice flame and complete the ceremony, paused, ready to rejoin the adult congregation, when with a gigantic *pop* the can cover flew to the ceiling—to the astonishment not only of the three- and four-year-olds, but of me, one who fancies himself at times a technician of the sacred. How miracles abound if only I, if only we, can harness that latent energy.

∾

Rev. Dr. Richard S. Gilbert is the parish minister of the First Unitarian Church of Rochester, New York.

Spreading
the Good News

REV. DR. M. SUSAN HARLOW

I find it striking that several entering theological students at
Meadville/Lombard Theological School report having stumbled
upon Unitarian Universalism by accident. Each student recounts
how she/he was searching for a religious community yet did not
know that a Unitarian Universalist congregation might be nearby
or that she or he would find fellow travelers for an open religious
search for meaning and values in such a church. Story after story
contains how once discovering a Unitarian Universalist congregation each student came to a sense of having arrived "home." This
newly found congregation provided acceptance for who each individual was; a community engaged in searching, exploring, and
growing; and a worshipping community affirming active work for
justice and social transformation.

Why do these students report that it was an "accident"
through which they ended up in a Unitarian Universalist congregation? How is it that Unitarian Universalism is such a well-kept
secret in many communities? How might religious education for
children, youth, and adults assist UUs in discerning the "good
news" of the liberal religious heritage? How might congregational
learning opportunities assist UUs in reaching out to those searching for a religious community of like-minded people? How might
religious education enable each child, youth, and adult to plumb
the depths of religious living?

As we move into the twenty-first century, liberal religious
education faces new challenges. Many of our methods and under-

girding philosophies were developed for a very different social, cultural, and religious context. As leaders, we need to explore these contexts in order better to chart future directions for our work and ministries.

Historical Forces Shaping Current Context

The twentieth century experienced enormous changes in the advances of technology, scientific knowledge, health care, travel, communications, standards of living for the United States and other "First World" countries, and in the unprecedented capacity to destroy the earth through nuclear weapons and environmental degradation. In *American Education: The Metropolitan Experience, 1876–1980,* Lawrence A. Cremin tells us that during this century, the United States moved from a rural nation to an urban and metropolitan nation. In 1890, two-thirds of the population of 63 million lived in small towns, villages, and rural areas. In 1980, three-fourths of 227 million U.S. residents lived in cities. Transportation capacities moved from the Model T Ford with its lack of shock absorbers which my father learned to drive in 1925 to the space shuttle that returns to earth after its flights out of the earth's atmosphere to be used again in the next space mission. In 1980 my mother took her first and only airline flight at age 59. (She decided she liked being in a car on terra firma a whole lot better.) I regularly fly from Chicago to Phoenix, New York, Washington, San Francisco, Los Angeles, Orlando, Boston, Salt Lake City, and other destinations for conferences, meetings, and to visit close and long-term friends who live in different cities and regions of the country. Computer and communications technology makes global communication available at such speed that the activists in 1989 protesting the Chinese government's domestic policies in Tiananmen Square could send facsimiles to Western news sources as the government troops moved to arrest the students and other protesters. During the U.S. Gulf War against Iraq, the Cable News Network (CNN) reporters covered the effects of U.S. bombing raids on Baghdad as they occurred.

Too often our discussions of religious education center on the church school and the interaction of a teacher with an individual learner. This approach to religious education was developed during the nineteenth and early twentieth centuries. The rationale for the Sunday school and classroom teaching originated when the United States was a rural nation, transportation was by horse-drawn carriage or railroad, communication consisted of hand-written letters that took months to arrive, and life was lived on a radically different scale than that of today. This approach to religious education was developed when the congregation was supported by an ecology of multiple institutions engaged in the religious education enterprise. Because this ecology was in place, religious education theorists and practitioners could emphasize innovations in certain areas of the enterprise and take for granted the supporting networks sustaining religious education.

John Westerhoff, former Duke Divinity School professor of Christian education, in his book *Will Our Children Have Faith?* identified six social institutions involved in religious education that were present during the first third of the twentieth century: community, family, public schools, church, media, and Sunday school. First, the typical United States community was relatively homogeneous, with most embodying the Protestant Christian worldview. Other ethnic and religious groups such as Roman Catholics, Jews, Amish, and others lived in their own homogeneous communities. Second, the family was essentially extended and less mobile than it is today. Westerhoff writes, "Most persons were nurtured, married, and died within a hundred miles of their birth."

Third, the public schools essentially reflected a Protestant Christian worldview with daily rituals of prayer, Bible reading, and textbooks that included lessons on Christian morals and religious values. Historian and former president of Meadville/Lombard Sidney E. Mead has noted, in *The Lively Experiment: The Shaping of Christianity in America,* that the state and its public schools have always taught religion as a way to foster shared values that support the nation and the state. In this way, the public schools in the United States took the place of the "established" or state-supported church. The Catholic community recognized this Protestant worldview early on and set up parallel Catholic parochial school systems.

The fourth institution engaged in religious education was the church. Each homogeneous community had local religious congregations that reflected its relatively stable neighborhoods. Families knew each other at church and in the neighborhood. The local church was a major focus of social life, and children, youth, and adults spent many hours at church functions, worship, potlucks and church dinners, educational events, choir activities and other musical events, and community outreach. Westerhoff observes that "persons were socialized in the shared understandings and ways of their particular denomination" through these church involvements. In *The Shaping of Protestant Education,* William Bean Kennedy, retired professor of practical theology at Union Theological Seminary in New York, observes that the ordained clergy also oversaw the religious education that took place within the church proper. Through sermons and teaching the catechism, often during the public worship service, the "learned" clergy instructed the youth and adults in the doctrines, beliefs, and practices of that church's tradition. In this manner, the clergy articulated the particular theological understandings of the church's heritage. Parents were able to derive deeper meanings for the catechetical questions and answers through listening to the minister's sermon. Through this sermon-based adult instruction, the parents could answer religious questions their children might have and engage in home-centered religious instruction.

The fifth institution engaged in religious education was the media. During the early years of the twentieth century, the primary media influencing public opinion were newspapers and periodicals, and later, radio. These sources provided the primary "entertainment" in homes and contained reporting and articles on religious themes and topics as central components.

Embedded in this context, the sixth institution involved in religious education was the Sunday, or church, school. This institution was "adjunct" to the local congregation in that it was lay led and served the function of teaching children the Bible and the distinctive traditions of the denomination, thereby bringing them into church membership as they grew older. The Sunday school, in its early years, did not provide educational opportunities for those already committed to membership and, in this way, Kennedy observes, made sustained efforts in adult education problematic. Westerhoff points to benefits to women, however, in that the emphasis on lay leadership opened up opportunities for women to become teachers and school superintendents. In the 1930s, with the move toward professionalization of teaching in public schools, women also found employment in newly created congregational educational staffs as directors of religious education. The "learned" clergy rarely became involved in the Sunday schools because lay men and women provided the primary leadership.

Today, this ecology of institutions engaged in the religious education enterprise is no longer in place. Many of the changes that have dismantled this ecology were extremely beneficial in eradicating the rigidity of church structures and oppressive cultural and religious practices. Nonetheless, the functions of these institutions were foundational to the whole process of religious education. Today, there are fewer and fewer institutions taking responsibility for religious learning or values and spiritual formation. Currently, the church school is perhaps the sole context in which children actively can pursue religious meaning and experience. The congregational service of worship is the sole context in which the majority of adults participate in religious growth and learning and ethical discernment. As we enter the twenty-first century, we need to move our attention from its exclusivity on one institution—the church school. We need to pay attention to the broad undertaking of how people, young and old, are formed in faith. We need to pay attention to the ways children, youth, and adults can be engaged in a lifelong process of religious growth and learning in community, rooted in Unitarian Universalist Purposes and Principles.

Approaches to Educational Ministry Design

Pioneering Unitarian and Universalist religious educators, such as Sophia Lyon Fahs and Angus H. MacLean, responded to the needs of their day and opened up unprecedented possibilities for liberal religious education. Building on her experiences at the Union School of Religion and the Riverside Church in New York City, Fahs contributed significantly to the design and production of the

New Beacon Series in Religious Education. In *The Unitarians and Universalists,* historian David Robinson argues that this collection of religious education materials helped bring about denominational "reinvigoration" and "renaissance" at a dire period in the life of the American Unitarian Association. During Fahs's eight years as part-time editor of children's materials, she produced fifteen books and teachers' guides that emphasized the inherent religious nature of the child and allowed each boy and girl to be the discoverer of his or her own religious meanings and truth.

Universalist Angus MacLean, professor of religious education and, later, dean at St. Lawrence Theological School in Canton, New York, was extremely influential as teacher and mentor to generations of Universalist ministers and religious educators. From 1928 to 1960, MacLean helped parish ministers comprehend that lifelong religious growth and learning was fundamental to their congregational ministries and that each minister needed to engage in religious education leadership for all ages. MacLean believed firmly that one's religious values must be operative in one's whole life and not present only in one's speech. He wrote in *The Method Is the Message,*

> Such values as we are concerned with cannot be communicated except as they are set in operation, given life, in the human relations in which teachers and taught are involved, that they cannot be, that they have no existence except as forms of human relations. Love exists only when someone is loved. Freedom exits when relations worthy of that name govern communication and action between persons. Such values are communicated only when "live," if I may borrow and somewhat distort a TV term. This is why I have so often said that a faith which is so largely a faith of dynamic ethical and intellectual values should make method the heart of its curriculum.

MacLean held that religious education occurred best when the teacher and student were engaged in "walking the walk," learning about democracy by participating in public and democratic processes, learning about religious freedom by venturing together in inquiry and critical questioning. He made pains to declare that he was not dismissing content or administration or other aspects of religious education. In emphasizing the "method," MacLean was advocating that the best teacher was one who lived what he or she was teaching.

Fahs, MacLean, and other Universalist, Unitarian, and Unitarian Universalist religious educators have provided pioneering leadership and given shape to present ministries of liberal religious education. We stand on the foundations constructed by these forebears who responded to the context and concerns of their day. What are the needs of our day? In what areas do we need pioneering work today?

Contemporary Challenges to Liberal Religious Education

I have identified at least five areas that need attention in the coming years as we chart the pathway of liberal religious education in the new millennium. First, we need to take religious education out of the Sunday school "box" and engage in exploring ways that the whole religious community is both the teachers and the learners. It has been quite enjoyable to read articles, pamphlets, books, and other materials written by Unitarian Universalist religious educators in order to prepare my thoughts for this paper. At various points in the past, UU leaders have called our attention to needs that are present with us still. Jean Starr Williams gave an address to the Unitarian Sunday School Society in 1979, entitled "Moving from Church School Classes to Living in a Religious Community." In this article, Williams, director of the Section of Education of the UUA from 1976 to 1980, argued, "Let us move away from the Sunday school classroom paradigm toward a paradigm of living in religious community." Unitarian Universalists had great success in developing content for religious education that allowed each child to be "an open, questioning, exploring, feeling, human being." However, Williams believed that the use of the classroom paradigm thwarted the potential of liberal religious education. The classroom paradigm isolated the children from the adults, inhibiting the child's sense of belonging to the community and stunting the adult's ability to grasp what it means "to live, . . .

companioned by the grace and glory of all the world's potential." Williams called for religious education to provide

> experiences which challenge us all to serve and know how to be served; which call us to struggle that all persons may experience justice; experiences which serve as well in expressing our rage at injustice, our devotion to truth, our repulsion from war, our urge to play our own part in creating a world at peace.

When we engage with one another in living as a religious community the walls separating the children from the "real" church come tumbling down. When we understand religious education as requiring all ages to live religiously, deeply grounded in the mystery of life and committed to values of justice and love, we move our task away from hoping that our children will grow to shape a better world than we were capable of shaping. We work together to shape our collective lives as a religious people and strive to leave a world of justice and love to the "seventh generation" of those who follow us and inhabit the earth.

The second challenge for religious education in the twenty-first century is that it must assist all ages in valuing "life." We live in a world where death is often the operative value. This is exemplified in the social, political, and cultural forces that foster physical violence, war as the solution to global conflicts, and the numbing of the soul through mass consumption, substance abuse, or solitary viewing of television and surfing the Internet. In *The American Evasion of Philosophy: A Genealogy of Pragmatism,* Harvard professor Cornel West categorizes this contemporary setting as a "world-weary period of pervasive cynicism, nihilisms, terrorisms, and possible extermination." He observes that "there is a longing for norms and values that can make a difference, a yearning for principled resistance and struggle that can change our desperate plight." In *Thinking about God: An Introduction to Theology,* German feminist theologian Dorothee Soelle observes that we live in a "culture of analgesics" that fosters a "narcotizing of life." The old ways of speaking about religion are increasingly problematic and ineffective. For Soelle, the cultural context and the impotent theological constructs provide "an opportunity to speak of God [the ground of life and its goal] in a concrete way, in a way related to praxis [the way in which one lives]." This opportunity to craft an existential faith and to critically explore "where we come from and where we are going" means, for Soelle, "bearing witness to God in a world dominated by death and oriented on death."

Liberal religious education needs to assist us all in bearing witness to life in face of all the forces that make wholeness, health, and quality of life problematic. An important component of our work will be to enhance the life of the gathered community of individuals so that each congregation pulsates with dynamic aliveness and is deeply involved in a free and responsible search for truth. This search requires the involvement of children, youth, and adults. All ages need to engage in studying the wisdom of the ages; the historical foundations of a liberal religious identity; the struggles throughout history to find theological, mythical, and symbolic interpretations for life's mysteries; and the life stories of women, men, and children who lived out of their religious convictions and commitments to make a better world for all. British philosopher of education R. S. Peters has defined education as a process that "involves the intentional transmission of what is worthwhile," a handing on to the next generations of our values. Given the global changes that have occurred in the twentieth century, many of us lack clarity as to what is "worthwhile." We ask questions such as: What is the point of this life I have? As long as I am growing, learning, and engaged in a search for truth, why do I need a religious community? Since Unitarian Universalists are open to all knowledge and experiences, are there any guides to assist me in making decisions and in striving to live a responsible life? Identifying what is "worthwhile" will engage all ages in constructing religious meaning, values, principles, commitments, and convictions to enable Unitarian Universalists to live full and authentic lives of service to one another and the world.

The third challenge to liberal religious education is that often we value "civility" over authentic human encounters and relationships. Well trained in etiquette and uncomfortable with conflict, we create distances between one another. Liberal religious education needs to assist the religious community through providing opportunities and processes whereby individuals within the congregation could develop deep interpersonal interactions of care, accompaniment, and challenge. These interactions would be of such quality and substance that the many walls that isolate one human from another would be torn down in these sacred encounters. Healthy relationships—between adults and children, adults and youth, youth and children, children and children, and adults and adults—would develop where alienation and segregation had been the case. Transformed by experiences of deep human connection within the congregation and equipped with skills in authentic communication, liberal religious people could provide leadership to create opportunities for such human to human interactions in the larger public of town, village, neighborhood, city, and world.

A fourth challenge to liberal religious education is to understand that worship is a central educating component of what it means to live religiously in community. In *Religious Education as a Second Language*, Gabriel Moran, professor of religious education at New York University, observes that classrooms and schools are excellent institutions for learning "about" religion. They are not the most conducive for learning "how" to live religiously. Instead of being the primary setting for religious education, our classrooms and church schools would understand themselves as auxiliary components of an integrated approach to education. As the predominant locus for the whole gathered people, the weekly service of worship as an educational setting needs our primary attention in terms of understanding the learning dynamics at work and intentional planning and designs for effective religious education.

And finally, a fifth challenge is to go beyond a focus on individual learning and growth. The individual is of infinite value, yet the global needs for moral witness and service far surpass the capacities of any individual. Liberal religious education must assist individuals and congregations to engage in the struggles to transform the injustices in the world and the violations inflicted upon planet earth. As long as any one human being's inherent worth and dignity is denied, our own humanity is desecrated. The defilement of planet earth becomes diminishment of our quality of life. Life demands that we move beyond our orderly human constructions of schooling, classrooms, and church buildings and engage with learning in and with nature. Justice demands that we learn from those living under domination and dehumanization and that we join in the struggle for transformation. Feminist theologian Rosemary Radford Ruether has observed that we live at a moment in time that is utterly unprecedented in human history. The human capacity and involvement in planetary destruction is occurring at such a pace that earth may not be inhabitable for any life form in the near future. These times call for radically new ways of thinking, sustained action in creating new ways of living on earth, and deep connection to the ground of all being and the source of hope and vision.

The priestly writer of the Hebrew book of Deuteronomy writes of God, "I have set before you life and death, blessings and curses. Choose life so that you and your descendants may live" (Deuteronomy 30:19). Liberal religious education has before it the ability to help us "choose life." May it rise to the challenge.

≈

Rev. Dr. M. Susan Harlow is the Angus MacLean associate professor of religious education at Meadville/Lombard Theological School.

Learning Types
and Their Needs

DANIEL HARPER

When I started mulling over the questions for the Essex Conversations, an old problem came back to haunt me. Why was it that some of our UU youth seem (to me, at least) to be further along in their faith development than some of our UU adults? As I reflected on this odd little problem, I began to see that the model of UU religious education that I inherited may not be a sufficient model for meeting the needs of all the learners I encounter in my programs. The more I reflected on the insufficiency of my narrow model, the more I realized how I, as a religious educator, was inclined to limit my conversations on religious education to conversations with other religious educators. And gradually, I began to realize that, if I were to move beyond the confines of my limited model, I needed to engage in conversations with a broader range of people, including parish ministers, lay leaders, theologians, scholars, families, and others.

But let me begin at the beginning. Let's go back to the problems with the narrow model of religious education I inherited.

In the past twenty or so years, developmental psychology has been one of the only concepts used by UU religious educators to describe learners and, therefore, to determine what material to present to a given learner. One of the fundamental insights of our progressive philosophy of education is that as children grow older, they are capable of learning different things. In the context of the Sunday school, this represents a huge advance over the nineteenth-century system of Sunday school teaching where there was one lesson for all grades. Sophia Fahs, our greatest UU religious educator, believed in developing closely graded curricula based on her understanding of developmental psychology. Fahs made extensive use of the developmental insights of Piaget, according to Robert L'H. Miller in "The Educational Philosophy of the New Beacon Series in Religious Education."

In my observations of individual learners, I find that developmental psychology does not give a fully adequate description of learners for the purposes of religious education. In *Religion in Childhood and Adolescence,* Kenneth Hyde writes, "there are not sufficient grounds for rejecting the idea of stages as a basis for the study for religious development, providing it is used as a performance rather than a competence theory and used with some caution." Referring only to developmental psychology, I should observe a fairly clear progression of educational tasks based primarily on the chronological age and/or developmental stage of the learner. Yet my observations of the real world show this is not so. For example, adults who come into Unitarian Universalism from unchurched backgrounds face some of the same educational tasks as young children.

Recently, I have found it useful to consider not only the developmental trajectory of the individual, a trajectory that considers the individual in comparison to idealized normative developmental stages, but also the trajectory of the individual in relation to a given religious community. John Cleverly and D. C. Phillips, in their book *Visions of Childhood,* wrote about defects in Piaget's work, pointing out that

> Piaget tended to regard the child as a solitary inquirer, as a young scientist engaged in single-handedly building his or her own cognitive structures so as to come into equilibrium with the environment. Other workers . . . have emphasized more the role of social forces in shaping the child's cognitive growth. For children do not develop alone; parents, teachers, older siblings, and peers indicate to the child what mental accommodations are likely to be fruitful, and they discourage the acceptance of other conceptualizations.

In *Growing Up Religious,* sociologist Robert Wuthnow says that "effective religious socialization comes about through embedded practices." An individual is embedded in a given religious community, and his/her faith development or moral development must be considered in light of the socialization of the individual within the religious community.

Let me give you an example. Let's say you grew up as a Unitarian Universalist, and you are now a middle-aged adult and have reached a fairly high stage on some standardized, objective faith development scale. But now you decide to become a Zen Buddhist monk. From the frame of reference of the religious community you are now joining, you might be considered a pretty special person (or not), but let's face it, you haven't memorized any *sutras,* you can't sit *zazen* for more than fifteen minutes, and *koans* give you headaches. I argue that similar things happen to people who come as adults to our UU religious communities. The problem may be especially acute for unchurched people; they may have as much difficulty listening to an entire sermon as the average seven-year-old UU kid, because they simply don't have enough practice.

I began to believe that developmental stage of the individual and socialization of the individual in the religious community do not necessarily have a strong correlation. For a given individual, the developmental stage may or may not predict relationship to and embeddedness within a given religious community. Within the context of a living religious community, developmental stage alone is an insufficient descriptor of a learner.

What I needed was a typology of learners that would allow me to better understand the needs of different persons so that educational programs could be tailored to meet their needs. To do that, instead of thinking in terms of a linear model (as most developmental models do), I began thinking in terms of two dimensions, a graph with an x-axis and a y-axis. Eugene Roehlkepartain uses a two-axis model for describing faith maturity in his book *The Teaching Church: Moving Christian Education to Center Stage.* While my model differs in most respects from Roehlkepartain's model, his two-axis model strongly influenced my thinking.

The x-axis represents developmental stage, and the y-axis represents what we could call degree of socialization, or perhaps faith maturity, or depth of faith. The phrase "faith maturity" comes from Roehlkepartain, who remarks that "any attempt to synthesize faith into a measurable concept is tricky at best, and treacherous at worst. Any construct inevitably reflects the perspective of those involved." And, inevitably, it cannot account for the nuances and specific emphases of everyone across the theological spectrum. The peculiar theological diversity of Unitarian Universalism makes our task particularly treacherous when it comes to talking about faith. The concept of degree of socialization is perhaps less problematic, though to my knowledge it has received little or no attention from UU writers on religious education.

But how to describe the position on the y-axis, the degree of socialization? Based on my observations of learners, I thought it was pretty safe to start with what I called new learners, people with a low degree of socialization to (and embeddedness in) a UU religious community. The 1997 Youth Programs Review Committee used a typology of new, mid-, and deep UUs: "Of necessity, much of our adult programming is aimed at new UUs. But our youth who have participated in YRUU have moved past that stage and need opportunities for religious depth . . . , opportunities which we have not been offering."

As new learners progress, they face a number of discrete educational tasks as they become socialized into a UU community, and eventually they may progress to becomes deep learners. I have found these educational tasks useful as markers, as a rough form of assessing where a learner stands on this axis.

This is a working model, developed to meet my needs as a UU religious educator. To be more useful, we need to better define what happens as someone moves along the y-axis. However, the model has helped me better understand how youth can appear to be further along in their faith development than some adults. The model has helped me to understand the conversion experience of older learners who join UU congregations, and how some long-term members gradually drift away from a UU congregation. Above all, it has helped me place children, youth, and adults in a unified model of lifespan religious growth and learning.

I'd like to introduce you to this descriptive method by presenting portraits (or very short case studies, if you will) of individuals who are characteristic of the different types of learners.

Young Children: Anne

Anne is a bright, complex girl who has just turned five. She comes to church with her parents nearly every week, and attends the first fifteen minutes of Sunday morning worship as do all children. Anne used to have trouble sitting through those fifteen minutes, but lately she has made real progress in learning how to sit still and be attentive. Her parents tell me that now she really gets something out of those fifteen minutes. Anne exemplifies a type we can call "young children."

Young children have to learn all the little things we take for granted: how to come to church once a week, how to sit still, and how to be respectful of older people ("no running in coffee hour!"). They have to learn what to do when it's time to sing a hymn (and what a hymn is), when it's time to pray or meditate, and when it's time to go to Sunday school classes. Young children have to learn how to do religion, learn the basic tasks of being in a specific religious community.

Children: Leslie and Carol

Leslie and Carol stand out in my memory as two paradigms of older children. They were best buddies and started coming to the church when they were each eight. They quickly learned where to go and what to do Sunday mornings. They quickly learned lots of stuff about Unitarian Universalism, Bible times, and world religions, and they liked to share their knowledge. By the time I left that congregation, Leslie and Carol were ten and often sat with each other and apart from their parents when they were in church. They were just beginning to find out that they had individual religious identities, separate from their families. Call this type of learner "children."

Children face two main educational tasks. First, they must continue to learn how to do religion; for example, how to sit through a whole sermon and maybe even get a little something out of it. Second, they are ready to learn about our heritage and the sources we draw inspiration from: What was it like to live in biblical times? If we traveled back in time to meet great Unitarians and Universalists, what would they be like? Some older children, like Leslie and Carol, may face a third educational task: discerning who they are as religious individuals. But children concentrate on learning about our heritage and how to do religion.

New Youth: Mary

In addition to long-term and deep youth, there are youth who are new to Unitarian Universalism. Mary, a friend of Bob's, began coming to youth group a few months ago. She hasn't come to a Sunday morning worship service yet. She's beginning to have some idea what this faith tradition stands for, but for now she's concentrating on finding her place within the small community of the youth group. Call Mary and those like her new youth.

New youth, while developmentally different, face much the same tasks that young children and children face. New youth have to figure out how this community works and how to do religion, and they have to learn something about the faith tradition and its heritage. According to the 1997 Youth Programs Review Committee, "Anecdotal evidence suggests that many religious educators, no doubt overburdened with the younger ages, continue to give a low priority to . . . the congregation's youth." Many people have noted that while we religious educators often do not adequately help new youth and long-term youth with the educational tasks that immediately face them, the youth themselves often do a stunning job of helping each other.

Long-term Youth: David

David, who is quiet and thoughtful, grew up in his church; he recently turned fifteen. He knows a fair amount about our faith heritage. He has begun to discern his religious identity: his individual religious identity, who he is in the faith community, and his role as a religious individual in the wider world. He has just begun to question why we do religion the way we do it, and he is struggling to find words that are adequate to this task. David exemplifies long-term youth, youth who have been a part of a UU faith community for some time.

Long-term youth have one main educational task: They have to figure out who they are. This task has at least three parts: They have to figure out who they are as religious individuals, who they are as part of a faith community, and who they are as religious persons in the wider world. As long-term youth wrestle with these questions, they often need to go back and learn more about our heritage. Like David, long-term youth may begin theological reflection as they grow into their UU faith, or they may discern that they really don't belong in the UU faith community. But discernment remains the chief task of long-term youth.

Deep Youth: Bob

Bob is seventeen, already a gifted teacher, indeed one of my best Sunday school teachers. He has already made a preliminary reckoning about who he is as a religious being. This year, he has been teaching the course "Why Do Bad Things Happen?" to fifth and sixth graders. While teaching this course, he has begun to reflect on why we UUs do religion the way we do, and he has had to come up with words to talk about what he's been reflecting on. This reflection is leading him to a deeper understanding of himself as a religious being and of his role in the wider world. I call young people like Bob *deep youth*, the deep indicating perhaps the depth of their growing embeddedness in their faith community, or the depth of their faith maturity.

Deep youth face new educational tasks. Long-term youth may have begun theological reflection, but deep youth have started to apply their beginning theological reflection to their lives. Appropriately nurtured, this in turn will lead to further theological reflection and further application.

Just as there are three types of youth, there are three types of adults: new, long-term, and deep. Again, there are distinct developmental differences, but in terms of the dimension of depth of faith, there are marked similarities between long-term youth and long-term adults, deep youth and deep adults.

New Adults: Diane

New adults come in at least three different varieties: those who have come to Unitarian Universalism from another faith tradition, those who come from no faith tradition, and those who stay with us for a while before moving on to another faith tradition.

"Come-outers" have come out of another faith tradition into Unitarian Universalism. These people constitute a large number of our adult members. Raised as Catholics, Protestants, Jews, etc., they already know how to do religion in some form. But their initial educational task is to learn how Unitarian Universalists do religion—little things like hearing members of the congregation reading their part of responsive readings in unison, or getting used to unfamiliar words sung to all-too-familiar hymn tunes. While come-outers face educational tasks similar to young children, there are two main differences: developmental differences and the complication of unlearning old habits.

Diane went to church all of two or three times as a child. When she reached adulthood, she felt some need for a spiritual home, but didn't know where to look. A romantic partner introduced her to Unitarian Universalism. She pretty much liked what she saw there. If asked what her religion is, she will probably respond that she's a Unitarian Universalist. But although she likes being able to identify herself a part of a faith community, she doesn't yet understand what it means to be a part of a congregation. For example, why do people waste a perfectly good sunny Sunday morning listening to a sermon? Diane has not yet learned some of the subtleties of doing religion.

Diane is a "come-inner." Come-inners weren't part of any faith tradition and have come in to Unitarian Universalism. Like young children, new youth, and come-outers, they must first learn how to do religion. In addition to developmental differences, adult come-inners lack the parental support of young children, the peer group support of new youth, or the background in religion of come-outers.

"Pass-throughers" stay for a time in a UU congregation, but wind up moving on to another faith tradition. Peter had been raised a mainline Protestant, discovered a UU congregation, and became very active there for a couple of years. As he better discerned who he was as a religious being, he discovered that he was not a UU. He went on to help found an evangelical Christian congregation. While we can't predict who is going to wind up being a pass-througher, recognizing their existence points out that we need to offer new adults opportunities to discern their religious identity.

Long-Term Adults: John

Long-term adults are quite similar to long-term youth. While they may become deep adults, often they remain just long-term adults, somewhat active in their congregation but avoiding greater depth of faith through discernment or theological reflection. John goes to worship services once or twice a month, does volunteer work in the congregation about once a month, and gives money each year, but that's as involved he gets. He doesn't demand much from his faith and doesn't want his congregation to demand much from him. Parish ministers and religious educators may ignore the educational needs of long-term adults like John because such individuals are so undemanding. The best way to reach such people educationally is through Sunday morning worship services and/or through rites of passage (marriages, child dedications, memorial services)—and here the educational role of the parish minister is key.

Deep Adults: Kathleen

When I knew Kathleen, she worked as the director of a child care center. She taught the preschool group in the Sunday school, served on her congregation's governing board, and had held many other leadership roles. Worship services and sermons fed her soul, and she only taught every other week so she could attend worship services. At the same time, she was deeply committed to teaching, and it, too, fed her soul. She also committed herself to promoting nonviolence and multiculturalism in and out of the congregation and saw her commitment as an outgrowth of her deep faith as a UU. She told me that the conversations she frequently had with others in the congregation (including the children in her preschool class)—about death, the meaning of life, deep conversations about everything under the sun—were in some sense life-altering and in turn continued to keep her deeply involved in the congregation.

Like Bob, the deep youth, Kathleen practiced her religion in various ways. This led her to reflect on who she was as a person of faith, and that reflection led back to further involvement in the faith community and the world. As you would guess, deep adults face similar educational tasks as do deep youth: theological reflection, practicing their faith, further discernment of who they are as persons of faith.

Having seen my descriptive model in action, you have probably figured out the five tasks I have used as rough markers of socialization into the UU religious community (movement along the y-axis). I do not claim that my list of educational tasks is complete; again, these are educational tasks that I have found useful as markers that help me know where a learner is along the axis of embeddedness or faith maturity.

First task: Learn basic UU religious skills; learn how we UUs do religion. Anne has learned how to come to church once a week, what a worship service is, what a hymn is, that we get religious inspiration from certain books and certain sets of words, and so on.

Second: Learn what it means to be a UU; learn and explore our faith tradition, our UU identity. Leslie and Carol learned lots of stuff about our Jewish and Christian heritages, other world religions we draw inspiration from, and our own UU tradition. Probably this task comes to mind first when thinking of the tasks of religious education.

Third: Learn to discern who we are as persons of faith, as religious beings. This task consists of at least three parts: discerning your religious identity as an individual member of this faith community, discerning your role within your faith community (which will change over time), and discerning your role in the wider world as a faithful person.

Fourth: Engage in theological reflection; think about how you do religion and how to find the words to talk about what you think. We often cede this educational task to the theological schools.

Fifth: Having discerned who you are as a religious being and gone on to theological reflection, establish and refine your religious practices. You might learn new techniques of prayer or meditation, learn a new role in the local congregation, engage in social action or learn how to find a job consistent with your faith.

These last three tasks can become an ongoing cycle leading to continued growth and deepening of faith. As you refine your religious practices, this leads you to further reflect on who you are as a religious being, and this in turn will lead to renewed theological reflection. This reflection/praxis/discernment cycle arises from the tension between theory and praxis, where theory and praxis are understood more in terms of philosophical hermeneutics. In his book, *Philosophical Profiles,* Richard J. Bernstein says, "One of the most important and central claims in Hans-Georg Gadamer's philosophical hermeneutics is that all understanding involves not only interpretation, but also application."

As we religious educators assist learners to face each educational task, we can begin to see whom we can consult for help. Parents and parish ministers can help us as we assist learners facing the task of learning how to do religion. Historians and other scholars of religion will give us invaluable aid as we plan to teach our religious heritage. Parents, parish and lay leaders, and youth advisors can help as we assist learners with discerning who they are as religious individuals; theologians, parish ministers, and lay leaders can help with learners who are discerning their roles in the faith community and the wider world. And, obviously, theologians will be a great help as we help people learn to engage in theological reflection. Whether or not the typology I have outlined in this essay proves useful, it is important that we religious educators continue to reach out to ministers, parents, theologians, scholars, and so on so that we may improve our ability to meet the needs of learners in our UU congregations.

It is my belief that we religious educators have become isolated from (and perhaps have isolated ourselves from) parish ministers, theologians, and scholars of religion. A funny thing: These groups all share a common concern for the religious growth and learning of individuals in our congregations. Why don't we religious educators engage in more conversations with parish ministers, theologians, and others? Think of Sophia Fahs and her groundbreaking work in curriculum development from 1938 to about 1960. As she developed curricula, Fahs engaged in conversations with theologians, biblical scholars, educational psychologists, religious educators, parish ministers, and others. Fahs's successors, at least up to Hugo Holleroth, did the same. Fahs even reached out beyond the tiny worlds of Unitarianism and Universalism and tried to engage other religious liberals in conversation.

But I believe we religious educators must do more than engage in conversations, enjoyable as those may be. We must also begin to question, and to modify, our own educational practice. For example, most UU religious education programs rely heavily on the technique of schooling for educating children and adults. But a person facing the task of discerning who he/she is as a religious individual will not be well served by yet another class. A retreat would be a better option, or perhaps the religious education department and the parish minister could sponsor discernment committees, similar to the clearness committees some Quakers use, or the mid-program review committees used in some theological schools. As individuals discern their roles within a faith community, schools and classes may help, but an apprenticeship or mentoring program might also work well. Howard Gardner, writing about children in *The Unschooled Mind*, says, "It is highly desirable for children to observe competent adults or older peers at work—or at play." And, I would add, at the task of doing religion. As we engage in continued praxis, and in a theoretical dialogue with our various colleagues, we may find that closely graded schools based solely on a developmental model of learning are not the be-all and end-all of religious education.

In calling for us to move beyond a paradigm of classrooms in schools, I am only echoing what others have said and continue to say. In *Fashion Me a People*, Maria Harris writes that one "misunderstanding gripping the educational imagination is the false identification of education with only one of its forms: schooling. In this view, the participants in education are always instructors or learners; the place of education is necessarily a school (or a setting that replicates a school); the stuff of education is books and chalkboards and lesson plans; and the process involved is mental activity."

Even within the context of schooling, we religious educators should question our current practices. Are our curricula based on the finest scholarship available, and have they benefited from the insights of the best liberal theologians? Do our teaching strategies meet the real needs of all learners (as opposed to perceived and/or politically expedient needs)? Do we support all learners as they face educational tasks? Do we have adequate assessment practices, such that we can know where learners stand? Do we fully realize that religious education programs cannot be separated from other congregational functions (at least, if we want to ensure real socialization into the religious community)? If we answer "no" to any of these questions, we are moving away from open conversation and toward the isolation and ghettoization of religious education. I want us to move toward open conversation.

I like to think that, along with individual conscience and freedom, cooperation and interdependence lie at the core of our UU faith tradition. It is my dream that in this next generation of UU religious education, we religious educators will reach out to—and deepen our conversations with—children, youth, and adults; parish ministers, theologians, and scholars; parents and guardians; lay leaders; and the wider faith community. In so doing, we can only get better at helping each other meet the challenges of our respective educational tasks and allowing others to help us. We can only get better as religious educators when we work together in a community of learners/instructors, a community committed to the continual religious growth and learning of all members of that community.

$\sim$

Daniel Harper is the director of religious education at First Parish in Lexington, Massachusetts.

What Youth Want

LOGAN HARRIS

You will make all kinds of mistakes, but as long as you are generous and true, and also fierce, you cannot hurt the world or even seriously distress her. She was made to be wooed and won by youth.

—*Winston Churchill*, Roving Commission

I did not grow up with a church community. I slept in on Sundays, basking in the glow of drowsy suburbia. I never really thought that church could be a good thing. "Church" was some sort of hellish place to which my friends were dragged off against their wills, taken away early from slumber parties for. I was thrust into adolescence having never gone to Sunday school, and I was pretty happy about it. As the child of a woman who was raised Unitarian and who currently describes herself as a "progressive independent thinker", and a man who was raised Catholic and now puts his faith in science and not much else, for most of my life I had no organized religion. Perhaps I was never religiously educated. In any case, I don't have very much to say about my experiences with religious education. I attended a local YRUU youth group for a very short time, and getting involved with Unitarian Universalism at the local level just never seemed as intriguing as working at the district and continental levels. It was through district and continental activities that I found my religion.

So if I can't reflect on my long history with religious education, what I can do is discuss and describe what I needed in a youth group that I didn't get from mine. But I wouldn't dream of trying to represent the YRUU community through just my opinions and the way that I viewed youth groups; I've talked to the members of my youth group (if I should even call it mine), members of youth groups in surrounding areas whom I've worked with on our district Youth Adult Committee, and a few other youth who I know from out of state. I tried to clump this potpourri of opinions and ideas together as best I could, but, alas, we youth are fickle creatures. Without a doubt there were some sentiments shared by almost everyone I talked to, but there was also some disagreement. Anyway, it's all here, or most of it's here, and I tried to show both sides, or all 50,000 sides, of the issue. I heard a lot from the youth I talked to. I heard about advisers, I heard about social action, about youth services and worships. I also heard about the times everyone laughed so hard that they spit soda across the room, and about the dance parties, and about the times everyone cried until they couldn't talk. What I learned from it all was what is important to youth when it comes to a youth group. And I learned something about why I didn't stay involved in my youth group, what I felt it was missing. And part of me wished that I had stayed involved, that I had evolved with my youth group, because they seem to have created something that is wonderful for all of them.

If I can't give my local youth group credit for keeping me involved in YRUU, I can give it credit for getting me involved in the first place. It all started freshman year. I had a friend who'd been raised UU, who knew the church and its congregation inside and out. She invited me to come to one of their Sunday night meetings. She told me they were fun. Little did I know what I was getting into. Youth group was fun, but I just didn't keep going back once I attended my first youth conference and became a part of my district YAC. Without a doubt, one of the problems was the advisers. They weren't bad people by any means, but I didn't feel like they were my friends. They weren't people who came to my mind when I wanted to talk to someone; they weren't the ones I was excited to see on Sunday nights. Of all the youth I've talked to, most of them mentioned good advisers first when describing the components of a good youth group. I know that I didn't want an adviser who made me feel like he or she was my superior. I strongly believe that for youth to become empowered, they need adults in their lives who treat them as equals, who respect their ideas, and who wholeheartedly encourage them to chase their dreams. It is often very difficult for youth to find these role models. More often than not, teenagers feel anything but comfortable talking to their parents. An excellent youth group adviser can mean so much to a struggling kid.

Several of the youth I talked to had quite disheartening experiences with their youth groups. All of them had advisers who they felt were entirely unsupportive. One told me about an adviser who simply seemed to not care very much about the group at all. She missed meetings and went on extended vacations without letting any of the youth know. Another big problem was advisers who were stuck in the role of being adults who were dealing with children, as opposed to people who were dealing with their peers. But enough of what's no good in an adviser; the important part is what makes an adviser good. When I interviewed my local youth group, we created Ms. X, the super-adviser. Ms. X loves youth and is excited to be working with them. She is patient and not easily fed up with meandering conversation and interruptions, but she is a skilled facilitator and knows how to get a discussion back on course if it is careening out of control. She is an active member of the congregation and tries to encourage the youth group to get involved in the services and in other church-sponsored events, as well as encouraging the congregation to involve its youth. Ms. X is creative and has ideas about what the youth group could spend their time doing, but she is also willing to listen to the suggestions of the youth, both to change the ideas she already has and to come up with brand, spankin' new ones. She is willing to work hard with the group to help them do what they want to do, whether it's to create a youth service or to build a ramp to make their church accessible. Ms. X is also comfortable with the youth. She is the kind of person who the youth feel they can talk to. They can approach her with their problems; they feel comfortable discussing their lives during check-in. She is responsible and quick to recognize behavior that could jeopardize the community within the group, but she can deal with it in a rational and compassionate way.

Pretty much, Ms. X is perfect. Don't try to be like her or find anyone like her. You'll probably die trying.

Perhaps even more important than the adviser is what the youth group actually does. High school youth groups can't function with the same kind of rigid curricula that can be used for younger kids. The youth I talked to all felt passionately that there were just some things a youth group has to do to be strong. One of these is to be active in the congregation. One of the best ways to do this is to plan a youth service. I recall the youth service I did with my youth group as being one of the things in my life I was proudest of. Most churches I've seen with strong youth groups have at least one service run by the youth group during the year. It's a great way to show what youth can do to a congregation who may not seem to know they exist. Many of the adults I've spoken to in the past look forward to the youth service as being one of the best all year. This is also a great way to get kids who don't enjoy church to try to think about how they can make it better, or "more fun."

There are, of course, other ways for the youth group to let the congregation know they're there. One friend of mine belongs to a youth group that has a bulletin board in the church's main hall. Active Youth Adult Committees within churches can empower youth to get involved in the church at more levels than just the youth group. Youth groups should attend church fundraisers and get involved with social action events. When the group needs to make some money, it can try to think of a fundraiser that will help its members get introduced to all the members of the congregation. This can be as simple as a bake sale during coffee hour, where everyone shakes hands and learns the names of the people who are buying cookies.

It is also important to work on social action issues. In my mind, there is nothing more empowering and nothing that builds a stronger community than making a difference while working together. There are, of course, thousands upon thousands of things a youth group can do to help the surrounding and global communities. What a group can do depends on its resources and how hard its members are willing to work, but even on a very small scale, working for justice is an amazing thing. Not every youth group is ready to go to Honduras to rebuild houses for hurricane victims, but cooking a meal once a month for a local homeless shelter might be within their reach. The variety of issues and projects that youth I talked to have tackled is astounding. These are some suggestions I got from youth: make a banner and march in a pride march, visit children's hospitals or nursing homes, attend rallies about issues that pique the group's interest, pick up trash around the neighborhood, create flyers about social action issues and post them around the church and town. The list goes on and on, including just spending a couple of hours talking about issues that affect us every day. Discussions about racism, sexism, homophobia, and ageism can lead to valuable realizations about ourselves and the people around us. Not only can discussions like this lead to great social action ideas and activities, they can help bring together the group emotionally as well.

Emotional bonds are the next element everyone feels is necessary for a strong and empowered youth group. Not that everyone in the group has to be best friends, but there are several exercises that can help a group share things with one another and become closer. Of course, before any deep, dark secrets are revealed, trust has to be established. Whether it's a verbal understanding or a written covenant, most groups, especially close ones, have a "whatever is said within these walls stays within these walls" policy. Whatever the group decides should be established at the beginning of the year, and new members should be aware of what's going on.

One way to get youth to share about even the most basic stuff is to have check-in at the beginning of every meeting. Check-in is just a simple way for group members to fill everyone else in on what's been happening to them in the past week. Whether popcorn style, or going around the room in a circle, everyone just shares what's been going on in his or her life. If you've really got to get down to business, limit check-in to three sentences. But if someone truly needs to get something off their chest, I say let them talk to the group no matter what. Youth group should be somewhere a kid can go and know that he or she will have a shoulder to cry on and a friendly ear listening. One youth told me that the most memorable youth group meeting she has ever been to was one in which everything that was planned was tossed aside and they checked in for the whole three hours. Kids ended up talking about all the stress they were under and began to feel comfortable sharing things with the group that they hadn't felt comfortable with before. Everyone ended up crying and hugging in the end, and the group has been very tight ever since.

An issue that relates closely to emotional bonding is worship. Most youth feel they need to express their religion in ways other than church services. Youth groups can worship and express their faith in numerous ways. It might be enough just to lower the lights and sing or chant together, or to go through a guided meditation. There are also tons of simple activities that can become spiritual if they're done in the right setting. The most important thing is for all the members to contribute ideas, talking about worships they've already experienced, or things that they've heard about. Find out what worshiping means to the youth, help them explore their inner spirituality. Several kids expressed to me that there are things that are spiritual to them, even though they might not fall within the expected boundaries of worship. Sharing these with their youth group has brought them all closer. For some it's walking in the rain, for some it's yoga in the morning, for some it's reading a certain poem over and over again. Bring everyone's spirituality into the picture.

Another component of an empowered youth group is a strong connection to both the district and the continent. This is not to say that everyone in the group should attend every single district conference, or every continental event, but there is so much to lose by not getting involved. There are so many youth in my district who don't even know what a conference is, who've never heard of the Youth Council or ConCon. There are amazing people to meet out there, across the state and across the country. There are amazing ideas to bring back to the youth group. District programming such as Leadership Development Conferences can bring born leaders out of their shells. These are the individuals who can give so much back to the group, when they never even knew they had it in them. It's easier than most people think for an adviser or youth member of the group to get information. All it takes is a few phone calls. All it takes is getting in touch with a few people. All it takes is signing some new people up to receive *Synapse*, or a district newsletter. Or just send an e-mail to the youth office to find out the number of your local Youth Council representative and call him/her to find out what's happening in the district. It couldn't be easier to make a youth group aware of what's going on outside the nucleus it creates for itself. It's a whole new world that everyone should be fortunate enough to discover.

Finally, you have to remember to have fun. At some level, we're talking about kids here. Sometimes all I really need is to sit around and tell jokes, to watch a cute movie, or to get up and "get down" to some funky beats. It's not all about creating the perfect environment; it's about creating the right environment. All these elements need to be balanced according to the group, but I believe that any group of open-minded people will be able to create something wonderful.

Any way you look at it, the youth of today are the leaders of tomorrow. We can do things that you never thought were possible; we can create things you never imagined could exist; we believe in incredible things; and we will make them happen, because we believe in each other. In a world that is changing so fast that we are all challenged every day by new forces, where technology and knowledge are expanding so fast that many of us cannot keep up, it will be the youth of today who face the wonders this growth creates and the problems that come out of it. Helping these youth become strong, proud, just, and responsible adults is far from easy. Growing up is a tumultuous time. We need somewhere to feel safe, somewhere to laugh and love and learn. We all share the power to change things and to discover things. It is in all of us, young and old, and we all need our unique, individual power to be recognized and nourished. A youth group can be both a haven of safety and protection and a place for growth to occur. But youth and adults must work together to create such a possibility. Neither group can do it alone.

~

Logan Harris is the dean of the 2001 YRUU Social Justice Conference.

Youth Groups
as a Model for
Transformative Ministry

Jen Harrison

Each of us brings a separate truth here,
We bring the truth of our own life, our own story.
We don't come as empty vessels
But rather we come as full people . . . people who have our own
story and our own truth. We seek to add to our truths and add
to our stories.
This room is rich with truth, rich with experience
All manner of people are here:
Needy . . . joyful . . . frightened . . . anxious . . . bored . . .
We all bring our truth with us.
May we all recognize the truth and the story in everyone's life.
And may we hear and honor the truths that we all bring as we
gather together.
Together we have truths.
Together we have a story.
Together we have community.

—Penny Hackett-Evans, "Separate Truths"

Since the dawn of time small groups have gathered. From the early
Christians who gathered to break bread, to the feminist
consciousness-raising groups of the 1970s, people have come
together for mutual support, spiritual understanding, and hope.
Women created covens, pagan groups that create rituals of affir-

mation, healing, and celebration. Salons in Europe during the Enlightenment created space where people came together in each others' homes to discuss philosophy and literature and share stories of their lives. The Mattachine Society, a secret society in San Francisco in the 1950s, was a place of support for gay men before it was safe to be out. Revolutionaries and organizers across the world have formed small groups for solidarity, protection, and networking.

In Africa, groups of women are organizing themselves into micro-economic groups and applying for small business loans together. At business meetings, they not only discuss the profits, losses, and success of their projects but also sing and dance and tell stories and build trust among each other so they can work more efficiently. (Wouldn't it be refreshing for UUs to sing about bank loans and credit in our churches? Maybe then it would be easier to talk about money). In church history we see the Wesleyan Revival in both England and America gathering groups of ten to fifteen people for spiritual advice, instruction, and community. The value of these small group meetings is expressed in a letter from John Wesley to his friend in 1748: "They began to 'bear one another's burdens' [sic], and naturally to 'care for each other.' As they had daily a more intimate acquaintance with, so they had a more endearing affection for each other."

The youth groups in our churches across the continent meet weekly to explore collectively each person as a spiritual being within the support of a loving community. It has been said that one cannot be a Unitarian Universalist alone. One of the deepest human longings is to belong, to be wanted as part of a group. Groups throughout history have gained solace and support by coming together. Communities of people have found ways to covenant, to be together, to search for wisdom and meaning, strength and support.

The type of bond building that youth groups do could benefit most people who are exploring their spiritual lives. People of all ages could benefit greatly from meeting groups that value their inherent worth and dignity.

There is much to be learned about building community from the model of our youth groups and their intentionality. We can also learn from other denominations about how to use small groups to grow large and successful churches. From these models we can adapt a shared, lay-led ministry approach to our religious education programs that will supplement the content-driven, curriculum-based programs for children and adults.

Many fundamentalist churches are adopting the small group model for religious education and ministry. While their reason for wanting small groups (the intimate environment is conducive to conversion) is theologically very different from our UU values, the structures of these small groups may prove to be quite useful to us.

Theological Foundations for Small Groups

When people come through a church door, they are usually searching for religious community, friends, shared values, comfort, meaning, and a place for spiritual exploration. People rarely come to church to get involved in a pledge drive or to join the committee for repainting the sanctuary. Folks who are most enthusiastic about finding religious community are immediately channeled into committee work and volunteering. While this type of involvement often fulfills some of the reasons people came to church in the first place, rarely does it give people the space to develop deep friendships based on sharing their lives with others. Nor does it give them a place to engage in the spiritual growth that brought them through the doors of the church in the first place.

According to Carl F. George in *The Coming Church Revolution*, new members have to make six friends in the first six months or they won't stay in a church. Seven out of nine people who come in the front door to worship end up leaving. The reverse is true with people who come into church through small groups. Small groups allow people to meet and bond. They allow people to find commonality in their lives and to celebrate their differences. At their best, our youth groups model this welcoming atmosphere and safe space for having conversation about what is meaningful and valuable in one's life. Ideally, a small group is a place where the focus is beyond intellectual stimulation—which serves the well educated and leaves our souls hollow—but where our joys and pains can be shared, so our minds are in the service of our compassion and humanity.

As we know from the Fulfilling the Promise survey, fifty-two percent of people feel the most important glue that binds us together as UUs is "our shared values and principles," with forty-two percent of the people weighing in with "acceptance, respect, and support for each other as individuals." It is within our communities that our values and principles are played out. It is with our minds and our hearts that we experience acceptance and support. Having small group ministries set up in our religious education programs means intentionally creating places for relationships to happen. It also means that no matter how many people come through the door, there always is a place at the table for someone new.

I have heard hundreds of stories from people who came to a UU church, met with a small group, and found for the first time in their lives that they were accepted for who they were, complete with their warts and self-perceived ugliness. I could hear the joy in the voice of the storyteller saying it was amazing to find people who loved them, not despite their oddities, strange ideas, or their troubled lives, but because of those very things. This kind of loving community should not be a privilege set up only for our youth programs.

Living Out the Principles

I think one of the most important reasons for small group ministry is that it gives people the experience of what it means to interact based on the Principles and Purposes of Unitarian Universalism. Across the denomination, UUs hold up our Principles as shared values; unfortunately, simultaneously we often find that our behavior does not model these same values. We are human. We get into conflict. We forget to listen and to be civil. We yell at people we don't know from within the safety of our cars. We profess acceptance of one another until someone adamantly disagrees with us. We don't know if we are doing justice when we give a homeless person a quarter. Every day we are presented with situations where we might forget to uphold our Principles when we act. The more chance we have to practice living out our values with people, the better we will get at it.

Experiencing Our Inherent Worth and Dignity

In small groups all people are considered valuable and each person's participation is cherished. All present are teacher and learners. Although each person may bring different gifts and roles, the key is creating a place where people experience being their authentic selves and having that be accepted and honored. In a group meeting, if someone asks you how you are you are not obliged by social conformity to respond, "Fine thanks, and you." You are allowed to express deep sorrow and exuberant joy. By giving people the respect of listening with an open mind and heart, the group can validate and dignify the struggles of others. With group compassion and empathy, each person knows he/she is worthy of love for just being who he/she is.

Creating a Place for a Free and Responsible Search for Truth and Meaning

Having the experience of people valuing your inherent worth and dignity creates an environment where truth and meaning can be explored. When do we have the time to explore truth in our lives? Why do so many people walk through the door of their therapist's office with questions about purpose in life? As UUs we are filled with questions but we also need to make time for the answers to form in our lives. In his *Letters to a Young Poet*, Rainer Maria Rilke asks us

> to be patient toward all that is unsolved in your heart and to try to love the questions themselves. . . . Do not seek the answers, which cannot be given you because you would not be able to live them. And the point is to live everything. Live the questions now. Perhaps you will then gradually, without noticing it, live along some distant day into the answers.

UUs need to make time to explore our questions about UU heritage, our values and the traditions we draw from. Each individual needs to explore his/her own cultural heritage and how it informs what he/she believes. Because so many UUs are new to the church, we need structures that allow people to make peace with the religious tradition they came from. People need time to develop a theology they can articulate about what it means to them to be a UU. Helping UUs become more theologically literate in a world where religious conservatives are dominating the public discourse would aid religious liberals in finding their voice and learning how to speak out. Speaking in the safety of a beloved community can build confidence and help shape an evolving belief system.

Our children need the consistency and intimacy a small group can bring, and a place to share what they think it means to be a UU. Many of our religious education programs leave children confused. We teach them the basics of other world religions, how to think critically and ask questions, and let them know we value and trust them to make up their own minds about what to believe. This was the religious education program of my childhood: a survey of world religions, a smattering of evolutionary theory, some arts and crafts, and some fun mayhem in the isolation of the basement. Some kids come away with the idea that they are supposed to pick a religious tradition and never gain a clear UU identity. I essentially learned that to be a UU was to question everything. (You've all heard the burning question marks jokes.) Well, it's not funny anymore. I have met many youth who have been raised in UU religious education since childhood and who cannot articulate their beliefs. I have met even more adults new to Unitarian Universalism who have this problem. We are getting better by using curricula that focus on UU identity. Many adults new to Unitarian Universalism are also challenged to say what they *do* believe, not just what they no longer believe from their previous faith tradition. It was only in my youth group and conference experiences that I learned how to articulate what it means to be a UU. There also is the opportunity for older UUs to share their identity-formation experience with newer members.

Learning to Accept One Another and to Encourage Spiritual Growth in Our Congregations

In our youth groups people get to really explore with their hearts and minds what it means to be a UU. Small groups give people a chance to develop an articulate core belief system. I think one of the reasons cynicism is so rampant among UU youth and adults is that we resemble Maya Angelou's saying, "There is nothing quite so tragic as a young cynic, because it means the person has gone from knowing nothing to believing nothing."

By supplementing our program-oriented adult religious education classes with small group meetings we can give people a place to contextualize their learning and to deepen their spiritual lives.

When faced with the enormity of eternal questions of what is it to be human, people often decide these questions are too scary, complex, or overwhelming to spend any amount of time on them. Heck, it is much easier to spend time choosing a wheat or rye bagel than pondering why I was born. What is my purpose and meaning here on earth? How do I relate to the Universe/God/Great Spirit/the Ground of Being/the Imminent and Transcendent Mystery, or whatever name I call the divine? These are big questions, often overwhelming questions, but they are at the heart of our spiritual quest. Sometimes in order to deal with things this big, we have to create smaller systems to make ultimate questions manageable and connected to our lives.

There is a story about a group of children standing at the ocean shore; the waves are immense, too big for them to play in. So they dig a smaller wading pool and let the waves wash into it, creating a smaller ocean they can play in. Gertrud Mueller Nelson writes about this story in *To Dance with God:*

> What is too vast and shapeless, we deal with in smaller, manageable pieces. We do this for practicality but we also do this for high purpose: to relate safely to the mysterious, to communicate with the transcendent. . . . We cannot head straight into the awe of the Almighty. Like the child before the ocean, we turn our backs on what is too much

and slowly create the form that will contain something of the uncontainable.

Small groups are a place where folks can spiritually explore some of these big questions. It is a way to explore the ultimate in an intimate setting.

We want the folks in our churches to learn what it means to be spiritual, both in the realm of individual spiritual practice and corporate worship. UUs often think they have to leave the church to do this work. Many UUs study Yoga or the Kabalah or do meditation outside our UU community to deepen their spiritual practice. Perhaps with small groups we can create spaces where people can deepen their spiritual experiences within the church. In small groups people might get the opportunity to experience what Mary Daly and Carter Hayward call *godding* (god used as a verb). It is a metaphor for creating, especially bringing forth the finest essence and power of human beings through right relationships. Perhaps the small group is a place where we can begin to explore what is holy, sacred, and divine in our lives.

Working for Justice, Equity, and Compassion in Human Relationships

Small groups can be places where people get the opportunity to break the silences that surround the injustices in their lives. In *Sister Outsider* Audre Lorde hit the nail on the head about speaking out:

> I have come to believe over and over again that what is most important to me must be spoken, made verbal and shared, even at the risk of having it bruised or misunderstood. . . . What are the words you do not yet have? What do you need to say? What are the tyrannies you swallow day by day and attempt to make your own, until you will sicken and die of them still in silence. . . . We can learn to work and speak when we are afraid in the same way we have learned to work and speak when we are tired. For we have been socialized to respect fear more than our own

needs for language and definition, and while we wait in silence for that final luxury of fearlessness, the weight of that silence will choke us.

When we break down the barriers around the pain of our own lives and find compassion for others and their suffering, it can heal us. When we are healed it makes us stronger, better able to be change agents for justice in the world. In order to have justice, one must have truth. And in order to have truth we must learn to speak out even when it is difficult. When we share the suffering of another person and find within us the desire to give aid, that is the root of compassion. It is a unique kind of love of finding empathy with the victim and the victimizer, for they each suffer.

In *Infinity in Your Hand*, William H. Houff tells this story of a peace-oriented church: A newcomer arrives who was a bomber pilot responsible for dropping bombs in the case of a nuclear war. People were anxious about his presence and felt that "something" should be done. But they had no idea what that something was. One day a gathering of congregants was discussing the situation when one of the prominent church members spoke out and said the pilot was not the sole cause of nuclear peril—that its cause arose from the paralyzing fear everyone had of nuclear war that prevented anyone from taking any action and that if the bomb were dropped, the pilot would be a part of everyone who caused it. The people then realized they needed look at themselves and not point fingers at the pilot. Small groups can be places where we get to know our enemies. Or perhaps a better way to say it would be "know of your oneness with your enemy."

I believe the foundation of justice, equity, and compassion is love, and while none of our UU principles speak directly about love, this is the glue that can bind a group together. In our youth groups I see people who may not love everyone in their groups but they sure do love the group. They experience what it is to be loved and to be treated fairly and to be held with compassion when things are tough. Once people have experienced this they expect other groups and individuals to be able to interact with that same level of integrity. Often after a conference experience youth are disappointed with the interactions of people in the "real world." But their con or youth group experience keeps them working toward that ideal, where all people act justly and work for equity and compassion in human relations.

Using the Right of Conscience and the Democratic Process

Small groups can set their own agendas and practice democratic principles in doing so. The group might brainstorm a series of themes they want to explore, then individuals might sign up to search for readings and facilitate a discussion. They can decide how big they want to get before they split into two groups. They can make decisions about the level of attendance commitment they want from the participants and ways to welcome new people. They can decide whether to let children attend the entire meeting or part of it or how to organize childcare. These choices allow the group to learn what it means to use democratic principles, knowing that one individual's contribution to the groups does make a difference.

Coupled with our quest for truth and meaning, as well as getting an experience of what it means to have right relations with one another, these groups may be the springboard for people getting involved in justice work in our communities. I have seen youth who have become empowered in their youth groups use those very skills in other settings. They start gay-straight alliances in their schools, organize animal rights groups, and start letter-writing campaigns for Amnesty International. We need to make places in our congregations for these empowered leaders to do meaningful work. Adults in our congregations could benefit greatly from joining a small group and exploring what it means to be empowered to speak out about the truth of their lives. They can explore beyond the family and work world and develop meaningful community.

Working toward the Goal of World Community with Peace, Liberty, and Justice for All

When working for world peace we must begin in our own families, neighborhoods, and churches. Our media focuses on conflict, controversy, and contradiction. Our TV shows are filled with violence. The average teenager has seen thousands of murders on TV. Youth are picked on in schools because they don't fit in, whether they are gay, a racial or cultural minority, or just a geek. Youth are bringing guns to school. We live in a violent society. Women are abused, raped, and beaten every day. It is estimated that three out of five women will have experienced some form of abuse at some point in their lives. Abortion clinics are bombed and doctors killed. Hate crimes take the lives of innocent people. Native people are still being run off their last bits of land. People of color are disproportionately being jailed for crime, and the incidence of police brutality during arrests is rising. We need to carve out enclaves where we can create cultures of peace. We need a place where people interact based on trust, violence is not tolerated in any form, and new people are welcomed and diversity is honored and respected.

If we want to work toward a world community, we need to deal with loneliness. People feel lonely even in church. Unless you are in a position of leadership, it is all too easy to feel that you are another voice in the crowd, singing the hymn or saying the responses to a reading. People in churches who belong to small groups know that they will be missed if they aren't there. The group dynamic will be different if they are not present. Our children and youth know this experience; our adults could learn so much from it.

Our society is experiencing epidemic proportions of loneliness and lack of self-esteem. UUs are particularly susceptible to the individualism that spawns these maladies. Small groups create a sense of family. This consciously created family can really practice Francis David's idea that "you do not have to think alike to love alike."

Respecting the Interdependent Web of Existence of Which We All Are a Part

Small groups can break down cliques, allowing relationships that might not otherwise form. Think of the ways we could learn from one another when we have a diversity of people sharing: elders, youth, rich, poor, children, people of color, white folks, young adults, people with disabilities, gay and straight people, and folks with a variety of religious views. We could learn so much by being in groups that include people who are unlike us. The hope is we might find some commonalties with people in these groups as well as celebrate our differences. Our youth groups elevate relationship over curriculum. No matter the task at hand, be it planning an overnight or leading a discussion on violence in the schools, what is most important is the way people relate to one another.

While our youth groups tend to be homogeneous because we are predominantly made up of white youth with similar class backgrounds, we have taken the first steps toward accepting all the youth who come through the doors. Jocks, goths, geeks, punks, and preppies all hang out together. As UU adults have more interracial adoptions and marriages, and our churches begin to attract more people of color, our youth groups are becoming more multicultural. YRUU is learning how to examine its own culture for racism and white privilege. The safe community of our youth groups is a good place to begin the hard work of becoming an antiracist organization. We also can set up groups in which people of different ages, theological perspectives, socioeconomic backgrounds, sexual orientations, races, and so on can share and learn about each other and begin to explore, break down, and link some of the systems of privilege and oppression in our culture.

Organization of Small Groups

The optimum number of members for small groups seems to be about ten. This includes the facilitator, the apprentice, and the host at whose house the group meets. When the group meets they always leave an empty chair (like Elijah's chair during Passover) to symbolize the group's openness for new members to join. The small group is not a class but a place to explore life issues in a religious context.

The empty chair can be filled by anyone. Someone from the group may invite a newcomer who might enjoy the group. The church staff may direct someone to the group. You might have a friend who would like to be part of this type of shared learning. This is a great way to invite potential UUs into our circle. Youth groups do this well. Many people attending our youth groups are friends of UU kids. Their parents may not be UU but they are developing a UU identity as they bond with the YRUUers.

The groups are designed to support a growing organization, so as the group grows it gives birth to new groups, opening up opportunities for new relationships. In order to make the small group work, people need to commit to attending for a period of time. The group can decide on the time frame. Once the group has become too large for deep and intimate sharing, the facilitator will generally take a few of the newer folks and start a new group and the apprentice will carry on with the old group. Whenever a new group starts, a new apprentice will begin training in each group. The new group encourages the newcomers to meet and bond with others, to be known and welcomed, and to be called by name. When there are no groups other than committees, the choir, and a few programs it is hard for new people to make friends.

The facilitators of the groups would meet regularly with coaches to help them work out problems or issues that come up. Each of these coaches would only meet with a maximum of ten people as well. This way the facilitators have their job modeled for them by the coaches. The coaches can help with problem solving, skills training in group dynamics, developing program content, and helping focus the facilitators on reflecting and learning from their experience.

The facilitator needs to have at least an orientation on how to run small groups, covenanting, creating safe spaces, confidentiality and disclosure, setting boundaries, listening, and allowing every voice to be heard. As the need arises, further skill building sessions can be built into the coaching sessions.

Youth Retention and Growth Issues

Small groups help retain our young people by ensuring there are places for their involvement when they leave youth group. There would be a natural and familiar place for a young adult to be involved in an adult group.

Small groups help with the problem of youth leaders getting involved in district work and leaving their youth group for more challenging leadership opportunities on the district or continental level. This would eliminate the leadership vacuum on the local and district levels. If our local youth groups were working on this small group model there would constantly be places for new leaders to be challenged by running new groups.

Creating youth groups and adult groups with this model in mind will prevent our youth groups from plateauing when they reach fifteen people or shrinking to five because we can't manage growth. Two-thirds of our churches have less than 150 people. If we create groups within our small churches, we will be able to grow without loosing the feeling of intimacy we enjoy. Creating small groups to go along with our religious education programs could abate the fear of the loss of community due to growth.

Meeting Content and Format

Large traditional Christian churches using this model of small group ministry often structure their meetings around short passages of the Bible to which people are asked to relate their lives. We Unitarians may draw from broader sources, but the key questions to ask the groups are virtually the same. What does that passage mean in your life? How would you apply its teachings? What is important is one's own personal understanding of the subject or writing. The goal of the group is not to debate, argue, or be abstract, but instead to dialogue about and share each person's understanding of the topic at hand. It helps to have a time at the end of the meeting in which people may do a process check or a round of affirmations and hopes. This gives the facilitator important feedback to assist with planning the next meeting.

MODEL AGENDA FOR SMALL GROUP

- Gathering and saying hello—ten minutes
- Opening reading and chalice—short
- Check in, or sharing each person's life—forty-five minutes total
    - Each person gets about four minutes without questions or interruptions
    - Reflect on check-in where anyone can talk—fifteen minutes

- Spiritual topic of discussion introduced by the leader—one hour
  - For the first several meetings, the topic will be given to the group. Depending how this goes, and what the group would like to do, subjects will be given to the group or the groups will pick their own.
- Likes and wishes—quick list of what people liked about the meeting and what they wish could have been.
- Closing reading or ritual

People need community in order to live. It is through our relatedness that we often come to better understand ourselves. I believe that small groups will strengthen our religious education programs and lead Unitarian Universalism into the twenty-first century. If our churches are to grow and thrive, retain our youth, develop theologically competent UUs, and work toward a more just world, we need to intentionally develop infrastructures that support relationship, spiritual questing, hope, and healing.

∾

Jen Harrison is the youth programs director at the Unitarian Universalist Association.

Religion as Relationship

REV. PATRICIA HOERTDOERFER

~

Although we are a part of Western culture and share the Judeo-Christian religious and moral heritage, we Unitarian Universalists have a different way of being religious and a distinct way of doing education. The constellation of beliefs, values, and techniques shared by members of our faith community is identified by a core of values, a method that binds us together, and a set of principles that encompasses our several theologies. Our Unitarian Universalist paradigm is twofold: one of content, the pluralistic beliefs of our membership, and the other of process, the way we *do* religion. Our individual theologies are growing and changing; our method of doing religion is constant and consistent.

Unitarian Universalists affirm the individual credo. In our religious communities we are free to and encouraged to create and develop our own core of meanings, values, and commitments. Our religion draws on many sources of our living tradition and lifts up our common affirmations. Our credos evolve out of the particular instances of our experiences which we generalize toward final truths that "are amplified into a coherent system and applied to the interpretation of life," to use A. N. Whitehead's terms for "religion in the making." Building our credo is our lifelong adventure that we do in our religious communities, our UU society.

Unitarian Universalists *covenant* together. It is our voluntary agreement with each other; it is our freedom to promise mutuality. It is our pledge of mutuality to respect "individual religious rights" and it is a commitment to action. Our covenant is a pledge to bond together to pursue common goals.

Unitarian Universalism emphasizes credo and covenant. Our UU paradigm is personal and communal as well as independent, dependent, and interdependent. It demands a harmony of individual and community, self and society. In response to our common principles and in partnership with others we are called to transform ourselves and our culture, to transform the negative effects of our culture in order for each self to become more fully human.

Education "draws us out" and takes us to new understandings, abilities, and ways of being in the world. Our education is religious because we bind together in a caring community to search for truth and to live lives of peace and justice, freedom and responsibility. Our religious education nurtures both roots and wings: the roots of community and shared values, and the wings of the free mind and creative spirit. Liberal religious education can lead us into living lives loyal to our deepest faith toward wholeness and ultimate commitment.

Religion Is Relationship

Religion is our quest for meaning and our ultimate commitment. By nature religion is relational. Our religious imperative is to live with ourselves, with others, and with our earth. These are the three inescapable relationships: psychological (self), social (others), and natural (planet earth). In *I and Thou*, Martin Buber wrote, "In the beginning is relationship . . . is a freedom together . . . one must commit oneself to a conjunction with the other—but it is not selfless—it is a maintaining of the self in mystic balance and integrity—like a star balanced with another star." He also wrote, "I become through my relation to the Thou, as I become I, I say Thou." This means meeting self, meeting others, meeting nature, and meeting the *mysterium tremendum.*

Growing into relationships is essential to becoming a person. We all exist within a vast interacting web of relationships and we are shaped by them. As we grow we become aware of their enormous variety and complexity. We begin with these qualities and experiences in the process of becoming a self. We start with our own bodies. Then we move to experiences with other people, building relationships with parents, siblings, extended family members, friends, and acquaintances. Equally important in our growing are relationships beyond other individuals—communities, institutions and ideologies, networks and systems, history, and time. We discover our relationship with the earth and all living things as well as our emergent relationship to the universe or *mysterium tremendum*.

All religion begins in experience; it is discovered. It is the emergence of a conscious awareness of sustaining and transforming relationships. Such a moment can come with the birth of a child or at the side of a dying loved one if we experience the awe that life and death are one and that each emerges out of the other. It can come with the loving union when two selves ecstatically flow into one. It can come in the midst of the urban center where we can experience the diversity within the multitude and allow ourselves to be swept up in the flow of humanity. It can come in the radiance of a splendid sunset when we can grow beyond the beauty and wonder and know that we are the same stuff as the sun and all the other stars.

The discovery of transforming relationships can come through a limitless variety of experiences, at any point in our lives. After the discovery come choices. We can consciously choose to seek to create the conditions that will make the experience of transforming relationships an essential and continuing part of our lives. Indeed, religious education is committed to this process, to this discovery, to these experiences.

Relationships that help us grow are characterized by the process Henry Nelson Wieman calls *creative interchange*. He identifies creative interchange at the center of our being and defines it as the attempt to achieve an appreciative understanding of the unique individuality of the other—another person, thing, or story. It is the process that introduces the unique in our experience, whether we call it revelation, God, intuition, or insight.

Education for Religion as Relationship

Our religious education is a lifelong adventure shared in a community of seekers. In *Pedagogy of the Oppressed*, Paulo Freire says, "No one educates anyone else; no one educates himself alone; persons are educated in communion with one another, in the midst of the world's influences." We discover, explore, and integrate many possibilities and we act on our examined choices.

Unitarian Universalist religious education aims to engage children, youth, and adults in opportunities that empower them to develop their own religious philosophies, thereby freeing them to be their own best selves and to become kind, fair, creative, and responsible persons. Our goal is to provide participants with dynamic, vivid experiences of the power of Unitarian Universalism and to help them develop life-enhancing relationships. The goals in our religious education programs are to provide opportunities to experience a depth of relationship with ourselves, with others, with the world, with the earth, and with the universe.

Imagine a spiral model of education for religion as relationship. As we explore our ever-expanding relationships, we nurture our religious values and ethical principles. We begin with the relationship with self and hold up the principle of a strong, healthy self-identity. Then we move to relationships with family, parents, siblings, extended family members, and support the values of love and sharing. In our relationships with friends and acquaintances in our peer groups and community life, we seek to foster a sense of belonging as well as the values of freedom and responsibility. In our Unitarian Universalist community we develop a relationship with its story and tradition and nurture our values of diversity and choice. As inheritors of the Jewish and Christian traditions, we honor the values of courage and continuity. Our relationship with other world religions engages our understandings of similarities and differences and fosters the principles of respect and tolerance. Our relationships expand to include all humanity and deepen our insight and practice of justice, liberation, and cooperation. Our relationship to the earth honors the interdependent web of existence and promotes the values of appreciation and stewardship. Our evolving relationship to the universe or mysterium tremendum engages our curiosity and imagination and values wonder, mystery, and reverence.

The UU Tradition of Religious Education

The Unitarian, Universalist, and Unitarian Universalist curricular efforts over the past half-century focused on distinct dimensions of religious experience. Sophia Lyon Fahs, editor of the American Unitarian Association curriculum materials from 1937 to 1951, was the principal leader in remaking liberal religious education. She replaced a Bible-centered curriculum with a child-centered curriculum. The goal of education was the formation of the whole child and the transformation and reconstruction of society. The educational process was one of creative discovery, intelligent exploration and free decision. The multimedia curricula era of the Unitarian Universalist Association of the1960s and 1970s had a wide-ranging focus. The curricula encompassed the humanities, science, and cultural anthropology with emphasis on the *process* of culture building, meaning making, and decision making. The goal was to provide a "university for children" that would facilitate their religious growth toward individuation and empower them to espouse liberal values and become religious citizens of the world. The work of the Religious Education Futures Committee influenced curriculum development in the 1980s and 1990s and focused our attention on our religious identity with the UU Principles and Purposes. The goal was to offer lifespan religious growth and learning through structured, developmentally appropriate, published curricula to equip each person to develop a redemptive philosophy of life for peace and justice and to promote UU principles.

Unitarian Universalist religious education in the twenty-first century needs to engage participants of all ages in developing, articulating, and living a comprehensive religious philosophy that addresses significant life issues and in discovering the sources and potentials of our Unitarian Universalist faith as an evolving global religion in a world community of diverse faiths. My vision of religious education includes congregation as learning community as well as worshipping community, caring community, and social service/action community that empowers religious liberation and socialization. Fundamentally, our religious growth and learning need to be concerned with relationships: our relationship to each other, to our living faith tradition, to the world we live in, to all of life, and to the universe in which we live and move and have our being. We need to offer experiences of belonging and a sense of purpose to those who believe and participate in our communities and educational programs that build these vital relationships.

We need to deepen our understanding and expand our engagement with these relationships of life. At the dawn of the twenty-first century our education for religion as relationship needs to address anew the biases embedded in human relations in our congregations and culture, the pluralism of the sources of our Unitarian Universalist faith, and the interdependence of spirituality and ethics in our reverence for life and for the earth. Our education must lead us to celebrate the differences of our global human family, to cultivate a dynamic interdependency of spiritual being and ethical doing toward our planet earth, and to celebrate the unity in the plurality of our theologies. The goal is to become more fully human and more faithfully Unitarian Universalist.

My vision for the twenty-first century calls on all of us as Unitarian Universalists and religious educators to pay special attention to three of our relationships: our relationship to the human family that engages us in lifespan antibias education and moves us toward social justice, wholeness, and celebration of the diversity of the world's people; our relationship to our planet earth that engages us as spiritual trustees and environmental stewards advocating for ecological justice, reverence, and wholeness; and our relationship to the sources of our living tradition that engage us in respecting the plurality of our UU story and in identifying with the particular history of our people over time.

Relationship to the Human Family

Our first two Unitarian Universalist Principles—the inherent worth of every person and justice, equity, and compassion in our human relations—call on us to be fiercely intentional in our antibias education. We need to acknowledge the endless array of labels (black, white, Latino, gay, straight, lesbian, female, male, transgender, old, middle-aged, young, white-collar, blue-collar, pink-collar, blind, deaf, disabled, etc.) that we use to categorize and judge people. Moving beyond this tendency of categorical thinking opens us up to new insights, new challenges, and new language. To transform our congregations and communities, we need to start with ourselves in dialogue with "others" and in taking the risks of personal change. Our commitment to a variety of intergenerational programs, social justice projects, and anti-oppressive, multicultural education holds the possibility for new religious authenticity and spiritual renewal.

Our initiatives with *Journey Toward Wholeness* and curricula like *Rainbow Children, In Our Hands, Race To Justice,* and *Weaving the Fabric of Diversity* need to be expanded and integrated into the fabric of congregational life. Children, youth, and adults need to acquire the skills to build relationships with people of different racial, ethnic, gender, cultural, sexual orientation, age, ability, class, and personal identities to transcend differences and find connections with the whole human family. With a deeper understanding of all oppressions we must call and empower one another to act for justice in our personal lives, our congregations, and our communities.

Relationship to the Earth

Our commitment to the "interdependent web of all existence" challenges our long-held assumptions about nature that are embedded in our Western worldview. A new relationship to the earth needs to move us beyond the assumptions of dualism (body and soul), materialism, consumerism, and technological "progress." The social, political, and economic concepts associated with deep ecology need to be taught in our lifespan education programs and practiced in our congregations and communities. Curricular endeavors committed to this ecological dimension would further our commitment to the development of ecological sustainability and our understanding of the equity of all living things and the interrelationships of the natural world. The earth is our only source of material sustenance as well as a major source of our spiritual nurturance. In our learning communities and religious education programming let us aim for a deep reverence for the earth and a greater understanding of human interdependence with the whole of nature.

Current religious education curricula addressing this ecological dimension are sorely limited. A primary goal for these programs around earth stewardship would be opportunities for religious experiences in nature guided by both reverence for and interdependence with nature. The *Haunting House* curriculum by Barbara Hollerorth touched on this thought:

It is sometimes said that we are born as strangers into the world, and that we leave it when we die. But in all probability, we do not come into this world at all. Rather we come out of it, in the same way that a leaf comes out of a tree or a baby from its mother's body. We emerge deep within its range of possibilities, and when we die, we do not so much stop living as our living takes on a different form. So the leaf does not fall out of the world when it leaves the tree. It has a different way and place to be in it.

Relationship to the Sources of Unitarian Universalism

The Unitarian Universalist Principles reveal an underlying unity in our faith. The content, or *credo,* and the process, or *covenant,* promote unity as a religious tradition. Our Unitarian faith statement from sixteenth-century Transylvania, our Universalist "liberty clause" from early nineteenth-century New England, and our 1985 UUA Principles and Purposes speak to our tradition of standing on a common ground of essential affirmations. They have nurtured a process of religious deepening and a commitment to lifelong religious education, common worship, social justice witness and action, and institutional extension.

Since the merger of the Unitarians and Universalists in 1961, we have affirmed and celebrated our shared liberal values, yet the different sources of our liberal religious traditions need to be remembered and brought to light. Our curricular efforts around our UU Principles are manifold. Curriculum development illuminating our sources demands equal commitment and endeavor. The six sources of our living tradition define our pluralistic faith. And the primary source of authority for Unitarian Universalists is each individual's experience in dialogue with others in community and in conversation with this tradition. This unique approach to the religious life originated to a large degree from our central tenet that the mysteries of creation are great and we must be in deeper relationship with the many streams of religious faith. We need to trust our direct experience of mystery and wonder; to explore the prophetic words and deeds of saints, sages, and forebears; to discover anew the teachings of the world's religions; to bring reason and science into our creative interchange; and to engage our whole selves—body and mind, heart and soul—in harmony with nature. Our pluralistic religious community calls us to balance the mind and heart, to integrate the individual with the community, to promote justice through inspiring deeds of love, to find harmony with the mystery that transcends us all, and to live the questions and know that we are at home in the universe. Our imperatives are to understand and celebrate our religious pluralism through "right relations" with fellow North American Unitarian Universalists and through intrafaith dialogue with global Unitarian Universalists. We are trustees of our living tradition and pioneers in the continuing revelation of truth that draws from our many sources.

It is our task in religious education to explore our relationship to the sources of our faith—through reason and love, intuition and science, passion and pain, wonder and creativity. We need to be rooted in and identify with our own particular history of our people over time. Our stories can lead to personal spiritual transformation and our vision can lead to an ethical transformation of society. In our learning communities we need programming initiatives as well as curricula and resources to engage with the religious pluralism that enriches our family life, our workplace, and our community. Within the UUA Religious Education Department we have envisioned a lifespan sources curriculum project. Conversations with colleagues in the field have begun; a survey on the six sources of our living tradition was introduced to ministers and religious educators. My passion and commitment to this curriculum project as it evolves is steadfast.

As the old proverb states, "A vision without a task is but a dream, a task without a vision is drudgery, a vision and a task is the hope of the world." My vision invites my involvement in many religious education tasks. My commitment obligates me to work in many contexts including children's programs and curriculum development, family and intergenerational program work and to seize opportunities and roles of responsibility to bring these visions into being. And I am not alone! There are many of us in religious education working as partners and companions in the evolution of Unitarian Universalist religious education in the twenty-first century. Together our collective growth and mutual learning can make a difference for the future of Unitarian Universalist religious education.

∾

Rev. Patricia Hoertdoerfer is the children, family and intergenerational programs director in the Religious Education Department of the Unitarian Universalist Association.

Building Strong and Radical Religious Communities

Dr. Jacqui James

If Unitarian Universalism is to be the vital faith needed in these changing and demanding years, we must do more than we have always done. And, in large part, we must continue those things that we do so well and create new areas of programming to meet the coming years. In particular we need to address ministry to and with families, justice making, increased support for religious education and religious educators, growing Unitarian Universalists, and functioning effectively in a more diverse culture.

This calls for a creative and visionary approach. The fast pace of modern life, the increase in uses of technology, increasing diversity, and the competing demands on families all call for changes in our language, our programming, and our perspectives. We must find ways to assure that the relatively few hours per year that families spend in church are more dynamic and fulfilling. Our task is to equip our constituents for meaningful participation in a rapidly changing world.

Ministry to and with Families

Since parents are acknowledged as the primary religious educators of their children, support for families is vital. If parents are to be effective primary religious educators, the intention of the church to be a place for lifespan religious education must become a reality. In addition to adult education courses on UU history, world religions, Judeo-Christian heritage, and so on, programs that help build strong families are essential. Parents must feel confident that they can answer many of their children's questions about life and its meaning and how we are to live as meaningful people in this world. As we well know, children do not save all of their "big" questions for Sunday morning.

These are challenging and uncertain times for families. The myriad demands—professional, educational, shrinking leisure time, the frenetic pace of modern life—challenge our religious communities to become strong centers for the "village" that it takes to raise a child. We must strengthen our church communities as intergenerational and multigenerational places for worship, education, and spiritual life.

Many of our families have so little time to be together, and our traditional ways of worshipping and educating perpetuate this separation of families. Creative and bold new initiatives for regular intergenerational and multigenerational worship and education are needed to address this traditional separation of the generations for the Sunday morning experience.

One of our challenges is to continue to expand our definition of family and to support the increasing variety of families that are part of our religious communities. Single-parent families; blended families; families with transracial adoptions; multiracial families; families with parents who are bisexual, gay, lesbian, and/or transgender persons; families with one or more members who have a disability—all of these bring specific as well as common needs. How well we honor and serve these families will be part of the way in which we measure our effectiveness and adaptability in the twenty-first century.

Justice Making

If we are to be true to our Principle of the inherent worth and dignity of every person, our religious education programs must fulfill the promise inherent in the *Journey Toward Wholeness* initiative. Samuel H. Miller reminds us that "only one kind of religion counts today, and that is the kind which is radical enough to engage in the world's basic troubles." Issues of oppression, prejudice, and stereotyping continue to plague us. Even in our liberal congregations, despite our many years of passing resolutions on issues of social justice, we continue in largely subtle, unintentional, and unconscious ways to oppress and exclude people. It's time we acknowledge that, in spite of our good intentions, we have learned and internalized some of the myths that used to separate and divide. Then we need to take the next step, which is to understand and accept that we have to struggle against our "isms" on an ongoing basis and to help our entire congregations understand that they, too, must engage in this vital and demanding task.

Achieving our *Journey Toward Wholeness* calls for all the creativity that our religious education programs can provide. First, we need to understand and affirm our individual and institutional identities. We must understand how identity informs our worldview and our actions, recognize the multiplicity of identities within individuals and groups, and begin to understand institutional identity as an outgrowth of personal identity. Understanding how our institutional identity has historically sustained oppression despite our liberal intentions is essential to our ability to transform our faith into one that is antiracist, anti-oppressive, and multicultural.

Acknowledging the many ways in which our society and our religious communities continue to separate and divide people based on their "perceived differences" is another of our tasks. It is so easy from our positions of comparative privilege to fail to see, to ignore much of what we do see, to feel that we have no way to intervene, to blame the victims instead of the systems that hold the various oppressions in place—to be part of what holds these systems in place instead of being about the business of dismantling oppressions.

Our task is to provide skills, tools, and attitudes that help to dismantle the various oppressions and build bridges between people. A large part of the task of the educating community is to prepare people for the lifelong nature of this work. There seem to be so many obstacles to creating effective social change. And change happens so slowly that it is easy to become discouraged, to begin to think that it's never going to happen, and certainly not in our lifetimes. It is the responsibility of our religious communities to equip people with ways in which to nurture and sustain themselves through this journey. The earlier we begin this equipping the more effective our transformation will be.

How do we genuinely honor and celebrate the many cultures that make up this planet? As a religion that acknowledges that "the living tradition we share draws from many sources," we have too often participated in reckless borrowing rather than appropriate cultural sharing. Our curricula and programs must acquire a clear understanding of how to differentiate between the two. Only when we stop taking a smattering of this and a bit of that and altering them to fit our theology will we be able to engage in genuine religious pluralism. If we hope to build a more diverse and multicultural religious institution we must be careful about how we treat the religions and cultures that many of these future members will come from.

Respect for the interdependent web of all existence summons us to cultivate ways in which we affirm the web of humanity, biology, and environment. Moving beyond simple fixes to institutional action is required for genuinely living out this principle.

We must teach and learn effective ways of engaging in social justice. Our actions should provide for sustained and consistent involvement with the larger community, cross-cultural collaboration in community service, and service programs that are linked to advocacy and systemic change. Our actions must focus on a positive, pluralistic, participatory vision. Moving from a paternalistic pattern of justice work to effective engagement and accountability with communities of oppressed people is absolutely essential to this work. Our work with both children and adults in this area must stress the importance of effective and sustained engagement and working with allies in combating social oppressions.

Increased Support

Too many of our congregations continue to look upon religious education as little more than babysitting while the adults participate in the important business of worship. Our facilities, budget allocations, and view of religious educators reinforce this view. Until congregations recognize that the entire church is responsible for the education of its members, we will continue to offer religious education that falls short of our vision. Religious education must be seen as one of the central tasks of the congregation, and that education must be offered in intergenerational as well as multigenerational ways.

Congregations must see the religious educator as a professional. Salaries and benefits must support that view. Support for continuing education and realistic expectations of the scope of the work and the time it takes to accomplish it are vital. Adequate support and acknowledgment of the professional status of religious educators will help to decrease their burnout and encourage them to remain in the profession for longer periods of time, resulting in stronger education programs.

Parish ministers and religious educators need to learn to work together in effective teams to promote the education, growth, and spirituality of our congregations. Religious education can no longer be relegated to second-class status. We will only achieve the kind of lifespan religious education that we yearn for when there is true collaboration of all areas of church programming.

Growing Unitarian Universalists

One of my goals is that we commit to raising our children and youth to become Unitarian Universalists in adulthood. If we do not show our children and youth that we respect and value them as Unitarian Universalists, how can we expect to retain them as members when they are adults? To do this we must build bridges between the generations, offer opportunities for intergenerational and multigenerational activities, and offer a vision of Unitarian Universalism that challenges them to be part of the living tradition of our faith. We must welcome them into our worship services on a regular basis, make space and place for them in coffee hours, encourage their service on committees and participation in congregational discussions, get to know them as individuals, affirm their spiritual quest, and help them understand our religious traditions.

My children, now grown, reflect on the love and acceptance they felt from most of the congregation in which they grew up. They remember fondly the teachers who cared enough to show up week after week and treat them with respect and acceptance. They don't always remember what the content of the lessons was, but they certainly remember the character and caring of the people around them. All of our children and youth deserve nothing less.

An elderly carpenter was ready to retire. He told his employer-contractor of his plans to leave the house-building business and live a more leisurely life with his wife enjoying his extended family. He would miss the paycheck, but he needed to retire. They could get by.

The contractor was sorry to see his good worker go and asked if he could build just one more house as a personal favor. The carpenter said yes, but in time it was easy to see that his heart was not in his work. He resorted to shoddy workmanship and used inferior materials. It was an unfortunate way to end a dedicated career.

When the carpenter finished his work the employer came to inspect the house. He handed the front-door key to the carpenter. "This is your house," he said, "my gift to you." The carpenter was shocked! What a shame! If he had only known he was building his own house, he would have done it all so differently.

So it is with us. We build our lives, a day at a time, often putting less than our best into the building. Then with a shock we realize we have to live in the house we have built. If we could do it over, we'd do it much differently. But we cannot go back. You are the carpenter. Each day you hammer a nail, place a board, or erect a wall. "Life is a do-it-yourself project," someone has said. Your attitudes and the choices you make today build the "house" you live in tomorrow. Build wisely!

What kind of religious education "house" have we built? Is it one in which each of us can be comfortable living and learning? Are we offering our children, youth, and adults shoddy workmanship and inferior materials? We must acknowledge that at times we have taken shortcuts and failed to deliver the best possible programs that we could. The time has come to radically transform how we educate in our congregations, so that each of us feels within the deepest part of our being, in the words of James Luther Adams, "the moral obligation to direct one's efforts towards the establishment of a just and loving community." This is the time to choose the best architect, the most enduring materials, provide the most creative and enduring attention to all of the details of religious education.

If we do this, it will change us in so many ways. It's hard to visualize what the end product might look like. We will probably learn to use our buildings and space in new and wondrous ways. When we learn to respect each and every individual in the fullness of their being, our interactions will be deeper and our spiritual lives much richer. We will understand that all of us have much to teach and much to learn. We will begin to understand diversity as the sum total of the potential to be found in any group of people because of their differences, and to know that when we welcome and celebrate diversity, it enriches the lives of all of us. We will build a religious home which is strong and radical enough to "engage in the world's basic trouble."

~

Dr. Jacqui James is the anti-oppression programs and resources director in the Religious Education Department of the Unitarian Universalist Association.

Building a Strong Community

ELIZABETH MOTANDER JONES

The core of our Unitarian Universalist faith for me is the community. Our faith community is the bedrock upon which we can stand to face the challenges that confront us in our rapidly changing world. It is the security of a community of love and caring with shared visions and values that gives us strength. As our communities and faith evolve, religious education must expand its vision from traditional classroom experiences to viewing all of the community's life as opportunities for education.

Our communities are what nurture our identity as Unitarian Universalists. In a world that is growing smaller and more connected by mass media, rapid travel, and instant communication, we have life-styles that foster independence and isolation rather than interdependence and community. We are losing the skills needed to build and maintain strong communities. An additional complication for us as Unitarian Universalists is our aspiration to create intentionally diverse religious communities. This creates problems for us as we seek to understand ourselves, share who we are with others, and develop our religious education programs. We must focus our religious education programs on creating, growing, and strengthening our faith communities. We need to develop courses and programs and materials to support that community.

In seeking ways to talk about this faith community—how it is formed, maintained, and strengthened—I began to visualize it using the model of the family. Today's extended families can be large, filled with many individuals at different stages of life, in different circumstances, with different beliefs and ideas, of different genders, from different races and ethnic backgrounds, and with different sexual orientations. The same is true of our faith communities. By looking at the elements that create and maintain strong extended family networks, we can learn how to apply those to our communities.

Roots and Wings

Today's families are created through acts of commitment and birth. So too are our faith communities. Some individuals choose to join a faith community and make public commitment to it. Others are born into such communities and grow into their own adult relationships with them. We speak poetically of families giving their children both roots and wings. This is true also for our faith communities. Using these concepts, we can begin to envision how our religious education programs can strengthen community.

How can we give roots to our communities and thereby to their members? We can share our stories. Our stories tell us who we are. They connect us to each other, and they connect us to those who have gone before.

We begin by telling our personal stories. Allowing individuals to share their own stories honors and affirms the worth and dignity of those individuals. It allows us insights into each person and helps us make the connections we need to form community bonds. We must intentionally structure opportunities for individuals to share their stories. Opportunities for sharing can be built into religious education classes. Small groups such as neighborhood gatherings, circle dinners, and support groups can be structured in ways that encourage the sharing of stories. We can provide appropriate opportunities in committee and board meetings for short sharings. Recognition of the significance of our stories can be made by providing a place within the context of our worship services for the sharing of religious journeys and faith statements. As each individual's story is heard and accepted, that individual's self-worth is affirmed and his/her story becomes part of the community's story.

We must also pass on our communal story. Telling our history and passing on our heritage helps to develop a sense of worth for the community and helps individuals realize that they belong to something greater than themselves. We can share these stories from the pulpit in worship and we can develop religious education curricula that pass on our history in engaging and thought-provoking ways. We must pass on not only the names and dates of our history, but the stories as well. We need to focus on the lives, motivations, actions, and significance of our Unitarian and Universalist foremothers and forefathers. When we can see within their lives and actions our own experiences, concerns, and abilities we can feel ourselves drawn into that living tradition and heritage.

Formal, intentional telling of this history and these stories gives them an importance and prominence in our communal life. We must also be able to share these stories in less formal ways so that we can connect this history to our lives. In order to do this we need to have a community that is well versed in our heritage. We need to produce materials—books, videos, cassettes, CDs, and websites—that can be used to educate our members at their own paces. These materials should be connected not only to our formal religious education programs, but also to all the other components of our communities such as social action and music. Our local congregations should be encouraged to honor and respect their own histories. Congregations need to be taught how to gather, store, and share their communities' stories through the development of archives, oral history programs, and simple methods for disseminating this information.

Shared values and beliefs also give the community roots. Within the context of our diversity of theological beliefs, political positions, and socioeconomic backgrounds we need to focus on those values that we hold in common. Our Unitarian Universalist Principles can be the focal point. We must first give attention to how principles differ from laws, rules, or commandments, and how those principles give us a vital, living faith. We need to find ways to make our Principles not just words on paper, but part of our daily lives. We then need to help individuals articulate the connection between their actions and their beliefs. We need to provide structured situations in which to share beliefs and values, and to provide support to one another in the process of living a life congruent with those values.

How do we give wings to our communities? In a family, when strong healthy bonds are created and a sense of self-worth is developed, individuals are then capable of reaching out beyond the family and into the world. Our faith communities can also give their members the wings—the strength and skills—they need to reach out. We need to develop good gifts-discernment programs to assist our members in understanding all aspects of their gifts and how they can be used not only within their faith communities, but also in their families, schools, work, personal life, and communities. Congregations can also teach by modeling skills and behaviors and through formal programs of leadership development, personal growth, and life-skills classes.

The next step in giving our members wings is to help them find their way in the wider community. Our congregations can do this in many ways. They can form intentional connections within the communities in which they reside, with other faith communities, and with social agencies that share their concerns and values. Joining with other groups to work together on issues such as homelessness, racism, health care, education, and the environment builds bonds throughout the larger community and multiplies the good that can be accomplished. Our congregations can also work to keep their members educated and informed so they are prepared to take action. Congregations can formalize social action/social justice programs to support their members' individual and collective efforts. As we assist our members in developing their values, beliefs, and skills, we must also encourage and challenge them to move out into the world to make a difference.

Building a Strong Community

While acknowledging the negative feelings some people associate with their family experiences, we can focus on the positive aspects of family. In their book *Secrets of Strong Families*, Nick Stinnett and John DeFrain share the findings of research that focused on self-identified strong families. In assessing these families, the researchers noted six qualities of strong families: commitment, appreciation, communication, time together, spiritual wellness, and coping with crisis and stress. We can build on those identified strengths as we extend the model of the family to our congregations.

COMMITMENT

Not only are families and communities formed through commitment, but a community is also held together by commitment. The sharing of our stories creates appreciation and bonds through which we begin to care about each other. Hearing our history, seeing in the lives of those who have gone before us similar needs and concerns, and learning about individuals who have struggled to live their values bond us to our heritage. And as with the formal unions that create families, we also have various forms of public commitment to our faith communities. These may take the form of "signing the book" or taking part in a membership service. Many of our congregations have other rites that mark stages of commitment. Coming of age programs, credo or faith statement groups, and mentoring programs all mark specific stages in an individual's personal growth and commitment to the community. We need to examine seriously how we formalize these stages and acts of public commitment in our communities. We can develop classes and rites of passage for many ages, stages, and transitions in life. We also need to encourage formal rituals and traditions that provide an opportunity for public commitment and recognition of an individual's assumption of responsibility through leadership positions within our communities.

Not only do individuals need to commit to the community, but the members of the community also need ways in which they can covenant with each other. The *Fulfilling the Promise* process exemplifies what needs to become an ongoing process of covenant and recovenant. Just as families revisit vows they have made to each other, so should our faith communities. As the community evolves the commitment we make to each other needs to be re-affirmed and new members brought into the covenant.

APPRECIATION

We need to create a culture of appreciation. We show appreciation through the process of sharing our stories, but there are many other ways that we can do this. We can build stronger bonds in our faith communities by formalizing our processes of showing appreciation for our members. All too often it is easier to criticize than compliment. When our leaders, both professional and lay, model voicing appreciation and saying thanks, as well as how to receive that appreciation and thanks, we begin creating a climate where all feel appreciated and affirmed. Knowing that there is a place where one is acknowledged, valued, appreciated, and loved is invaluable. Our communities can assist that process by offering workshops to teach people how to write thank-you notes and notes of appreciation and by creating guidelines for when to do so. We can recognize accomplishments in newsletters and through verbal sharing of joys and concerns to let individuals know they are appreciated for all they do, not just what they do in the congregation. We can acknowledge births and deaths, birthdays, and passages within small groups and as a whole community to develop bonds and provide support. We can also present formal awards for special accomplishments. Finally, we can show our appreciation by offering individuals of all ages the chance to use their skills and abilities and to stretch themselves in new and challenging ways.

POSITIVE COMMUNICATION

Good communication skills are essential to the development of a healthy community. We need to learn to speak and write clearly, to disagree without arguing, to settle conflicts peacefully, and to speak to each other respectfully. It is important that the lay and professional leadership of a congregation model this. Formal courses on leadership skills, communication, and conflict management can assist in the development of these necessary skills. Providing such instruction not only to adults but also to our children is important in growing and developing a healthy community. Giving appropriate attention to the processes and the methods we use to communicate is very important. Positive communication includes not only the active process of communication, but also the ability to really listen. Too many communities are torn apart by an inability to communicate positively and appropriately with each other. Along with teaching skills, congregations can establish policies that encourage positive communication and provide formal processes for grievances and for dealing with abusive situations.

TIME TOGETHER

Spending time together is an important mark of a strong family. Congregations can help to build strong community by planning many opportunities for time together. We need to begin to visualize all we do as opportunities to develop community. Some of these opportunities will be formal and structured. Others will be informal. Some will be designed for the whole congregation and others for small groups. We need formal symbolic times together, such as our worship services, that not only provide opportunities to be together, but make a statement about who and what we are as a faith community. We also need times to deal with community issues in venues such as forums and congregational meetings. District meetings and General Assemblies provide opportunities to expand the community beyond our own doors and make the connections we need to the larger Unitarian Universalist movement. We should also encourage time together that is less goal-oriented and more focused on the opportunity just to be with one other. Eating, playing, singing, sharing, and working together gives us the shared experiences that build the bonds of community.

We must also provide formal and informal opportunities to gather in small groups. This can deepen connections between individuals and build lasting relationships. These small groups can be classes, committees, neighborhood gatherings, or interest groups. They can be intentionally diverse and mixed groups or they can be specifically defined groups such as adults, children, men, women, musicians, neighbors, or any other defining characteristic or interest. Each time we gather together is an opportunity for developing community.

SPIRITUAL WELLNESS

Spiritual wellness seems an obvious part of being a faith community, yet much can be done in this area to strengthen the community. Families develop strength from a sense of who they are and how they relate to each other, the world, and a greater good or power in life. Our communities need this as well.

Worshipping together is the symbolic heart of our community. We also need opportunities to worship in ways that speak specifically to our individual needs and concerns. These could take the form of worship aimed at adults or children. We might find times and places for individuals to worship in smaller groups and in styles that speak to them, such as silent meditation, movement meditation, singing, or dance. Worship opportunities can be created for special needs, such as services of healing, memorials, special rites of passage, blessings of animals, and celebrations. We can develop opportunities for individuals to take active roles in creating worship for themselves and others. Worship can also be incorporated into other gatherings, such as meetings, meals, or work parties, so that we are reminded of who we are as a faith community.

Spiritual wellness means more than worship. It also means paying attention to the spiritual development of individuals. It is important to create classes and support groups to assist individuals in their own searches for truth and meaning as well as offering them opportunities to articulate their beliefs. Our communities will be stronger when our members are comfortable to explore and discuss their religious beliefs and questions. Our religious education programs should continue to teach about other faiths and traditions to assist our members in living respectfully with those around us and to give us the foundational knowledge to develop our own beliefs. We must also provide one-on-one support for individuals in this process. This can be done through pastoral counseling and mentoring. Additionally, we can educate and encourage individuals in the understanding and use of spiritual disciplines.

Coping with Stress and Crisis

A strong healthy community, like a strong family, must be able to cope with stress and crisis. Like families, communities must learn to view stress and crisis as opportunities for growth. How a congregation deals with stresses (money issues, loss of key leaders, changes in size and demographics, or changing communities) and crises (disasters or current events) is critical to the stability and strength of its community. Practicing healthy processes and communication—and learning to deal with and grow from minor stresses and inconveniences—provides the skills and attitudes needed to deal with major issues if and when they arise. Providing training for leadership in dealing with stress and crisis both as individuals and at the community level will create the solid core necessary to withstand the destructive pressures that such issues bring. We can also provide support and counseling for individuals when the community or individuals are in crisis. Well-trained professionals and paraprofessionals within the community are important at such times. Peer support groups also provide needed help for individuals. Times of stress and crisis are often turning points in the life of a community. Learning to approach such critical times in the community's life with hope and expectation for success creates strength.

Unitarian Universalist religious education must maintain its traditional components—Unitarian Universalist identity, world religions, social justice, ethics, and spiritual growth and development—and present them in new and engaging ways. We must also expand our vision of religious education to include the whole of our communities' lives. In this way we can work to build the strong bonds that form our core.

∾

Elizabeth Motander Jones is the director of religious education at the First Unitarian Universalist Church of San Diego, California, and a member of the Board of Trustees of the Liberal Religious Educators' Association.

The Children's Fire
Is the Community Fire

GINGER LUKE

Our Vision

As we enter the twenty-first century, I envision the goals of religious education being to create and maintain a human environment and atmosphere where people of all ages can find and create a just community, grow and develop skills and the confidence to live their lives wholly, find and give comfort and solace, and celebrate life. This vision requires institutional support (staff, research, communication and inspiration). It requires the realization that each goal is connected to the others. It requires a commitment to seeing human beings as both individuals and as a part of the community. It requires an expectation that the vision is achievable, reasonable, and possible. For the vision to be realized, we will need to claim it as *our* vision.

Components of the Vision

Community comes in many shapes, and I mean all of them. The glue that holds community together is love—love of each other, love of a cause or a passion, love of the dynamic of being together and belonging, love of the possibility the community offers. The intimate group to which you belong—your family, your Sunday school class, the children's choir, your committee, your activity group—is an important part of community. The environment that recognizes and values your skills and contributions is an important intimate community. The grounding, security, or centering created by this kind of community is essential for human well-being.

The intermediate community, such as the church community, stretches beyond just one's intimate friends. It is larger. It provides a sense of belonging. It is a gathering of people one has chosen to join. It is an environment where the community has power to do things that individuals would not be able to do by themselves. All good religious education always nurtures this kind of community.

Global community may stretch us outside ourselves and our usual environment. It is the place where we work on the "us" and "them" concepts. Interestingly, all the pieces of this global community have a direct effect on our individual selves and the more intimate forms of communities. Social justice—a just community—can be an issue in all three kinds of community. To be treated respectfully, to be empowered, and to be allowed to grow are important characteristics of a just community in any form. Collective approaches to addressing social justice often involve articulating one's oppression or being in solidarity with the oppressed.

Growth and learning address the needs of the individual. They can happen, of course, in community, but they are most often designed for the individual and individual experience. This is the component of the religious education vision that stretches and informs the individual. It is the component that builds self-esteem, trust, and respect for oneself. It is where an individual first realizes or confirms that she/he is really able to be a contributing member of the community. This individual learning and growth often feeds into individual growth and learning that can only take place in community.

Healing—finding and giving comfort and solace—is held together by hope. Religious education programs continually are confronted with opportunities to promote healing. Classes that deal with life issues, such as loss, grief, pain, fear, death, diminishment, or simply change are all "healing" classes. Because these conditions of human vulnerability are present in any community, we must be able to address them. People come to religious communities because they do not know how or do not seem able to deal with these vulnerabilities alone. In these communities they discover other people dealing with similar human struggles and the power of community in healing is realized.

Many of these human vulnerabilities are part of everyday life. Even children, youth, and adults who are not in crisis encounter loss and disappointment and pain and fear. And people who are in crisis are often among us. The loved ones in our lives most certainly will encounter some of these hurts and we will want to console them.

It is in the healing component that we find spirituality. Preventative maintenance is a part of healing; keeping oneself well is a kind of healing. Spirituality and our involvement with it keep us well.

Celebration is most often a collective activity. Celebrating life is a way of being actively grateful for life. It is held together and fed by joy. Celebrations can be small individual rituals, family rituals, worship services, holiday events, life passage events, a walk through the woods, or playing a piece on the piano. Celebrating the joy of being alive and enjoying being alive can be very energizing. It is acknowledging the moment and appreciating it. This is also a form of spirituality.

It takes all four components—community, growth and learning, healing, and celebration—to make up religious education. Many people in our congregations think of religious education as Sunday school classes and maybe adult education classes too. Certainly classes are primary components and continue to need development and extensive focus, but they do not exist alone. Classes exist in conjunction with these other components. It is very important for the leadership of churches and those who are creating and nurturing religious education to understand that Sunday morning worship, pastoral care, and the condition of the building and grounds are also part of religious education. Sometimes it is so obvious and so much a part of a church's culture that it is not an issue. Other times, it may require orchestrated advocacy efforts to point out the breadth of religious education within the church community to the decision makers and participants alike.

Religious Education and Unitarian
Universalist Faith

Community is grounded in social justice and an awareness and respect for diversity. Our Principles of inherent worth and dignity; justice, equity, and compassion; the use of the democratic process; world community; and the interconnected web all serve as a seat for the grounding of community.

The growth and learning component is grounded in our historical connection to the value of intellectual growth and rational thought. It is grounded in our Principle affirming "a free and responsible search for truth and meaning."

Healing is grounded in spirituality. We see this grounding in our Principle on "the encouragement to spiritual growth in our congregations."

Celebration is grounded in the emphasis we place on Sunday morning, rites of passage, and the growing cry within our faith for intergenerational worship, social justice, and play.

Two of these components—community (diversity) and healing (spirituality)—especially affect the core of our evolving Unitarian Universalist faith in significant ways. The issue of *diversity* within the community component of religious education is pushing edges on the evolution of our faith. This issue of diversity has many faces. One face is simply the *racial and cultural diversity* of the children in our Sunday schools. About 10 percent of the children in my Sunday school are multiracial and/or multicultural children. Many of these children are here because of international adoptions. Work is being done within Unitarian Universalism to help religious education programs become sensitive to multicultural and multiracial images, language, and assumptions. We are beginning to realize this is not only to help us understand and work with "other" people, but to work with ourselves. Sometimes working with ourselves is harder. When we make mistakes it hurts more obviously. In our language about diversity there is little or no acknowledgment of the presence of the diversity our international families provide. It is as if they are invisible to the entire congregation. People go on talking about what a shame it is we have no diversity within our church. We are working on revising who the entire congregation considers "us." Not long ago in my church, during a forum on immigration, some disparaging words were made about Latino teenagers. One of the fathers stood up and said, "In a few years will I hear words in this church like that about my son from El Salvador?"

Our world is more culturally and racially diverse. We also need to be able to recognize the diversity in the larger communities of which we are a part. Making some people in the larger community invisible is especially harmful, and we do it regularly. I go into the grocery store and hear Spanish spoken in every aisle. I go to the checkout counter and two-thirds of the clerks are Latina or African American. I go to church later that very same day and hear people say, "We just don't have any people of color in our neighborhood." Children pick up on our marginalizing people. They see that totally ignoring a group of people is inconsistent with our Principles. We need to do better.

The *theological diversity* within Unitarian Universalism is again coming around as an issue. Many new faces are bringing in more theological language. New ministers use more theistic language than they did twenty years ago. Our humanists are uncomfortable with some of this. Some parents aren't sure what they believe themselves, but they would like something solid and unwavering for their children. Many of our teenagers sound more humanistic than the new members of the congregation.

Recently I heard a teenager in my church say, "The most spiritual experience of my life was working on the burned church rebuilding project last summer." There are many teachers in our Sunday schools and some children who are looking for more language about "spirituality without God." I've spent a lot more time trying to redefine "God" as relationship, love, interconnectedness, process, and the whole of the universe than I have trying to define spirituality as breath of life, mystery of life, life-giving force, and spirit of life. Perhaps I should rethink this concentration of effort. It is clear that there is more interest in spirituality—in that experience of being more or being connected to more than we are as individual people. That more can be other people, nature, perhaps even our dreams and our passions. And for some it is the divine within each of us. This engagement in spirituality is affecting the core of Unitarian Universalist faith because it hasn't found a common ground or a common language with which to experience or reflect upon spirituality.

Implementing the Vision

Learning *who we are* and discovering *how to be* in the twenty-first century will require religious education programs to model what I have just identified as the components of our vision. We need to model a balance in living. The context within which all this may happen needs some examining. There are characteristics of the twenty-first century that will influence the substantive ways we address religious education:

- People are too busy.
- Many parents are spending less time with their children than their own parents spent with them. Few families eat every evening meal together—or any meal, for that matter.
- Children's schedules are busier.
- Almost all volunteers, other than retirees (and some of them), work outside the home during the day.
- More information is available than is possible to absorb, but it keeps on coming.
- Adults and children alike have so many choices it sometimes immobilizes them.
- Families come in all kinds of shapes, and they are experiencing constant changes.
- Generations are more isolated than ever. Fewer children interact regularly with their grandparents, and fewer grandparents interact regularly with their grandchildren.
- More children and youth are living on prescribed drugs to control their behavior and their concentration.
- Children with special needs are present in almost every Sunday school.
- Children are accustomed to being entertained.
- Children are from more diverse cultural and racial backgrounds.

The goals haven't changed. We need community, learning and growth, healing and spirituality, and celebration. How we do it gets more complicated when you take into consideration the preceding characteristics. How we do it gets more complicated when these characteristics are true about many of us working in religious education and to some extent true about many of our religious institutions as well as those in our congregations.

To model our vision requires knowing the terrain. It requires focusing. It requires making choices. It requires having compassion and not expecting perfection. It requires holding up the quality of life in the doing as well as in the vision.

PEOPLE ARE TOO BUSY

How does that affect the way we train our religious educators and how we provide support for them on the continental level?

First, our religious educators need to be taught how to define and understand their jobs in clear and simple terms. We need to be able to visualize and say what it is we are doing. This, of course, doesn't mean that we are limiting creativity, but we are focusing.

Second, religious educators need to be taught how to review activities and help committees identify what is really important and what can be simplified. For example, we can set timelines so we can address an idea or issue, but we don't have to do it all at once.

Third, networking must be nurtured in churches so those in the religious education department know which part of religious education is their responsibility and those running other church programs understand that their roles include a form of religious education. For example, choirs are a form of religious education. Worship services are often forms of religious education. Social justice task forces often engage in religious education. Religious educators and volunteers involved in religious education must not think they are responsible for everything.

Fourth, work needs to be ongoing concerning defining reasonable jobs for volunteers, and training and recognizing volunteers in this busy age.

Finally, use of the arts may be a way of decreasing the anxieties created by being too busy. As economy measures, the public schools have eliminated much access to the arts. Religious education may do for art in the twenty-first century what it did for teaching reading to children in the eighteenth century.

There Is Too Much Information

The Unitarian Universalist Association Religious Education Department, the Liberal Religious Educators' Association, and seminaries can be especially helpful in this area. Having too much information doesn't mean the information is no good. It means many people do not have time to find it or process it. These institutions can review much of the information out there and compile lists of items that may be extraordinarily valuable to a specific circumstance in a specific church. I don't have time to even read all the reviews on children's books about death. I do have time to read a summary of those books which the UUA Religious Education Department recommends highly. Filtering resources and informing us of the gems is a valuable service. I hope money is allotted to make more of this happen.

E-mail lists are potential resources. Sometimes, however, the e-mail information gets so extensive that it discourages people with little time from using it. We need more help learning how to access information via our computers in the most useful way.

Training on and group purchasing of expensive computer projection equipment might be ways to take advantage of the tremendous resources available on the Internet for class use. Religious educators need more training in the technology available to convert the individual experience of operating a computer into a class activity.

Our People Are in Need of Community

People are going through more geographical changes in their lives. Their jobs are competitive and their neighborhoods are often isolating. There are very few experiences where young and old encounter each other. The best way to be in community is to feel you are a contributing member of that community. That is why intergenerational worship and child and youth participation in the Sunday morning service are so important. There are remarkable adults and children in our congregations. It is a gift for them to experience each other. This experiencing includes intergenerational classes, mentoring programs, social justice activities, worship creating, holiday celebrating, and sometimes the sharing of our confusion and pain over sickness or death.

I am reminded of the Native American stories about the "Children's Fire." Whenever the council made decisions the last question asked around the fire was the grandparents' question, "Is this good for our children and our children's children?" We need a "Community Fire" story for the twenty-first century. With every decision we make in our churches we need to ask, "Is this good for the building of community?" Many Native Americans knew it was the same question; if only we did too.

May we all be demanding and yet patient with each other as we create a religious education program for the twenty-first century that finds and creates a just community, grows and develops skills and the confidence to live our lives wholly, finds and gives comfort and solace, and celebrates life.

~

Ginger Luke is the director of religious education at River Road Unitarian Church in Bethesda, Maryland, and a seminary student at Meadville/Lombard Theological School.

The Principle
Behind the Principles

REV. FRANCES H. MANLY

Religious education presents a particular set of challenges in the liberal church. Committed as we are to theological diversity and to the ongoing search for truth and meaning, how can we honor that diversity and emphasize the search while still giving learners something solid to grow on? How can we offer learners the security of being grounded in a centuries-old tradition without limiting their spiritual horizons to a particular set of ideas and beliefs? How can we offer the wisdom of many religions without losing the sense of a tradition that is uniquely ours? How can we teach people that they must find their own truth and meaning without giving the impression that all values and beliefs are equally admirable? How can we inspire our children and adults to live lives of compassion, caring, and commitment to justice without a framework of moral absolutes in which to ground them? Underlying many of these questions is a deeper one which is of critical importance at this time in history, namely, how can we nurture in both children and adults a deep and abiding sense of their interdependence with all of creation and still affirm the inherent worth of every individual?

There are no easy or final answers to questions such as these, and there never will be. Several generations of religious educators have wrestled with them, emphasizing different questions in different periods and proposing different kinds of answers. Those of us who seek answers for today may draw upon their experience, and yet we must also identify the questions most critical for our own time and construct a new set of provisional answers that respond to, and address, the historical and cultural context in which we find ourselves.

As I have phrased them, and as we often approach them, these questions sound like methodological ones. My concern here, however, goes beneath the "how" to the "why." On what basis do we even ask such questions as I have posed, much less answer them? The time has come to take the next step forward in articulating the theological ground of our approach to religious education. This is not to negate what has gone before, but, one hopes, to take it deeper than we have yet done. For the past decade and a half, our curricula and our overall approach to religious education have tended to be grounded in Principles of the Unitarian Universalist Association, adopted in 1985. I am proposing that some of the answers we seek today may be found by moving to a deeper level in our use of the Principles in religious education, and I offer here a more complex and holistic reading of the Principles which would allow us to do so.

My focus here will be on the last of the questions I have raised because I believe that it goes to the heart of what we are about as an educating community of faith. I start with the assumption that the goal of education—and particularly religious education—is, simply, to help people to become more fully human. But if this is the case, then immediately we have to ask what it means to be human. The traditional liberal answer, and the answer most deeply embedded in American culture, has been that the human being is first and foremost an autonomous individual who comes together with other individuals to form community. As long ago as the early part of this century, liberal philosophers, theologians, and educators like John Dewey and George Albert Coe spoke about interdependence as a counter to what they saw as a dangerous overemphasis on individualism. But the idea of interdependence never made much headway against the powerful force of individualism in this country and culture. At best, it gave rise to the liberal view of human society as an organization of interdependent but at the same time autonomous and self-reliant individuals. As Robert Bellah put it in his address to the 1998 General Assembly, "We start from an ontological individualism, the idea that individuals are real, society is secondary." What Bellah argued, and what some of us have begun to realize, however, is that if anything it's the other way around. The great web of inter-relationships in which we exist does not come into being because we in our individual worth and dignity have chosen to participate in it. To the contrary, we have individual worth and dignity not because of our separateness, but precisely because we are first part of the whole, a part, in Emerson's words, of "the wise silence, the universal beauty, to which each part and particle is equally related, the eternal One." It is this view of what it means to be human that I am calling "the principle behind the Principles."

I dare say that for many, if not most, UU adults, this may be an important and even moving idea, but it is not a description of how they most deeply experience their relationship to the world. Individualism is deeply ingrained in us by our culture and by the liberal religious tradition, and it is hard to leave it behind; at times it is hard even to recognize its presence because we are so embedded in it. Our real hope for a broad-based new under-standing of what it is to be human lies not with ourselves, but with our children.

As I see it, our greatest challenge in religious education in the coming decades is to create a context in which we and our children can experience the fullness of our humanity as profoundly, radically relational individuals, a context in which we and they can experience this not as an idea but as a felt reality. In such a context we and they together can learn to live in ways that most fully embody that experience.

One of the most valuable tools available to us in this work is the Principles of the Unitarian Universalist Association—if we read them in such a way as to reveal and emphasize the "principle behind the Principles." I propose that we look at the Principles as a single complex statement, rather like a poem. When we do so we find that the whole conveys a coherent meaning greater than the sum of its seven constituent parts, and each principle in turn derives an important layer of meaning from its relationship to the whole.

As I read them, the overall structure of the Principles reflects the fact that as human beings we are always in dynamic tension between separateness and connection, between individualism and community, between autonomy and interdependence. The poles of this tension are represented, as has often been noted, by the first and seventh Principles: the inherent worth and dignity of every person at one end, and the interdependent web of all existence at the other. What has not been generally recognized, however, is that as we move from the ends toward the center, paired Principles balance one another, expressing related concepts but reflecting a different point on the continuum from separateness to connection, a different resolution of the tension between the two poles. The second and sixth Principles, for example, both address the issue of justice; but one sees it from the more individualistic perspective of justice, equity, and compassion for each person, while the other offers the perspective of community, affirming peace, liberty, and justice for all. A similar, though less obvious, balance exists between the third and the fifth Principles, where acceptance of one another as individuals corresponds to the right of each person to speak and act publicly—that is, in the context of community— according to his or her conscience; and the encouragement to individual spiritual growth corresponds to the affirmation of democratic process as the means by which the community itself can grow toward its greatest potential.

In the center of the Principles, at the point where individualism and interdependence meet, is the "free and responsible search for truth and meaning." Thus, by their very structure the Principles not only affirm the search for meaning as central to the human enterprise, but also suggest that the very meaning we search for, the meaning of human existence itself, is to be found somehow in the fact that we are at once separate individuals of worth and dignity and interdependent parts of an indivisible whole. Moreover, that same structure also suggests that a "free and responsible" search for truth and meaning does not mean a purely individual search because none of us is a purely individual being. Rather, it is inherently something we carry out both in the privacy of our own souls and in community with others.

A view of humanity that starts with interdependence and that holds individuality and relationality in such dynamic tension is profoundly countercultural—perhaps at any time, but certainly in our own. On the one side in our culture are powerful dehumanizing forces that grow out of and reinforce an unreflective, narcissistic individualism, an attitude of "I've got mine, never mind anybody else." On the other are the equally dehumanizing forces that, at least for the vast majority of us who define ourselves as middle class, would turn us into a homogenous mass of indistinguishable people eating the same fast foods, driving the same cars, watching the same television shows, and thinking the same thoughts. (I oversimplify and caricature, of course; I mean only to suggest, not to offer a thorough analysis of contemporary culture.) On neither side is there any place for the true and rich humanity that represents our deepest understanding of what it means to be human. There is no place for acknowledgment of the radical interdependence that is the most fundamental aspect of who we are and that therefore grounds the individuality that makes us human.

This way of defining what it means to be human is not really new; it is grounded in science (particularly in evolutionary biology), in theology (particularly process theology), in psychology (for example, in the work of Robert Kegan and Carol Gilligan), and in many other disciplines. It is already implicit in much of what we are now doing in religious education, as well as in antibias work and other initiatives of our Association. What I am suggesting here is that the time has come to make explicit what has been implicit.

The popularity of the Principles clearly speaks to the need of many UUs for a statement of who we are and what we stand for. Perhaps we sense that there is more there than meets the eye, but we have scarcely begun to tease out the depth of meaning the Principles contain. Too often we use them as not much more than seven separate hooks to hang our lessons and sermons on, and by doing so we close off important layers of meaning and fail to take full advantage of their power to ground and support our educational goals and claims. As I read them, they are more theologically coherent and more complex than is usually recognized, and the view of humanity I am lifting up here is integral to them. We urgently need to understand and to use the Principles in this more holistic way which will make clear—first to ourselves, and then perhaps to the wider world—that what we teach and preach is grounded in something deeper and more solid than just seven nice things we happened to be able to agree on.

The incorporation of the Principles into most UU curricula written in the past fifteen years is an important and useful change in our approach to religious education and helps to address some of the questions I raised at the beginning of this paper. Without in any way limiting or denying our children's freedom and responsibility to choose for themselves, we now recognize more clearly the need to give them a sense of belonging to an identifiable, vital tradition as they grow up. Without limiting our commitment to freedom of belief, we communicate more clearly that there are values and ideals that Unitarian Universalists agree to affirm and to work toward. This movement toward a greater focus on the Principles and on UU identity has begun to bring religious education more closely into alignment with the central meaning of the Principles by focusing on the development of the individual as part of a religious community. That is, we understand that while our children, like all of us, must eventually decide *for* themselves what they will believe, they do not have to (and indeed cannot) decide entirely *by* themselves.

Now I am suggesting that we need to go even farther in this direction. We need to take our use of the Principles to a whole new level, based on the reading I have outlined and focused on the "principle behind the Principles." The change I am proposing would not be trivial, superficial, or merely cosmetic. If fully implemented, it could mean as great a change in the direction of UU religious education as was the Futures Era or any of the other major shifts in our history. The proposed change would require us to

- encourage further reflection, by many people, on the meaning and structure of the Principles, leading in some cases to alternative and perhaps even more persuasive readings.

- rework old curricula and write new ones, not just to add on a new way (or ways) of seeing the Principles but to ground all our teaching in them.

- rethink teacher training in relation to adult education in general, seeing all adults as teachers and providing contexts for deeper exploration of, and reflection on, the Principles.

- rethink how we present the Principles to children to find ways that leave openings to grow into the complexity of what the Principles stand for; our current "children's versions" tend to be more simplistic than simple.

- become really serious about seeing the whole congregation as the locus of religious education, working together to create a truly intergenerational community where the "principle behind the Principles" would be fully experienced in the life of the congregation.

- become very intentional about helping both adults and children to understand the covenantal nature of the Principles— that they are not statements of belief but in fact a solemn promise we make with one another, with our human community, and with the interdependent web of all existence, about how we will live our lives.

- use all the resources available to us to turn our whole congregations into lab schools where people learn together to live that promise.

If what I am proposing means so great a change, why should we do it? I see two kinds of reasons. The first is that people in our congregations are hungry for this kind of grounding. The current generation of newcomers are not come-outers in search of an alternative to religion but come-inners seeking an alternative religion. They have adopted the Principles as their own in a way sometimes astonishing to long-timers among us, but many are still seeking more depth. Religious education committees, often composed primarily of these relative newcomers, are seeking the same kind of grounding in our religious education programs and curricula. Too often I have seen this kind of questing brushed off by someone saying, in effect, "The Principles are not a creed; you can't use them that way." It's true that they're not a creed, but I submit that if we take them seriously enough, and reflect on them deeply enough, they can meet a significant and now largely unmet need among our members.

The second and more compelling reason is that using the Principles in this way gives us a powerful tool for presenting the relational view of humanity and of human meaning which is the most important thing we need to teach in the next few decades. The ontological individualism that has so strongly characterized our religious movement and American culture has run its course. Although it is still strong in both, it can no longer take us in the directions we need to go, and in fact is leading us in increasingly dangerous directions. The success of many of the initiatives we are now undertaking in religious education and in our movement as a whole—interreligious dialogue, anti-bias work in all its forms, ecology, etc.—depends on our learning to experience ourselves in a new way in which we feel our connectedness with all people and all of life as strongly as we feel our individuality.

It will not be easy to make this shift at the deep level it needs to be made, and perhaps many of us who are now adults may never quite get there. But some of us will, and our children will, if we offer them the possibility. To do it, we will need to use all the resources at our disposal: stories, songs, and metaphors; new ways of being together in community; and good old-fashioned reason and logic. Ideas and theory alone can't effect this kind of change, but they are an essential part of the process. They can help us find the words to articulate what we are coming to know, they can hold up the ideal and point us in the direction we need to go, and they can ground what we are learning in a shared language and under-lying principles. For now, I know of no better place to look for that language than in our Principles and in the "principle behind the Principles."

∽

Rev. Frances H. Manly is the minister of the First Unitarian Universalist Church of Niagara in Niagara Falls, New York, and director of the Renaissance Program at Meadville/Lombard Theological School.

Practicing the Scales
of Rejoicing

REV. JOHN NEWCOMB MARSH

I believe we need to teach people how to express themselves in religious language. I believe this requires introducing them to a vocabulary of words, stories, poetry, music, movement, and other forms of expression. I believe we should imbue people's calendars with celebrations and invite them to practice daily spiritual disciplines. I believe in religious education programs with form and content.

When I was preparing for the Ministry of Education I learned that the method used to teach something is just as important, if not more important, as the content of the lesson. As religious educators, our primary role is not to teach but to model how to learn and thereby instill a love of learning. I learned that it is important to offer choices to students, both in recognition of different styles of learning and as an exercise in democracy. Our goal is to produce critical thinkers. *Haunting House* was my favorite curriculum.

At the time, our country had just emerged from a great evil, the Vietnam War. Those who shied away from critical thinking and relied on respect for authority and rote answers to complex problems were regarded as a part of the problem.

Seven years later my partner and I had our first child, and I began my journey toward increased respect for rote learning. I have not abandoned the goal of producing critical thinkers. Nor have I fully embraced the idea of children as empty vessels waiting to be filled, but my understanding and emphasis have changed. I still like the *Haunting House* curriculum, but I also want my children to learn what is taught in *The Old Story of Salvation* curriculum. When our eldest reached the age of four I started offering bribes as a reward for rote learning. Seven years and two more children later, there are no signs of turning back.

My partner takes charge of most of the responsibilities concerning our children—clean clothes, meals, sleep times, homework, etc. I do backup and music education.

An old upright oak piano serves as an altar in our home. I see it as a place of daily ritual; a place where the temporal meets the eternal; where, in the words of the poet W. H. Auden, we "practice the scales of rejoicing" and sometimes encounter the holy. My children are just as likely to view it as a place of human sacrifice, where the precious moments of their childhood are torn from them and offered to a god about whose goodness they harbor many doubts.

I am not much troubled by their protests. I figure that we are destined to have arguments. They might as well be over things I consider significant.

Some of the parents in our church are surprised at this enforced discipline.

"Did your child choose to play the violin?"

"Yes. No. Sort of. He was given the choice of which instrument he would choose to study. He argued that he did not want to study any instrument. He came up with some very convincing arguments about why it was a bad idea. We simply kept repeating that studying no instrument was not an acceptable choice. His choice was to pick which instrument to study."

I interviewed potential teachers. One confessed that as a child she had rarely practiced between lessons herself. Another joked about producing a concert star. Finally, one said, "My goal is to produce good citizens through music education. I insist my students need practice only on those days on which they eat food."

"Yes!"

One of the things I like best about the study of music is that it provides the opportunity for correction without reproach. Most children's art projects can only be celebrated. The goal is self-expression and there is no place or need for correction, only encouragement to further exploration. When our children exhibit unacceptable behavior we correct them as mildly as possible, but there is still an element of reproach. This does not prevent them from attempting to justify their behavior, a skill they are developing to a high degree.

If they miss a note, or play the wrong note, it does not mean that they have been inconsiderate or greedy or that they acted out of anger or lied about the truth; it simply means they have hit the wrong note and need to try again. The trying again can be trying on their patience, but they can also hear and understand improvements in their playing. Learning how to benefit from correction is no small accomplishment.

My children would rather spend their time playing computer games. I can understand the appeal of such games and even concede that such games may be educational. In these games my children travel through jungles, construct incredible machines, and manage townships. In many of the games you spend time playing on one level until you accomplish a set of tasks and then move on to the next level. The computer games do not annoy by saying, "You hit a wrong note"; they simply kill you and then give you a new life and invite you to start over. The computer games give a sense of power and accomplishment that is not based in any reality outside of the game and can only be shared with others who play the same game. After spending time playing these games my children are often cranky. Repeatedly going over the difference between an E and an E-sharp during music practice also produces grumpiness, but at the end of the practice time there is more likely to be a sense of satisfaction. Perhaps it is merely relief that the dreaded practice time is over, but often there is a warm feeling of mutual accomplishment at the end of music practice that almost never exists at the end of computer game playing, even on those occasions when we play computer games together. Knowing that difference between E and E-sharp provides a balance to the world of fantasy and freedom.

That our children have developed into critical thinkers and readers has been more caught than taught. There are books around the house. They see their parents reading. They listen to their parents discussing (arguing). They quickly learn that formulating a good argument will often (though not always) be rewarded in our household. They are young and impressionable. Things take hold. They also see me practicing at the piano. I take lessons from the same teacher as my middle child. I hope this helps to make lessons more palatable for them, but I am not sure.

Just as learning how to make music requires clear structures and expectations in our home, so I believe that learning our religious heritage requires clear structures and expectations in our churches.

It should be all right to expect children to attend Sunday School regularly and to make up for a missed lesson. It should be all right to ask our children to sometimes do things they consider boring. It should be all right to expect our children to be familiar with a body of knowledge about our religious heritage by the time they reach a certain age. "And which of these passages from our hymnal are you going to choose to memorize?"

At the First Unitarian Universalist Church of San Francisco we are currently discussing structuring our curricula around a set of core stories that our children would be expected to explore repeatedly at ever deeper levels of understanding as they travel the different levels of our religious education program. Most of the stories would come from our Judeo-Christian and Unitarian Universalist heritage. Stories from other sources would also be included. The adults would also hear these same stories woven into the preaching at their Sunday morning worship experience.

Some of the proposed stories celebrate values I do not share: Abraham's willingness to sacrifice Isaac, Jesus being born of a virgin, Arjuna's considering pacifism and then rejecting it. Contemporary theologians provide beautiful poetic interpretations of these ancient narratives. I enjoy the poetry. I also believe that our world would be a better place if these stories had never been given so much airplay. If I could give my children a world without such stories, I would do so in a hyperspace second.

Given the world we inhabit, however, ignorance of such stories does not seem a blessing. Rather, I would tell the stories, allow for multiple interpretations, and also share my own concerns and reservations. The stories are part of who we are. Like the inequities in our economic system and our use of the death penalty in our penal code, they represent a brokenness, a fragmentation I protest and work to change but ultimately must be prepared to leave to the next generation.

In the decades ahead, people will encounter ever greater amounts of information. Our task as religious educators will center less and less on providing people with information, and more and more on helping people to sort through information and discern the wheat from the chaff. I believe that a grounding in enduring stories will be a useful tool.

One famous music teacher claims that he never practices making music, but is always making music whenever he plays his instrument. I confess that often my children and I engage in mere practicing. There are moments, however, when the melody engages and my children, in spite of themselves, are glad of the moment. The practicing of the scales of rejoicing falls away and all *is* rejoicing. I live for these moments and pray that my children might one day share similar moments with another generation. At the same time, I know this is not the end of our story. The end of our story belongs not to me, but to them.

Every generation creates a form of musical expression that confounds and frustrates its elders. I do not expect the next generation to prove an exception. We provide structures so that they might have a place from which to begin their explorations. They will create music of which we have not yet dreamed—harmonies and disharmonies beyond our imagination.

∼

Rev. John Newcomb Marsh is a co-minister at the First Unitarian Universalist Society of San Francisco, California.

Doorway
to the Sacred

Rev. Makanah Elizabeth Morriss

We are not here to judge people,
we're here to unlock them.
In unlocking people, you will discover
a vast amount of simple goodness.

—*Swami Chetanananda,* Songs from
the Center of the Well

I believe that Unitarian Universalist religious education is all
about unlocking people—unlocking doors of creative possibilities,
unlocking minds with new ideas and the permission to think for
oneself, unlocking hearts that may have been hurt by life's experiences so that healing may occur and joy and compassion may be
experienced more fully. Our Unitarian Universalist Journey
Toward Wholeness, the sacred journey to which we have committed ourselves at this point in our history, has at its core the need to
unlock people. Liberal religious education can offer such a doorway to the sacred.

One of the most transformative moments I experienced while
on the UUA staff occurred one summer day in 1994. I got a call
from Helen Zidowecki, now an MRE but then a DRE and part-
time religious education consultant for the Northeast District.
Helen had called to chat about a variety of things. She had just
returned from religious education week at Ferry Beach. She talked
with enthusiasm about the interactions, the conversations, the new

learnings. And then she shared something that opened a new door for me in understanding the core of our Unitarian Universalist faith. Helen mentioned that there had been a lot of talk about the "six Sources" of Unitarian Universalism listed in our Principles and Purposes:

> The living tradition we share draws from many sources:

> Direct experience of that transcending mystery and wonder, affirmed in all cultures, which moves us to a renewal of the spirit and an openness to the forces which create and uphold life;

> Words and deeds of prophetic women and men which challenge us to confront powers and structures of evil with justice, compassion and the transforming power of love;

> Wisdom from the world's religions which inspires us in our ethical and spiritual life;

> Jewish and Christian teachings which call us to respond to God's love by loving our neighbors as ourselves;

> Humanist teachings which counsel us to heed the guidance of reason and the results of science, and warn us against the idolatries of the mind and spirit;

> Spiritual teachings of Earth-centered traditions which celebrate the sacred circle of life and instruct us to live in harmony with the rhythms of nature.

It had occurred to the participants of that conference that these six Sources perhaps should come first in our Principles and Purposes, followed by our Principles. It seemed to these folks, and it definitely seems to me, that in actuality our seven principles have come out of our individual and collective experiencing of the wisdom and insight of the six Sources.

The six Sources are what offer to me the sacred attraction to be a Unitarian Universalist. It is our inherent pluralism as a religious people that attracts most if not all folks to our liberal religious path in a culture where more mainstream denominations pursue only two or three sacred sources at the most. Ours has been a religious heritage open to many streams of religious and spiritual insight. In our Principles and Purposes we clearly proclaim this heritage and this gift to our followers.

I believe that the core of our evolving Unitarian Universalist faith is our use of these Sources of sacred wisdom. These Sources will offer to us current answers and continuing questions as we grapple with life's basic issues. These Sources invite us into dialogue with the past, with the writers and teachers through the ages who have pursued each path. They invite us into an experience of the present as we engage in the different spiritual disciplines each has to offer. They open us to visions of the future as we look for ways to create a world of justice, equity, and compassion. These Sources speak to the multiple intelligences we know are important to tap in religious education. They open doors of understanding to the varied perceiving and judging functions of our human psyches: sensing, intuiting, thinking, and feeling.

How do these six Sources interface with each other? How can we use them as individuals and as an association of congregations to articulate our always evolving theological perspectives? How can we use them to help us open the doorway to the sacred?

Last spring I came across a remarkable book entitled *The Heart of Learning: Spirituality in Education,* edited by Steven Glazer. It is a collection of presentations made at a conference at the Naropa Institute in Boulder, Colorado. The spectrum of presenters included people like Parker Palmer, His Holiness the Dalai Lama, bell hooks, David Orr, Ron Miller, Huston Smith, Rabbi Salman Schachter-Shalomi, Vincent Harding, and many others. These wise and insightful people discoursed on what was most critically needed in education at this juncture in history. They suggested three objectives, which seem to me to fit well with our needs for our religious education as we move into this new century:

- To establish the understanding that true learning requires openness to the unknown, to mystery.

- To establish awareness and wholeness as important necessary goals for education.

- To help people understand learning as a process of transformational growth that requires dynamic interpersonal and interactive work in the world.

The Naropa Conference suggested that sacredness can be understood as growing out of two basic qualities of human experience: awareness and wholeness. Awareness is our ability to perceive, experience, and know. A sense of awareness can be cultivated (or enhanced) through mindfulness or attentiveness. The development of awareness enables us to bring a greater sense of presence to the repercussions and meaning of our lives. And wholeness is the inherent, seamless, interdependent quality of the world. Our seventh UU Principle speaks well to this. Through awareness and wholeness, we begin to establish our individual and shared views of the sacred.

As Glazer suggests, "Sacredness as the ground of learning asks us to consider the possibility that the sacred is here and now. It challenges us with the questions: Can we see this world as sacred? Treat everything and everyone as worthy of respect? Can we open our minds wider and our hearts wider too?"

Our six Sources offer such education—the invitation to awareness and wholeness, the invitation to experience the sacred. Our six Sources invite each of us with our inherent worth and dignity, our individual gifts and talents, our unique perspectives and sensitivities to experience the "spiritual," the "diverse ways we answer the heart's longing to be connected with the largeness of life." It is from our sense of the direct experience of transcending mystery and wonder, from our knowledge of the words and deeds of prophetic women and men, from wisdom from the world's religions, from Jewish and Christian teachings, from humanist teachings that counsel us to heed the guidance of reason and the results of science, and from the spiritual teachings of earth-centered traditions that we each can find such universal connections.

My vision of Unitarian Universalist religious education for the next century is that it consciously and conscientiously become a doorway to the sacred, which calls us to acts of radical compassion and transformation. By utilizing our six Sources as the core of our curricula, programming, and preaching, we will be able to help our people of all ages to know and touch a sense of universal connection that is sacred. We will be able to speak to the wondrous variety of perspectives present in our classrooms, youth groups, and sanctuaries each week.

My goals would include developing curricula and program resources that offer students, in age-appropriate ways, seeds of information and understanding related to each Source. How and when did this Source become important to our religious tradition? What are the spiritual disciplines it invites us to follow? How does it call us to be active agents of change in our world?

The reality of lifespan religious education, especially for our children and youth, is that in our religious education classes and groups, we only have time for the planting of seeds—seeds of possibilities, seeds of interest, seeds of potential spiritual journeys. Each individual will grow these seeds in his/her own way and time, both individually and within religious community. This is the way we can continue to nurture the free mind, which is the cornerstone of our faith. As William Ellery Channing wrote, "I call that mind free which jealously guards its intellectual rights and powers, which does not content itself with a passive or hereditary faith; which opens itself to light whencesoever it may come; which receives new truth as an angel from heaven."

I firmly believe that we need to plant and nurture such seeds every year so that with each new year of physical, emotional, cognitive, and spiritual growth our students will be introduced again to the sources that nurture our Unitarian Universalist tradition. My vision for our religious education includes finding new ways to empower our teachers to tap their inner creativity so that sacred moments of creative interchange can occur in our classrooms, with learners and teachers sharing in the incredible joy of new insights gained and doors opened. My vision includes ways to offer parents education in the six Sources both as spiritual nurture for the challenging calling of parenthood and as help in providing the spiritual food to help the seeds of our teaching germinate in our children and youth. My vision includes pan-generational learning events and fun events and worship events where each of the six Sources is celebrated and experienced as a whole community.

My vision includes intentionally bringing the five components of our current youth programming—community building, social action, worship, learning, and leadership development—into the goals of programming for the whole congregation, from our elementary age children on through our lay leaders and our elders. My vision includes helping our people know in every fiber of their beings that spirituality is not solely mystical or otherworldly; helping them instead to recognize that spirituality and human service are one by engaging our folks of all ages in hands-on activities that bring love and healing to the communities in which they live.

What then are the vital components to such a Unitarian Universalist religious education? I believe a core component needs to be the development of a lifespan thematic curriculum based on the six Sources. By this I mean that each year the same themes would be presented which would consciously connect the learners with our six Sources. The increasing use of the "pillars" or theme approach to religious education in our congregations across the continent tells us it is time to develop such materials. In this approach, congregations have developed units on three to five core themes or "pillars" of learning for use in their church school programs. Each theme is offered every year for six to eight weeks at a time.

I personally had the good fortune to volunteer as a Sunday school teacher during my years on the UUA staff. I taught a "pillars" curriculum for six years to a group of students as they grew from second through sixth grades. I watched firsthand as their understandings of these pillars grew each year because they were exposed to them each year. I also have observed how our folks are much more excited about teaching when a particular pillar or theme resonates for them in their religious journey. These teachers offer to students an embodiment of that pillar or Source. To have our young people being taught by Unitarian Universalists who know and follow specific Sources is a way to offer our students extraordinary mentors.

A curriculum that begins in the early elementary years and offers units through adulthood will open new doors of theological understanding and acceptance in our congregations as well. Basic units on each of the Sources for adults will of course be supplemented by increasingly in-depth courses so that the wisdom, disciplines, and call to action of each Source can be tapped by our adult members. Peter Richardson's insightful book *Four Spiritualities* offers adults an in-depth understanding of individual ways of perceiving and judging in the world (sensing, intuiting, thinking, and feeling) and leads us to follow one of four spiritual journeys: the Journey of Unity, the Journey of Devotion, the Journey of Works, or the Journey of Harmony. Our Unitarian Universalist faith can and needs to offer nurturance and acceptance for these four journeys. We need to offer chances for our adults to dialogue about these paths and we also need to know that for some of the journeys, our religious approach may not be sufficiently helpful.

A vital component of this new curriculum is its ability to be easily shaped and reshaped by local teachers and congregations as well as by the UUA. A new curriculum will need to be at least on disk if not online, with individual users able to "enter" the lesson plan and move it around, adding their own resources and activities that they believe will work well with the particular group they are teaching.

Teachers need to be empowered in new ways to tap their creativity, to bring in related stories, games, and crafts they enjoy and believe will enhance a lesson. One of the most exciting times for me is when I watch the Sunday school teachers arrive early to set up their classrooms with the special resources they have developed. Teachers need to be encouraged often throughout the "presented" lesson plan to "think of a story that might work better for you" or to "chose a different game or craft, one you maybe enjoyed at this age and can shape to today's theme."

Teacher empowerment is a vital component of a religious education that will be a doorway to the sacred. Enthusiasm is very contagious. Enthusiasm is a channel for the sacred. An enthusiastic teacher has a 95 percent chance of having a very successful class session. We definitely still need lesson plans as starting points and as guides as to how to create a structure for a morning. But we need to help our folks become freed from what has always seemed to me a rather surprisingly rigid attachment to following a lesson plan down to the last detail. No lesson plan as published will work unless it has been reshaped by the loving and creative hands, mind, and heart of an individual teacher.

We need a curriculum development resource book and work-shop or Renaissance module so that local Unitarian Universalists wishing to enhance and develop their own curricula know what goes into solid, effective, holistic, liberal religious education program resources. By encouraging a higher quality of local curriculum development, we will create a much larger pool of potential curriculum authors continent-wide. This particular component is one to which I would give the highest priority. We have a great deal of "raw" talent in our congregations that will benefit from such resources.

Parent resources, stories that reflect the six Sources, greater dissemination of magazines like *UU & Me,* and development of other Unitarian Universalism at-home resources (including computer resources) are critical if we are to help our families become centers of liberal religious living.

Youth programming needs to include a component about the six Sources so that youth at various points on the theological spectrum will be welcomed and included. We need to make sure that during what are some of the most formative spiritual years, none of our young people feel excluded because of their need to explore more or less traditional paths than their peers. Courses on ministry to adolescents and young adults would be important additions to our theological schools and would offer our ministers and religious educators a stronger foundation for creating healthy and vibrant programming.

Commitment to our shared Journey Towards Wholeness needs to weave its energy through all the curricula, programs, and resources. We need to make sure that we are offering places of true dialogue where individual insight and perspective can be shared openly and safely. We need to affirm and strengthen our young children's innate ability to accept everyone for who they are and to watch and learn from the sacred energy we can see and feel in their interactions. We need to offer tools and spaces for increasing clarity so that individuals can release the old baggage of prejudice and shame, often deeply buried, and claim a new sense of wholeness and connection. We need to make sure that the historical thread of this journey, with all of its knots of disappointment as well as its times of progress, is known so that our present will build upon but not repeat our past.

Three vignettes underscore the need to honor our theological diversity.

A mother in a New to UU course writes,

> People often turn to religion when they are really down and need some hope to grab onto. In more defined, orthodox religions this is usually their beliefs or dogmas. What does the Unitarian Universalist church offer in these situations? In other words, in having my children attend church here will they leave with something to see them through the bad times?

An eight-year-old who is a Myers-Briggs sensing-thinking type comes home to his UU intuitive-feeling-type mother and asks, "What exactly is wrong with the Ten Commandments?" He didn't understand all of them and didn't agree with a few, but on the whole he liked having everything spelled out and he liked knowing what was expected.

After listening to two guest speakers talk about their Wicca beliefs a sixth grader confided to his Church school teacher that what they talked about was what he believed also. He asked, "Does that mean I am a Wiccan and not a UU?"

Unitarian Universalism's six Sources offer a response to each of these concerns as they offer a doorway to the sacred. A religious education based on these Sources can help folks understand differing options, perspectives, beliefs, and visions. A religious education based on these Sources can help our people experience the sense of universal connection, their sense of spirit, in ways that will offer sustenance in times of suffering and celebration in times of joy. A religious education based on the call of each of these Sources to committed and loving action will help change the world.

∽

Rev. Makanah Elizabeth Morriss is a co-minister of the Unitarian Universalist Church of Cheyenne, Wyoming.

The Teacher as Spiritual Guide

REV. DR. ROBERTA NELSON

*Only kindled souls can really do religious teaching, for they
must lead children, youth and adults to the threshold of those
great experiences which bring a feeling of the overpowering
beauty, the majesty, the awfulness of the world in which they are
living. Only they can teach, who have first beheld; and only they
can teach who, having beheld, find their souls under great com-
pulsion to share what they have seen.*

—Frederick May Eliot,
ordination sermon for Dr. Ernest Kuebler

As of June 2000 I have worked in religious education for forty
years. For forty years I have struggled in a variety of ways with a
wide range of models to convince the church community that the
teacher is the curriculum. The books, guides, tapes, videos, music,
stories, and field trips are supports and strategies that are important to learning, but it is the teacher who is at the heart of our programs. It is the teacher who listens and hears, who affirms and
challenges. It is the teacher who questions and encourages questioning. It is the teacher who is the spiritual guide.

I come to this conclusion from my classes with Dr. Robert
Miller, who taught religious education at Crane Theological
School; from Dr. Abigail Eliot, a professor at the Eliot Pearson
School at Tufts; and from Barbara Patterson, my preschool intern-
ship supervisor at Parents Cooperative Nursery School in Cam-
bridge. I do not believe that any of them articulated this message

as clearly as they modeled it. Each in their own way taught from the heart. Each nurtured and supported, challenged and affirmed, accepted and guided us on our journey toward becoming. They related to us as people first, not as students who had much to learn. Each of them had faith in the process of transformation.

I can point to many teachers who heard and responded to the call, and in some cases were already spiritual guides. Resistance to teaching from the heart has come from teachers and parents who want answers to every question, who do not want to be embarrassed because a child cannot answer the question "What do Unitarian Universalists believe?" It comes from people who see teaching as a duty rather than an adventure. It comes from religious education committees struggling to fill a list of teaching vacancies; it comes from those who think/believe that "anyone can teach." It comes from those who think that one hour a week does not make a difference. It comes from those who are unwilling to fund programs of value and substance. It comes from those who do not value or understand our rich heritage.

Angus MacLean wrote *The Method Is the Message* in 1951. In it he says, "I place method in the heart of our curriculum because methods determine so largely the human relations that prevail in our work with children. . . . I place method at the heart of our work because the methods of address to life and people are at the heart of our liberal faith."

I grew up on the New Beacon Series and I later taught several of the curricula. The series was still in use when I began my career in 1960. Many of the books and teachers' guides that accompanied the curricula dealt with important issues: birth and death; God and prayer; wonder, awe, and mystery; stories and myths from around the world; biblical figures; and other religious traditions. Unitarian Universalism was implicit, not explicit. The methodology encouraged expression and exploration of ideas and values. However, the materials and the teaching guides never mentioned the role of the teacher as a mentor or guide. I never participated in any sessions where this area of teaching was emphasized.

In 1965, when the first Unitarian Universalist curriculum kits were published, we moved into an era that explored the "search for meaning" amid the many complex, ambiguous, and difficult areas of living. In *Relating to Our World,* Hugo Hollerorth stressed the following goals:

- To help children and young people become aware of and comprehend the multitude of powers within the self as well as those that impinge upon them from the world.

- To help children and young people discover and become skilled in using the process which is the Unitarian Universalist religion.

- To help children and young people use the process which is the Unitarian Universalist religion for relating to and dealing with the ways they are affected by the world.

The "kit" era introduced a new approach to teacher training. Interdistrict weekend modules often introduced the leaders to the process, philosophy, and materials in the curricula and how they related to Unitarian Universalism. In spite of their success, lack of finances, overworked Association staff, and the decision that the new materials did not need such intensive training led to the abandonment of UUA sponsored trainings. Even so, some districts continue to offer teacher-training workshops.

I am most familiar with the *About Your Sexuality* and *Haunting House* trainings because I am a trainer for both. I have observed the changes in attitudes and feelings about teaching that take place when people "catch" the role they play in opening new vistas of understanding for themselves and their students. In both of these trainings, my co-leaders and I have consciously introduced our Unitarian Universalist Purposes and Principles and helped the teachers to explore the religious and spiritual dimensions of the curriculum. We have tried to make what is implicit explicit.

In the development of *Our Whole Lives,* the connections to faith and spirituality have been made very clear and are woven into the curriculum and weekend training. I suspect it would be a rare individual who did not make the connections.

Sexuality education is extremely important and deserves the time, attention, and money that we are spending. There are other areas of religious education that deserve a fairer share of our resources. There are many issues—diversity, social justice, theology, values, faith, decision making, history, and heritage—that our leaders need to explore if they are to guide themselves and others through and over the sometimes rocky terrain. In *Fashion Me a People,* Maria Harris writes, "Teaching is the creation of a situation in which students are handed over to themselves, allowing content to emerge, discourse to occur, ideas and insights to develop."

Teachers are artists who hand on clues. This kind of teaching creates a place to ponder the known and unknowable and nurtures our attempts at answers from the mystery and awe at the center of our being. As Frederick May Eliot wrote in "Our Kindled Souls," "Only kindled souls can really do religious education." It is our responsibility to provide the nurture that will kindle our teachers.

I serve a large suburban church in the Washington, D.C., area. I observe and listen to families struggling to contend with ever more limited time. The demands made on them, as well as on their children, tax their minds and spirits. People feel frustrated, exhausted, and inadequate to the many tasks they are assuming: career, school, family, volunteer work, and travel. Robert Kegan names it in *In Over Our Heads,* which is about the adult capacity to cope with an ever-changing and complex world. He says,

> All adults in contemporary America share citizenship with people whose skin color, gender, age, social position, sexual orientation and physical capacity differ from their own. These activities present us with a vast variety of expectations, prescriptions, claims and demands. Even the ever-accelerating flow of information to our eyes and ears, information competing for our attention, our allegiance, our money, makes a claim on us to do something with it, to decide about it, since there is no possible way we can do even a fraction of what we are asked.

Add to this isolation from larger extended family; increased mobility, commuting, and job travel; two-career families; some job insecurity; life-style changes; and single-parent households. There is continual anxiety over child care. Given these factors, I realize that we (churches) have also become part of the problem because we need some of their time in order for our congregations to function. In addition, schools, sports, and Scouts also vie for the limited time that adults have.

I have come to believe that we must change the cultural attitudes about religious education and teaching in church. We need a vision that engages teachers in their own spiritual search. I believe that people are seeking a richer spiritual life. Our task is to make manifest what we know happens when teacher-guides engage with young people, their co-leaders, and themselves. They become co-creators of a pilgrimage that goes ever deeper and feeds their souls. Christopher Logue's poem "Come to the Edge" expresses this call:

"Come to the edge."
It's too high.
"Come to the edge."
We might fall.
COME TO THE EDGE.
  And they came,
  And she pushed them.
    And they flew.

In *Fashion Me a People,* Maria Harris quotes this story, written by Susan Lukas:

Mauve, I suppose you'd call it, and double strands of imitation pearls that matched their silver-blue hair. And for assembly days, black dresses with white collars and cuffs pinned on with tiny gold safety pins.

  For those first six years they all seemed the same. "Miss" this or "Miss" that. Turn-of-the-century relics. Genuine virgin Victoriana. Theirs was not a "career," it was a refuge from the shame of spinsterhood. They ate their two and a half minute eggs because they were good for them, and the translucent whites slithered down their throats without any taste at all. Just like the knowledge they sought to impart.

  Miss Hull could have been their daughter. Chronologically, that is. Beyond that, the image won't hold.

When she laughed, you could hear it, and she never covered her mouth to hide her amusement—or wore shoes that laced. Or sent home notes that said "Compliments of Susan" and carried neatly penned admonitions about my "deportment."

The other sixth grade boys giggled and looked with envy on the boys in Miss Hull's class. And the boys in our class learned from her anyway. So did I. I learned every use of the comma known for the first time and came home knowing there was someone on this planet who understood there was more to me than met the eye.

Who is your Miss Hull? What did she do for you? What do you remember about her?

Most of us have had a Miss Hull in our lives. It is important to recall their impact on our lives. Many of these people invited us to come to the edge and when we hesitated, they invited us again and again and finally we flew. Marian Wright Edelman, in her book *Lanterns: A Memoir of Mentors*, writes,

O God, I thank you for the lanterns of my life,
who illumined dark and uncertain paths,
calmed and stilled debilitating doubts and fears
with encouraging words, wise lessons, gentle
touches, firm nudges and faithful actions along
my journey of life and back to You.

We learn from the voices that support us; we learn from the voices that denigrate. We learn from the voices that ask us to question. We learn from those who ask us to challenge and risk. But how we are treated when we are being asked to cross boundaries makes a difference. The way in which a teacher's life tells us something about our own lives is a connection—it is a message within us, from someone who likes us, informing us about ourselves.

A few years ago in a local church newsletter, the minister wrote about the return of a young woman in her thirties who had entered the Unitarian Universalist ministry. In her sermon she told the congregation that they had "saved her life." A young man then wrote in response to the column, saying,

Someone asked me why I remember religious education so fondly or what my favorite curriculum was. I had to reply that other than *About Your Sexuality* (which was truly memorable), I didn't remember much of the curricula. I do remember being nurtured in a way that I was not nurtured elsewhere in my life. I remember it as a place that showed what school should be like. I remember the church as a safe place even when my family was not. I remember talking to the minister when things were bad. Our talks reinforced my self-esteem. I think the church saved my life also.

These teachers were spiritual guides who taught from the heart.

Mary Elizabeth Moore, in her book *Teaching from the Heart*, speaks of the heart as part of a complex system, warning us not to be simplistic and to realize its relationship to the body, continuously giving and receiving. She continues,

Teaching from the heart has to do with sending forth energy to every part of the body—it has to do with receiving depleted energy, not to hold onto it or judge it bad, but to send it out again for renewal. Teaching from the heart is a gift beyond measure.

This rich metaphor is about transformation and transcendence. The "hidden curriculum" is that which is not written but which deeply touches us all.

Teaching from the heart has to do with sharing oneself and getting to the essence of critical issues. Both are necessary for the nourishment of religious growth. Education is religious. It is about calling forth, drawing out; it is about revering that which is known and that which is to be discovered.

In "The Spirituality of the Religious Educator," Thomas Groome describes education as a "passion for the people, a deep passion and caring for the well being of those we would presume to educate." To revere is to recognize the sacredness of the educational drama and its participants. In *Whitehead, Process Philosophy and Education*, Robert Brumbaugh discusses teaching as "giving the student a feeling of being together with the teacher in a shared creative time."

In his recent book, *The Courage to Teach*, Parker Palmer writes, "Mentors and apprentices are partners in an ancient dance—the old empower the young with their experience and the young empower the old with new life, re-weaving the fabric of the human community as they touch and turn."

I think of teaching as a living tradition because, like any truly human activity, it emerges from one's inwardness. Teaching is an invitation, an opportunity for diving in and wrestling with all that is available to us. It is an exhilarating experience in which more than our own creativity is operating. Teaching creates an environment where "students and teachers are sacraments to one another; they are co-creators," writes Maria Harris in *Fashion Me a People*. Therefore, at the heart of teaching must be an invitation for all persons to engage in a process of transformation, the process of moving over, going beyond, across, or through real or imagined limits. "Return to the deep sources, nothing less will teach stiff hands a new way to serve," writes May Sarton in "Santos: New Mexico."

Teaching from the heart is revering others in their wholeness and brokenness, in their joys and sorrows, in their contemplation and action. Parker Palmer writes, "The courage to teach is the courage to keep one's heart open to those very moments when the heart is asked to hold more than it is able so that teacher and student and subject can be woven into a fabric of community that learning and living require." To revere is to recognize the sacredness of the educational process. It is an honest transforming relationship.

In a religious community we have the opportunity to reshape ourselves. To accept life in community is to affirm life itself. In community we share some vision of the mystery of existence and life itself. Teaching in such an environment is rooted in Groome's idea that

> education that is religious is clearly a transcendent activity. Its ultimate goal is to liberate persons to fulfill their potentialities for authenticity and creativity. It is guided by a vision that urges people to interpret their lives, to

relate to others, and to engage with the world in ways that they perceive to be ultimate.

When I contemplate the questions put before us, I am reminded of one of my favorite quotes from William and Barbara Myers' book *Engaging in Transcendence: The Church's Ministry and Covenant with Young Children:* "But of deepest concern for all of us is the development of a sense of faith that invites and permits children, parents and all adults to learn and to hope—to lean and move with expectancy into our future." For me, it could be about people of any age. This sense of faith cannot emerge in a vacuum. It grows, develops, and is nurtured in a community of the faithful. It is rich in Frederick May Eliot's kindled souls. It is dependent on relationships that are cultivated. Maria Harris, Padraic O'Hare, and Gabriel Moran urge us to consider education as a complex pattern of relationships between persons and within communities through which we strive to be faithful, to learn faithfulness from others, and to instill faithfulness in others, especially those for whom we care. The communities of which they speak will share a common vision of the way of life—a path of faithfulness. Faith is not a state to be attained or a stage to be realized. It is a way of being and moving, a way of being on a pilgrimage.

The development of curriculum is critical, and it is formidable, but we will not succeed in nurturing people to "lean and move with expectancy into our future" if we do not have "kindled" souls in our classrooms and pulpits, and on our boards and committees. The whole congregation needs to take seriously its role in developing a faith community. Myers and Myers challenge us with this idea in *Engaging in Transcendence.*

The ongoing dynamic of transcendence suggests a new understanding of *curriculum.* A curriculum in tune with transcendence cannot be purchased from canned resources of a denominational publishing house. Denominational literature can inform the ways we plan for children, but this "curriculum of transcendence" emerges from the experience of life itself—for example, when adults require children to encounter new events like beginning preschool, accepting the arrival of a sibling, sustaining the absence of a loved one, going on a lengthy trip, or being in the hospital.

These children are being involved in experiences of transcendence. Experiences are transcendent not because they fit within certain categories of organized religion, but because children have been asked to move beyond the known into the unknown. "Those who teach must be able to take that giant step to move from the known to the unknown, to cross over the real or imagined boundaries."

The challenge before us is daunting especially in light of the stress and fragmentation of modern life. However, the future of our Association demands that we act now to change the culture so prevalent in our movement about religious education for all ages.

The Reverend Richard Gilbert, in his paper "The Galloping Gospel According to Angus Hector MacLean," quotes MacLean as saying, "I've never seen a curriculum so good that a teacher couldn't ruin it. I've never seen a curriculum so bad that a teacher couldn't redeem it." I say Amen.

A while ago a ministerial intern working in one of our classes said to me, "I would never teach that way" (referring to the teacher in the class he was working with). I asked him, "What are you observing?" He said, "The teacher loves the material and her students; she plans exciting lessons. She relates the material to newsworthy materials; she plans exciting trips; she invites her students to her home to bake pie and make candy." I asked him what he thought the young people would remember or learn from the teacher. He was not sure. We then explored what was really happening in class: relationships and connections, trust and affirmation, excitement and caring about the subject and each other.

As Mary Boys writes in *Educating in Faith*, "Research has been unable to prove that any single way of teaching is inherently better than any other. No one 'right' way of teaching exists. Nor is there a model of the 'perfect' teacher. There are only people who believe so much in the power of the traditions that they are willing to risk learning to teach."

Our challenge is to find those who are willing to risk learning to teach. These are our tasks:

- To change the limited view of religious education.
- To focus our creativity on the role of teacher as spiritual guide.

- To develop materials for our teachers that help them explore their own spiritual journeys and their impact on how and what they are teaching.

- To make a more conscious effort in the Association and our congregations to affirm the importance of religious education and the role of those who lead, be they lay or professional.

- To convey to everyone how seriously we take religious education, so we don't just fill the spaces or take second, third, or fourth options.

- To interview our teachers in order to clarify goals and expectations and to explain what we are doing and why.

- To develop orientation sessions for all our curricula (like those for *Our Whole Lives, About Your Sexuality,* and *Haunting House*).

- To encourage teaching teams. They provide continuity for students and teachers and, of equal importance, they contribute ongoing nurture and spiritual growth for teachers. (*Haunting House* provides an excellent model.)

- To develop ongoing support systems and networks that help teachers keep their spiritual lives alive and well.

- To ask ourselves where our teachers experience worship, renewal, and support.

I do not have a magic wand to make some or all of this happen, but I believe it is urgent that a commitment be made to teacher training in all our future curriculum development. I want all of our teachers to have adequate paid education about all aspects of being a spiritual guide (and child care if needed). I want every new curriculum to have a training component and a public relations program that makes clear our expectation that leaders will attend. (*About Your Sexuality* and *Our Whole Lives* led the way.)

We need to develop some mentoring teacher models that provide nurture, support, and ongoing skill building for our leaders. All our professional and lay leaders need to recognize that worship, fun, friendship, and sharing enrich the spiritual life of our teachers.

There are no easy answers. I offer a hope that if we begin here in this space and at this time we will gather the courage to ask not only why but why not now and move toward a place where teaching and spirituality intersect.

In 1936, Frederick May Eliot wrote in an article entitled "The Personal Enrichment of the Teacher" for the *Christian Register,*

> Unless the teachers in a school of religion find their own lives enriched by what goes on there, unless they find that their own spiritual insight and awareness are continually growing as a result of what happens in the school, there is practically no chance that the pupils will be getting much that is valuable for their religious lives. I should say that the personal enrichment of the teachers is the first test of the value of any institution that is carried on in the name of religious education.

≈

Rev. Dr. Roberta Nelson is a minister of religious education at Cedar Lane Unitarian Universalist Church in Bethesda, Maryland.

Seven Reminders

Rev. Dr. Tom Owen-Towle

Our Mission

The mission of Unitarian Universalist religious education is to create and sustain an intergenerational community of truthfulness and service, holiness and love. This imperative should undergird and guide our social action, liturgy, and stewardship as well.

Unitarian Universalist religious education is neither book- nor guru-centered. It is not adult- or even child-centered. It is congregation-centered, wherein all ages cooperatively engage in what Starr Williams called "a cycle of nurturing." Hence, our educational perspective must be grounded in sound ecclesiology— unswerving focus upon the welfare of each local Unitarian Universalist commonweal.

Seven Reminders

I suggest seven unprioritized and overlapping reminders for revisioning our religious education as we transition into the new millennium. These are familiar notions, but since when is *novophilia* a virtue? On the contrary, Unitarian Universalists would concur with Samuel Johnson, who wrote, "We don't need to be informed so much as reminded." My reminders will be of a theological and evocative nature.

These reminders comprise qualities of a healthy religious education curriculum. The word *curriculum* originally signified the course for a foot race usually held in the great amphitheater. We hold no races (other than relay races at picnics) in our religious educating, but courses to be sure. Our "curricula"—the courses around which our children/youth/adults move—center on courageous, wise "bonds of union." And the amphitheater of religious education is as spacious as the worlds both around and inside our souls.

Toward fulfillment of our intergenerational nature, Unitarian Universalist congregations might consider co-creating each year a core curriculum wherein adult worship and religious education classes, as well as all intergenerational events, are intentionally woven around spiraling reinforcement of our bedrock Principles and Purposes. This proposal would diminish the oft-gaping gulf between liturgy and classroom, children and adults, religious education and pastoral professionals.

Our beloved communities are both blessed and robust whenever participants of all ages are religious, remembering, recreative, responsible, respectful, renewable, and reverent pilgrims.

I choose the term *pilgrim* because I perceive the educational venture to be more akin to sauntering than scholarship. Saunterers are literally "holy-landers," youngsters and elders who treat every step as a conveyor of sacredness. Pilgrims search, not merely for, but with, our very own stories and struggles, remaining ready resources for fellow travelers along the journey. Pilgrims, despite dull stretches and dry spells, are distinguished as persistent plodders—ever trekking toward the next horizon of religious growth and learning.

We Are Religious Pilgrims

It is prudent to recall that a major recommendation of the *Religious Education Futures* report in 1981 hinted that the erstwhile education wing of the UUA be renamed the "religious" education department. This constituted a rather radical notion back in the 1960s and 1970s when our curricula were not UU-specific in content and our resource products (e.g., *Man the Meaning-Maker*) were shaped and marketed for the secular world as well as local churches.

As parish minister Earl Holt aptly phrased it, "We are not an alternative to religion but rather a religious alternative." Yes, and moreover we represented a bona fide religion with grand histories and mutual affirmations—a responsibly free faith immersed in profound mysteries and governed by ethical imperatives. We have grown to affirm that Unitarian Universalism is undeniably religious, albeit a version of religion oft-considered weird, even "cultic," and rendered outcast by ecumenical purview.

Amidst the shifting sands of contemporary culture, the very word *religion* urges earnest pilgrims to "bind ourselves together again." The twenty-first century will demand that Unitarian Universalists yoke together in cooperative quest for abundant meaning, but our religious joining must extend beyond horizons of comfort and familiarity to embrace the larger community, our entire association—the interdependent web of which we are a part. In a world of rampaging fragmentation and discord, our version of religion must practice its fundamental mission of binding people—furnishing fasteners and coherence—tying the totality of existence together.

Unitarian Universalism is not merely a personalized *spiritual* quest undertaken by lone souls but rather a communal *religious* venture that is secured to and aligned with an association, local institutions, pressing causes, and unmistakable imperatives. Private spirituality may soar skyward—unrestrained and unattached—but genuine religion simply can't. It is earthbound, incarnated in kinship circles of empowerment. While clearly undogmatic, Unitarian Universalism remains doggedly committed to penultimate claims. We negotiate the fine line between creative and destructive bonds, harboring an open, not an empty, mind.

Ours is a religious enterprise that points to those resources and realities that bind us together again and again within ourselves, among neighbors, throughout the entire ecosystem, and with the elusive yet nourishing divine mystery Sophia Fahs referred to as the "Universal Living Unity." We are a full-fledged religion because we want our children, youth, and adults to foster mature allegiances and grow enduring loyalties to the true, beautiful, and good.

WE ARE REMEMBERING PILGRIMS

It is increasingly incumbent in our fast-paced, narcissistic society, which is fixated on the here and now, for thoughtful Unitarian

Universalists to honor the gifts and sacrifices of our spiritual ancestors. Our religious education curriculum will falter if ungrounded in the peculiar resources of our UU heritage and identity. No child should ever be unclear about the linkage between our history and Principles and what transpires in their programs. Similarly, no adult religious education class need duplicate what is already available in the larger village.

All who walk the ways of our Unitarian Universalist faith must catch and be caught by our vision: namely, that every unit of existence is inherently worthwhile and to be treated as such and that the governing nature of our interdependent web is love and that we are held by and stirred to act in the name of that eternal love.

One rightly hears about being trained Jewishly. We must think and school one another in a particularly Unitarian Universalist way while cultivating necessary interconnections with other faiths and the secular world. We are not simply religious, but religious as Unitarian Universalists.

We may choose to be Buddhist or Christian or humanist or existential or mongrelized Unitarian Universalists, but our various theological persuasions are modifiers; the noun, our primary institutional allegiance, should be Unitarian Universalism. We and our offspring must learn to speak and act directly from the soul of our historical evolution without ever growing precious or arrogant. We dare not romanticize our roots in order to expand our diminished egos. This will prove a critical challenge especially for our young who are often the religious minority on life's playground.

Four pivotal questions are perennially engaged by every pilgrim in our UU religious education curriculum: Who are we? (Identity); Where did we come from? (Roots); Who are we traveling with? (Companions); and Where are we headed? (Destination).

WE ARE RECREATIVE PILGRIMS

A nineteenth-century church school policy statement of a mainline faith declared, "We prohibit play in the strongest terms. Let this rule be observed with strictest nicety. For those who play when they are young will play when they are old." It is hard to believe that any American religion could have ever been so stifling. Yet when one remembers even in our own lifetimes that laughter, dancing, and fun have all been labeled "sinful" (especially in the church), one is not surprised.

On the contrary, Unitarian Universalists affirm and promote a religious growth and learning pathway that majors in noncompetitive times of playfulness, good will, and good humor. We take seriously (not grimly) our place as full-fledged partners with the Creator whenever we engage in recreative endeavors. We want our little ones to frolic early and keep on doing so all the way to the grave.

In German the word for blessedness is *seelisch*, which is etymologically related to our word *silly*, reminding us all that to be holy we are beckoned to become irrepressible practitioners of silliness, therewith entering the realm of God—becoming not childish but childlike. This is one reason why our religious education requires an intergenerational atmosphere—a living-together process where we mutually engage in worship and play, service and learning. Together as youth/children/adults we will make masks as well as garden on church grounds, march and meditate alongside one another. Without children around we adults are prone to debate or swim amid abstractions when sending up balloons is called for, labor tediously amid policies when frolicking is in order, fall into the role of grim crusader when the healing balm of zaniness would profit everyone.

Our memorial wall at First Church in San Diego contains a verse from Isaiah proclaiming that amidst the sorrows and losses of life, our eyes must stay focused on the prize of joy—a reality more expansive than happiness and more enduring than pleasure. The passage reads: "And you will go out with joy and be led forth in peace. Before you the mountains and hills will break into cries of joy, and all the trees in the countryside will clap their hands." That's our vision indeed: that all ages might not only leave life with a sense of joy but leave our houses every morning with the assurance that life is full of wondrous surprises, that we are worthy, and that promising things await us.

WE ARE RESPONSIBLE PILGRIMS

Unitarian Universalism affirms that you and I are responsible for the well-being of every common bond we create. While limited, we are not immobilized by history or biology. We are choice-makers. To paraphrase Gandhi, we can and must become the changes we wish to see accomplished in the world.

Our Principles assist our responsible journey with two references. First, "we covenant to affirm and promote a free and *responsible* search for truth and meaning." Ours is a *solidary* not a *solitary* quest: we are responsibly free creatures—without freedom, accountability becomes slavish, yet without purpose, freedom is anarchous. This is what educational psychologist Robert Kegan means by his keen term *embedduals:* we are not wholly autonomous persons, but individuals embedded in bonds of meaning and communities of purpose. Such was the founding direction of our *About Your Sexuality* program wherein young people have been challenged to make decisions *for* but not *by* themselves.

Second, our "Sources" declare that we heed "the Jewish and Christian teachings which call us to *respond* to God's love by loving our neighbors as ourselves." Hence, our responsibly-free faith summons us to respond to the Love that brought us into existence and will not let us go. We return the Eternal One's favor through compassionate deeds. We are collaborators in the restoration of the world's brokenness. Our congregations exist to serve beyond their own walls. Healthy religious education claims that "truth is in order to goodness"—informing minds and transforming souls so that we might more wisely and bravely reform society.

WE ARE RESPECTFUL PILGRIMS

As we move into the new century, Unitarian Universalists must advance beyond mere tolerance to vigorous respect: respect for ourselves, the natural world, neighbors and strangers, and God/Goddess. Being respectful creatures denotes what the Buddhists mean by "right relationship."

The Unitarian Universalist practice of respectfulness starts among all ages of the beloved community in which we live, move, and have our beings. It means neither warehousing nor worshipping our littler ones but holding them in high regard, treating them as beings of equal value to ourselves, lest our faith communities degenerate into adultist empires. Our goal is to ensoul both inter-generationally and globally the message of hymn #302: "From you I receive, to you I give; together we share, and from this we live."

Two other mandates ensue from being "respectful" pilgrims: resistance to evil and reconciliation among differences.

Unitarian Universalists dwell squarely in the Protestant tradition because we are summoned to *pro-test:* literally, oppose wrongdoing by testifying on behalf of what we consider to be the righteous and holy. We rage for impact not injury. Our naysaying dwells in service of justice building and peace making.

We want religious education pilgrims to be well schooled in the "words and deeds of prophetic women and men which challenge us to confront powers and structures of evil with justice, compassion, and the transforming power of love." The litmus test stands when we speak truth to power, especially when we hold it—knowing well that the majority of UUs are privileged and harbor considerable power.

The partnering value to resistance is reconciliation, equally important to be cultivated in our holistic religious education curriculum. As reconcilers we resolve conflicts through compromise not bullying. Creative compromises don't always mean giving in to the other side, but they do mean giving up being right all the time. As reconciling pilgrims, we dare to bridge chasms of otherness. Our faith reminds us that all differences among opposing viewpoints, genders, races, and religions are reconcilable ones. Our mission is to create an intentionally diverse community of ever-widening embrace.

WE ARE RENEWABLE PILGRIMS

The foundational phrase in our heritage derives from our sixteenth-century Transylvanian roots: *semper reformanda*—always reforming. Growth is the evidence of life, and we never stop evolving as religious travelers. We are not limited by past mistakes or present prejudices. Ours is a lifespan journey. We die somewhere in the middle of our trek. We are pilgrims.

While Unitarian Universalism is neither a pessimistic nor an optimistic faith, it is hopeful. A mature religious education curriculum maintains a passion for the possible. It is spiritual treason to succumb to cynicism, so we keep the faith, keep the love, keep the hope. We are counted among those who, as Adrienne Rich says in *Dream of a Common Language*, "age after age, perversely, with no extraordinary power, reconstitute the world."

Semper reformanda means that we are resilient not rigid beings, that "consistency is the hobgoblin of little minds," to second Emerson's warning. It signifies that since we learn racism and sexism, we can unlearn them. We can repent: literally, turn ourselves inside out and change course.

WE ARE REVERENT PILGRIMS

The heart of our Unitarian Universalist awareness is maintaining a primal sense of awe, gratitude, wonder—reverence for the unspeakable, gracious gift of existence. As David Bumbaugh said in a sermon, "My faith is not rooted in knowledge, though I lust to know all I can know; my faith is rooted in awe and wonder, in a world so mysterious that it forever escapes the net of words with which I attempt to ensnare it."

To be religiously educated beings is to remain bathed in the sense of mystery. Whenever a congregant has died, during our Sunday worship service we ritually extinguish our flaming chalice, then light a candle, and offer these simple words: "We are born in mystery, we live in mystery, and we die in mystery."

It is dismaying when modern UUs keep turning eastward or to New Age fancies to locate a current "spiritual" discipline. While it is worthwhile to draw from other traditions, Unitarian Universalist wayfarers need not beg for or borrow mystical resources. Our heritage is a treasure trove of both rational and intuitional insights. As Unitarian President Louis Cornish voiced in 1937, "We belong to the mystics."

Our religious education curriculum is incomplete unless it is brimming with illustrative material from the transcendentalists and mystics among us, from Edith Hunter to Jacob Trapp to Elizabeth Tarbox. Our Hymnbook alone, containing a superior sampler of our sacred scriptures, furnishes ample nourishment for cultivation of the reverent spirit.

In summary, may these seven reminders—to be religious, remembering, recreative, responsible, respectful, renewable, and reverent pilgrims—assist congregations in fulfilling our twenty-first century religious education mission and produce abundant (both many and life-affirming) objectives in alignment with our Unitarian Universalist principles.

∾

Rev. Dr. Tom Owen-Towle is co-senior minister of the First Unitarian Universalist Church of San Diego, California.

Education as Liberation

Rev. Dr. Rebecca Parker

The core of our evolving Unitarian Universalist faith is humanistic concern that every being have its chance at life. The goal of liberal religious education is the unfolding and liberation of life in cooperation with revolutionary grace present in the heart of life. The vital components of such an education are practices of critical reception and creative engagement in the world. Education is a spiritual practice that produces social change.

The Purpose of Education

The purpose of education is *humanization* in the context of *dehumanizing* forces and realities, and the abiding presence of healing, sustaining, and transforming grace. To humanize is to release the full powers of human life. Its opposite is dehumanization. Dehumanizing forces and realities operate in social systems and are internalized within the psychodynamics of individual persons and intimate relationships. They oppress, deny or constrain the fullness of human life. They kill the soul.

Expressed in traditional religious language, the purpose of education is to save souls. The soul dies when a person is cut off from fully and vividly receiving the world. Likewise the soul dies when a person loses her/his capacity to make a response to the world, or surrenders to passivity. A soul is saved when the flood of feeling is restored. Sensitivity comes back into the eyes and the ears, life's touch and feel is renewed, and energy for active engagement and response is reclaimed. When soul-denying culture leads to a debilitation of soul, lust for life—the longing and energy that is within each of us to come back to life—urges us into the transformation from dull to vibrant feelings, from helplessness to passionate involvement. Education creates a fresh and healed relationship to the world, through the relationships of teachers and students to each other and together in relationship to the wider circle of life.

To speak of the abiding presence of healing, sustaining, and transforming grace is to say that even when dehumanizing forces hold sway there is something in life that will not allow life to be suppressed. It resists, protests, mends, and creates change. It is restless. If we ignore it, it will wake us with nightmares and dreams, confront us with dead ends that we can't get around, or charm us with beauty.

To be an educator is to cooperate with revolutionary grace in the work of sustaining and restoring soul.

To speak of the abiding presence of grace is to witness what is observable in the world. It does happen that injustices are protested and repaired, that broken hearts are mended, and broken relationships healed. It does happen that fresh creativity and commitment bring an end to destructive activities and replace them with new forms of beauty. Swords are beaten into plowshares; children play in fields that were once the site of war; the hungry are fed and the grieving comforted. These things happen. It is not guaranteed, by any means, but the force of grace—regardless of how its source or ontological origin is understood—does operate in the world. Its presence is relevant to education.

If we educate without a sense of the abiding presence of grace our modes of education become overly defining and controlling of people. Education seeks to determine the shape of people's lives within a horizon of despair. We begin to believe that without the educator people will never become what we want them to be. This is a form of faithlessness. There is little confidence, trust, or respect for what is *in* people.

Those who educate with a sense of the abiding presence of grace know that to teach is to cooperate with forces of growth, transformation, healing, change, discovery, creativity, and revolution that are not of the teacher's making. This makes education a religious activity.

At the heart of this approach to education is trust in the intrinsic goodness of life, respect for the powers of human life, and care for souls—care that the soul of each person born into this world have its chance at life. As Rumi puts it, "An eye is meant to see things./The soul is here for its own joy."

Roots

During the first half of the nineteenth century, William Ellery Channing advanced a theologically grounded, humanistic philosophy of education. In "Remarks on Education," he wrote,

> The true end of education . . . is to unfold and direct aright our whole nature. Its office is to call forth power of every kind—power of thought, affection, will, and outward action; power to observe, to reason, to judge, to contrive; power to adopt good ends firmly, and to pursue them efficiently; power to govern ourselves, and to influence others; power to gain and to spread happiness.

Channing's educational ideas are grounded in his theology. Human beings are created with a rich and interwoven set of faculties or powers. Our affections, reason, will, thought, and power of action are aspects of the *imago dei*—the image of God in us.

For Channing, the unfolding of human powers is growth in likeness to God. To be godly is to be virtuous, moral, loving, helpful, good, and true—but also, to be logical, critically thoughtful, emotionally empathetic, aesthetically responsive to the world as well as productive and creative in it. As the second-century Christian theologian Ireneas said, "The Glory of God is a human being fully alive."

Education develops full aliveness. Education's purpose is more than acquiring knowledge or adapting to society. Education is for the unfolding of our powers, the full realization of our human-ness, the full growing of a soul into our God-given, divine nature. Thus, the spiritual practice at the heart of Unitarian Universalism is education.

Channing's theology of education holds humanism and spirituality together. The two need not be divided. Religion is a human undertaking that serves an earthly end: fullness of life for all. When life attains to a full unfolding, divine presence is more fully manifest in the world.

Channing's theology goes beyond isolated individualism, or narcissistic self-absorption. Channing conceptualizes fullness of life as *participation in the world*. The powers of the soul that must be unfolded are powers of relationship, connection, interaction, and creative productivity.

The unfolding of our powers is the unfolding of our interactive life as recipients and creative participants in the world. Any unfolding of the self that is not about engagement with the world is not an unfolding of the fullness of our powers, our likeness to God. By keeping soul and world intimately interconnected, Channing's theology makes spirituality and education inseparable from social justice. Religious education fosters active human agency in the creation of a just society by fostering fully alive human beings.

Social Justice

The social implications of Channing's philosophy of education are easily apparent: Any system that prevents the full unfolding of human powers is evil.

Channing saw the implication of his philosophy for economic issues in his time. He was concerned that manual laborers were being treated in the economic system as means to an end, and not human beings of intrinsic worth. His address on *Self-Culture* was delivered to "those who are occupied by manual labor." He said,

> He who possesses the divine powers of the soul is a great being, be his place what it may. You may clothe him with rags, may immure him in a dungeon, may chain him to slavish tasks. But he is still great. . . .
>
> Self culture [is] the care which every man owes to himself, to the unfolding and perfecting of his nature. . . .
>
> I do not look on a human being as a machine, made to be kept in action by a foreign force, to accomplish an unvarying succession of motions, to do a fixed amount of work, and then to fall to pieces at death, but as a being of

free spiritual powers; and I place little value on any culture but that which aims to bring out these, and to give them perpetual impulse and expansion.

I am aware that this view is far from being universal. . . . But the ground of a man's culture lies in his nature, not in his calling. His powers are to be unfolded on account of their inherent dignity, not their outward direction. He is to be educated, because he is a man.

To deprive human beings of the opportunity to exercise their powers is to dehumanize them, to treat them as if they were not created in the image of God. While Channing did not see the implications of his thinking for the lives of women in Boston society, he clearly saw the implications for slavery:

Declare a man chattle, something which you may own and turn to your use, as a horse or a tool, strip him of all right over himself, of all right to use his own powers . . . except what you . . . deem consistent with your own profit, and you cease to look on him as a man. . . . The great right of a man is to use, improve, expand his powers, for his own and others' good. The slave's powers belong to another, and are hemmed in, kept down, not cherished or suffered to unfold.

What is the end and essence of life? It is to expand all our faculties and affections. It is to grow, to gain by exercise new energy, new intellect, new love. . . . It is to hope, to strive, to bring out what is within us, to press towards what is above us. In other words, it is to be free. Slavery is thus at war with the true life of human nature.

To be an educator is to counteract social systems that dehumanize people.

Our Time

In Channing's day, self-culture corrected the negative view of human beings found in Calvinistic doctrines of predestination and total depravity and replaced them with a strong vision of human capacity, inherent goodness, and responsibility. It grounded these capacities religiously in an *imago dei* theology and gave impetus to habits of social activism and public engagement by religious liberals that lasted well into the twentieth century. It countered, as well, some of the dangers of dualism emerging with the Enlightenment while embracing the Enlightenment's emphasis on the use of reason in religion. It contributed to the development of progressive educational practices that were humanistic, holistic, and undergirding of democracy.

The struggle in our time is different. We live now in the context of a highly individualistic, consumer-oriented society. Liberal education finds itself in thrall to self-concern for personal healing, or personal growth and enrichment. Such education does little to unfold the capacities of engagement with the world and social responsibility. Self-culture easily accommodates to a culture of self-interested consumerism.

There is a great hunger for soul among us. I think it is because we have souls made small by a dominant economic system that defines us as merely self-interested consumers. In this smallness we have lost the public world and have been domesticated into a narrow sphere of interest in which we are numb to the fullness of our own being and hungry for the bread of an engaged and meaningful life. No amount of enrichment education or personal spiritual practice will suffice to fill the void created by our loss of the public world and the diminishment of knowledge of ourselves as history-making beings.

What we do in the educational programs of our congregations and our theological schools must address us at this point of our dehumanization. We can accomplish a new approach to religious education by trusting the abiding presence of revolutionary grace, which blesses and disrupts our lives. Our task is to cooperate with this grace as it emerges and disrupts our small worlds and wakes our souls to the wild, wild world in which we meet more fully our neighbors, encounter the divine energies afoot, and find, in our engagement there, our deepest selves—the restoration of our souls.

Pedagogy of the Oppressed Meets Self-culture

Paulo Freire—a humanistic educator whose pedagogy does more than "nurture" the faculties of soul—can assist us in defining the purpose of education. A consideration of his pedagogy, formed among the Third-World poor, shows a way beyond the limits of narcissistically bound liberal religion and culture.

For Paulo Freire the purpose of education is humanization, "the struggle to recover lost humanity." In *Pedagogy of the Oppressed* he writes, "Dehumanization, which marks not only those whose humanity has been stolen, but also (though in a different way) those who have stolen it, is a distortion of the vocation of becoming more fully human." In his foreword to *Pedagogy of the Oppressed*, Richard Shaull says that to be fully human "is to be a subject who acts upon and transforms . . . [the] world, and in so doing move[s] towards ever new possibilities of fuller and richer life individually and collectively." Dehumanization cuts us off from experiencing the world in a vividly conscious way and interacting with it creatively. The dehumanized are submerged in the world, passively shaped, controlled, determined, and used for the purposes of others—but they are not active in the world.

The purpose of education, as Freire proposes it, is to liberate people's capacity to be vividly and critically aware of the world. Simultaneously, education enables their capacity to act in the world as engaged participants in shaping history and society. According to Richard Shaull, "Education becomes 'the practice of freedom,' the means by which men and women deal critically and creatively with reality and discover how to participate in the transformation of their world."

Freire emphasizes that "the pursuit of full humanity . . . cannot be carried out in isolation or individualism, but only in fellowship and solidarity. . . . Attempting *to be more* human individualistically leads *to having more* egotistically." Freire continues,

Education as the practice of freedom—as opposed to education as the practice of domination—denies that man is abstract, isolated, independent, and unattached to the world. . . . Authentic reflection considers . . . people in their relations with the world.

The educational practice that leads to the release of human capacity to be in the world as a critical and creative participant is grounded in profound respect and trust for people. Freire writes that the revolutionary teacher is "imbued with a profound trust in people and their creative power." Such a teacher teaches by engaging students in dialogue. Dialogue is the practice by which teacher and student are side by side in seeking to critically know the world and creatively act in it. "Dialogue," Freire writes, "cannot exist without love, and dialogue is a form of love." Radical trust in people, Freire says, is at the heart of revolutionary teaching.

The liberation of humanness is not simply a matter of casting off an oppressor. It involves re-collecting, re-discovering, and re-engaging powers of the soul that have been silenced, suppressed, split off, or denied by dehumanizing social systems. Such reparation can be the work of a lifetime, an ongoing, unfolding process of claiming and manifesting the power of life within oneself. Feminists speak of the liberation of women as a recovery of soul or self. This recovery is a reclaiming of the powers of soul—the power to speak, to feel, to think, to act for oneself and in the world.

In our time, the challenge is to form educational programs in our congregations through which people develop their capacities to experience the world critically, and engage in it constructively, for the sake of greater fullness of life for all people. When we do this, we begin to emerge from the smallness of soul that characterizes consumerism, and re-emerge as fuller embodiments of divine presence in the world.

A Model for Congregationally Based Social Action as an Educational Practice

The following process requires very active educational leadership from the minister(s) and from lay persons with responsibility for the congregation's educational work and/or social action work. People will emerge from within the congregation with energy and insight to move the process forward. The task of the educational leaders includes recognizing and calling on those people.

STEP 1: PAY ATTENTION; POSE A QUESTION

Pay attention to what is happening in the lives of people in the congregation, the community, the nation, and the world. Notice where fullness of life is being constrained. In response to observations or critical events that occur, pose a question that expresses a problem to be solved or addressed.

This step is done by the educational leaders in the congregation as they critically reflect on their observations, and as they keep their eyes and ears open to questions that are actually being asked by people within the congregation or community. Example: In response to two murders in the neighborhood, the question is posed: How can we respond to these murders in a way that will prevent people in our neighborhood from becoming fearful and isolated?

STEP 2: MAKE A GROUP DECISION REGARDING THE QUESTION

Present the question to the congregation and determine through a democratic process whether the question is one that the congregation feels is important and is willing to take on. This step can include the preparation of position papers by members of the congregation, arguing for or against the value of addressing this question. During this step, the statement of the question may be recast through a process of congregation-wide discussion and dialogue. The educational leaders guide this process, and participate actively in it. Example: In the case of the previous example, the church board discussed the importance of the question and voted to pursue it.

STEP 3: CONDUCT AN INVESTIGATION INTO THE QUESTION

Work with the congregation to design and carry out an investigation of the question and possible actions. The people in the congregation will have knowledge, professional skills, tools of scholarly research, life wisdom, experience, and imagination that can be called upon in finding an answer to the problem posed. The educational leaders bring their experience and knowledge to bear as well. The ministers give particular attention to identifying theological questions at the heart of the problem and lead an inquiry into these questions. They engage people in study of religious, ethical, and theological texts and themes relevant to the question. People from beyond the congregation—neighbors, community leaders, scholars, artists, social workers, etc.—may be invited to participate in the investigation.

The process of investigation produces an educational program of courses, forums, field trips, research papers, public meetings, consultations, etc. Through the process of investigation, possible actions in response to the question are clarified.

Example: In response to the question regarding murders in the neighborhood, the congregation studied approaches to crime prevention, consulted with the police department and the community council, and reflected on religious and ethical questions such as, What does our religious heritage teach us regarding the establishment of peace and security in human affairs? The congregation called a series of community meetings to present information, options, and recommendations.

In the course of the study process it became clear that there were two basic approaches to crime prevention. In one, people try to protect against crime by acquiring weapons, installing expensive security systems, putting bars on windows and doors, and requiring increased police presence. This option is expensive for people and for the community and deepens a sense of fear. In the other, people build stronger bonds of relationship, mutual care, and concern and accept responsibility for the well-being of the community. This option asks something different of people—time, attention, and caring. It costs less, and it deepens a sense of joy.

These options were articulated at a neighborhood meeting. Research made available by the police department showed that the second option was more effective in reducing crime.

The choices for action were becoming clearer.

STEP 4: PREPARE TO TAKE ACTION

Present identified courses of action to the congregation. Position papers may again be prepared to argue the pros and cons of different actions. Consider the resources available for any given action, and the likely consequences of the action for people and for the community. Present a recommended action and set a time table for a vote.

STEP 5: TAKE ACTION

Take a congregational vote on the recommended action. Implement the chosen action. Once taken, the action will yield deeper knowledge and awareness and pose new questions. These questions will lead to the next phase of educational endeavor as the process circles back to Step 1 and begins again.

Example: In response to the murders in the neighborhood, the congregation decided to form a coalition with other churches, the community council, and the police department. Block meetings were organized on every block in a 100-block area, led by church members and community council leaders. People on each block covenanted to assist one another. They helped each other make use of simple, low-cost home security measures that were taught in a series of workshops held at the church. People promised to help keep one another safe by getting to know one another and by watching out for one another.

The congregation's study and action led the neighborhood to create security rooted in relationship and care. Crime went down 50 percent within a year. During the process, the congregation developed a deeper knowledge of the sources of crime. They discovered that most of the neighborhood crime was committed by teenagers from the neighborhood. The question emerged: What is happening in the lives of our youth that leads them to commit crimes? To answer this question, church members visited the family of the young man arrested for one of the murders. They discovered a family deeply stressed by poverty and in need of compassionate support in a time of great pain. Church members sought to be of help to the family. A new question emerged: What needs to happen so that this family and other families in our community have the resources they need for their children?

This question sets the stage for the next round of study and action.

This seven-step method was developed in 1980–85 at Wallingford United Methodist Church in Seattle, Washington, by members of the congregation. Carl Slater and Robin Moore-Slater were responsible for the congregation's educational work during much of that time. I was the parish minister. The method exemplifies practices proposed by Paulo Freire's pedagogy of the oppressed, but was developed independently as a successful grassroots experiment. It shows that Freire's principles can be discovered and applied in a North American congregation in a way that leads to concrete action for a humanized world. At Wallingford this practice enabled the congregation to overcome an individualistic approach to social action. And, it made it clear that, when practiced as a dialogical, democratic, interdisciplinary process of posing questions, study, and action by people whose questions are the voice of their humanistic concern, education is the embodiment of love.

～

Rev. Dr. Rebecca Parker is president of Starr King School for the Ministry in Berkeley, California.

The Core of Our Evolving Unitarian Universalist Faith

REV. MEG RILEY

~

As I think about the transient and the permanent in Unitarian Universalism, I am drawn to these words from May Sarton's 1955 novel, *Faithful Are the Wounds:*

> "What's happened to us, Edward?" and this time there was a plaintive note in her voice.
> "Nothing's happened to us, nothing at all. We're just what we always were. That's the trouble . . . it's a liberal organization, Grace, after all."
> "It used to be a fighting organization."
> "The trouble with liberals is that they see *all* sides. It paralyzes them. . . . It was quite all right to be radical twenty years ago—at least in these parts. Now I frighten my students if I mention the New Deal. Actually they've never heard of the Spanish War—even the best of them. They're not interested in politics."
> They stopped in the final moment here in the open space before Beacon Street grows dark with office buildings. . . . This Boston may look sedate, ancient and settled to an outsider, but to Edward Cavan and Grace Kimlock, standing on the corner, its tradition was a living one, a tradition of reform, protest, fierce belief in the rights of minorities. Not for nothing was their final glance for the corner where Robert Gould Shaw stood in bas-relief leading his Negro regiment into battle.

As we enter the twenty-first century, I believe that Unitarian Universalism will continue to be a liberal religion with disgruntled radicals at its edges, and will vacillate between bold action based on our beliefs and regular retreat into processing the perennial, if seemingly minute, disagreements among us. I am one of those frustrated radicals, and so a large part of me wishes that what was at the core of our faith was "a living tradition of reform, protest, fierce belief in the rights of minorities." There was a time when I did. However, in my middle age, I have come to accept that our Theodore Parkers and our James Reebs—the real prophets among us—have always been institutionally marginalized, and ever will be. I have also come to believe that a liberal institution with radical fringes has a great deal to offer the world in the twenty-first century.

Temples of Pluralism

Seeing all sides of things is both a blessing and a curse. Seeking decisive, consistent action from a liberal institution is extremely frustrating. However, if our religious education programs could create congregations where the religious impulse itself is to savor pluralism—not only to allow but to encourage creative tension, our congregations would be a great gift for the United States and the world in the twenty-first century. I believe this is a difficult but achievable goal.

Vital Components

The tired old joke goes that given a choice between going to heaven and attending a discussion group about heaven, UUs choose the latter. The same, I think, is mostly true about pluralism. We'd rather talk about it than live it. What would it mean to equip people to live what we speak about pluralism? I believe there are seven components of religious education programs that could equip us to do so.

These components are very largely directed at the adult members of the congregation. It has always been my experience that the real curriculum for children is the lived experience of the adults. We have never had a problem coming up with vital, engaging, relevant hour-long weekly programs for our children about peace making, world religions, sexuality, justice, etc. The problem is that they experience these curricula, for the most part, in a vacuum of intergenerational community or focus. That is what my components are centered around.

The components are

- commitment to and immersion in embodied religious practice
- affinity and accountability groups based on religious identity
- civility squads who teach and maintain guidelines for positive interaction
- real time together in community
- the cultivation of stewardship as religious education
- respect for the passion and wisdom of those who bring energy and juice to the congregation
- opportunities for close relationships across affinities, self-identities, and ages.

Embodied Practice of Religion. Congregational members make a commitment to engage in actual religious experience, not just to approach all the world's religions with an equal amount of disassociation and consider it detached equanimity!

For example, I grew up UU and was exposed to many religious beliefs, and I always felt deep in my heart that Native American beliefs were most resonant with my own. Imagine my surprise when, as a seminarian, I was invited to a Lakota ceremony and found myself, in terror and desperation, trying to maintain detachment as lightening bolts zinged around the dark room, birds flew and wolves howled, and other 'impossible' events took place. ("It's electromagnetic forces," I told myself in a pseudo-reassuring voice. What I knew about electromagnetic forces was about equal to what I knew about the spirit world, but it was where I sought my reassurance!) When the ceremony was over, the medicine man observed, "It was a good service despite the presence of an anthropologist." I knew he was talking about me. I realized that despite my intellectual familiarity with the interdependent web and all that, I was not a bit comfortable leaving my zone of "knowing what's going on." (Amazingly, I continued to be invited back into the ceremonies of the Lakota people and continued to accept the invitations for over a year, until I realized that the invitations spoke volumes about the spiritual generosity of the Lakota people, but really said little about my own spiritual gifts except that I was willing to learn and willing to be welcomed into another culture!)

As my own religious journey has progressed, I have chosen to leave the mode of the "religious anthropologist" which I was raised to be in a UU fellowship and become open to and eager for actual religious experience. I have moved through my terror in a passionate and zealous Christian congregation and in regular week-long silent Buddhist meditation retreats. I am now more comfortable in those metaphor systems than I was, though neither feels exactly mine. My own deepest spiritual path seems to be maintaining real relationships, standing in awe before the power of our interconnectedness. I don't say all of this because I think a religious education program would have to provide total immersion experiences in all world religions for all congregants. However, some immersion—and especially the experience of moving through fear—would be necessary!

Sunday services are not a likely place to experience what I am speaking about. Forums and guest speakers can only introduce people intellectually to new belief systems. Music or dance can go a little deeper. But in order to move out of our heads about our faiths and into the true humility that comes from embarking on the impossible task of embodying our greatest ideas without perpetual failure, we also need to take spiritual risks. This will not take place for us when we sit mutely in the role of an audience.

Opportunities for immersion and risk could include social service activities, such as the street retreats led by the Rev. Kay Jorgensen in San Francisco. They might include classes in meditation, with the encouragement to practice it daily and with periodic weekend or week-long intensives. They might include taking interfaith action with those religious people we find the most frightening, fundamentalist Christians. They might include regular healing circles or prayer groups.

The specific content of immersion groups would vary depending on the needs and interests of each congregation. It would be necessary for their effectiveness, however, that they involve risk and action in the center and reflection and discussion off to the side. Such risk, and taking action despite fear, would need to be understood as central to the religious life of the congregation and individuals. (And there would need to be several choices for members about where to become immersed. Without such choice, most UUs would bolt into rebellion against authority and need to discuss what is wrong with the congregation for the next thirty years!)

Small Groups for Intimacy and Accountability. These are different from immersion experiences. Rather, they are home groups, touch groups, family groups, cell groups. However, I think they are strengthened by being centered on some part of religious identity that is a current focus of attention, rather than by being randomly assigned. For instance, parents of young children or parents of teenagers are struggling to incorporate this new identity on the deepest levels. Families of people with life-threatening illnesses are reshaping their identities, religiously and otherwise. People who want their work to embody their deepest passion for life are struggling with religious issues. People are trying to simplify lives and slow down.

Too often, "support groups" in our congregations might just as well be run by anyone and have little to do with the religious lives we aspire to live. Ongoing support for the perpetual struggles of our marriages and partnerships, single status, family lives, work lives, and activist lives could be deep sources of spiritual strength in our congregations. Howard Thurman (and I paraphrase out of desperation, having sought the quote fruitlessly) wrote, "Once we're at home anyplace in the universe, we're at home every place in the universe." These groups would locate people inside congregations.

Civility Squads. Cultivating and maintaining a cadre of people whose special task is the maintenance of civil community is, unfortunately, an increasingly necessary task. This is because the culture, the media, and even our families are teaching us less and less about it. "Civility" does not mean that everyone should suddenly become Minnesotans and worship "niceness." It does mean that there are acceptable and unacceptable ways to disagree and differ. It does not mean that people's feelings won't be hurt and there won't be anger and disappointment. It does mean that there will be more safety and a sense that everyone is accountable to the same set of angers and disappointments. In some congregations, where passive aggression has ruled for centuries, civility squads may have more work to do in eliciting people's engagement in real, healthy differences than in mediating out-of-control conflicts.

Real Time Together. This is increasingly important as our lives are lived in the spin cycle of busyness. People need to make a commitment to be together overnight, all day, not just for an hour here and there. In the small fellowship where I grew up in West Virginia, there were three church retreats every year. I don't have a clue what the grown-ups did all day. At night we all danced, held talent shows, and made music together. Because of these retreats the kids formed a community that held us across the several hundred miles from which we commuted to the fellowship.

As our lives speed up and undivided attention is harder and harder to come by, we need even more to hold regular, intergenerational retreats in relaxing settings. For most families now, once a year might be more likely than three times. The ministers and their families need to be part of these retreats and model their value. The programming needs to include worship, fun, and focused presentations. "Why We Should Pay Our UN Dues" is probably not the right kind of focus. Rather, more relevant issues would be related to faith and family and personal identity, with all participants helping the community through meal preparation and shared leadership and music and worship.

Religious Education about Stewardship. The congregation's money, building, and gathered community are precious commodities, to be cared for as part of religious life. Such care can't be relegated to tiny committees but must be taught as central to faith.

Tithing, cleaning and gardening, and sorting nursery toys could all be done faithfully or with no care and attention. On Buddhist retreats, vacuuming, washing dishes, and preparing meals become as central and vital to meditation life as sitting and walking do. You end up feeling privileged to do them, which of course you are. Mindfulness about stewardship of money can't be carried out in a pledge drive and then abandoned with relief for another nine months. With good facilitation, tending to stewardship as a religious education process offers fertile ground for discussions about class privilege, scarcity and abundance, fairness, representative democracy, our expectations of each other, entitlement, generosity, and other profound issues.

Most religious education programs with which I am familiar have little to do with conversations about church finances and funding. Rather, it is as if the "heads of the family" make the budget and then offer an allowance to the "dependents." Putting religious educators, and families, in the center of funding the congregation's life would radically alter the way money was discussed and handled.

Most Passionate Vision in the Center. Even though, for most congregational members, the center of church life may be coffee hour and potluck dinners, the visionaries in the group need to be given good attention and taken seriously. I don't mean here the zealots, the relentlessly driven activists for particular causes. I mean the sources of passionate energy. Often they are young adults and older teens, but sometimes they are new members, newly retired elders, and even ministers!

What could this mean? It might mean regularly holding up a vision of what the congregation could be if excluded groups were to be invited in and addressing the barriers to such invitations being accepted. This has happened with very positive effects in our Welcoming Congregation program, with less success in our racial and cultural diversity work, and probably with least effect of all in our work around accessibility.

One of my most abiding and passionate convictions about what our denomination needs is the creation of a residential leadership training center for UU faith-based activism. I see it in Washington, D.C., with about eight UUs committing a year of their time to its mission: embodying UU values in the world. I envision young adults as the primary constituency, but also an occasional new retiree, displaced middle-aged seeker, lonely community minister. I see them engaged in regular worship, meditation and reflection, and a great deal of activism and direct service on behalf of our movement—learning all the ins and outs of advocacy. I think this would add a great deal to our movement in a variety of ways. Young adults, whether they were part of the actual life of the center or not, would know it was there, a concrete commitment to their living faith and a concrete acknowledgment of their talents and gifts. Eight committed full-time activists could make an amazing difference in terms of UU visibility and effectiveness. And a new generation of leaders, grounded in a shared immersion process, would live out our spoken commitment to justice.

Opportunities for Intimacy across Barriers, Self-Identities, Ages, Interests. Probably nothing transforms our viewpoint as radically as an authentic relationship with someone who is different from us. Any of us who has stayed in a relationship for more than a year or so can attest to this! But we tend to gravitate toward people who are within our comfort zones or to maintain superficial and inauthentic relationships with those who are not. I believe our congregations need to engage in encouraging guerrilla relationships that shake up our preconceptions and give our systems a jolt.

For instance, we regularly pair up adults with young children in "secret friends" programs, which are deeply rewarding to all. The following are thoughts about how such programs could be expanded:

- Pair up e-mail or snail-mail buddies and give regular assignments of topics to share thoughts about via the Internet or U.S. mail. (This would be ideal for teens and seniors, elders and new parents, workaholics, and the homebound.) Assign topics that demand increasing vulnerability, encourage people to write stream of consciousness for half an hour, demand that participants pledge never to share what another has written. Those who do not believe the Internet is safe for confidential communication can choose the snail-mail option.

- Have secret friends among adults. Youth regularly do this at conferences. It makes you look at the whole room differently, wondering who's sending you love letters and noticing what you're doing so attentively!

- Have coffee hours with assigned topics. Discourage discussion of professional life. Encourage discussion of more risky topics: hell, redemption, sex, money, death, suffering, joy, marriage—and encourage each person to talk with three people they ordinarily wouldn't speak to.

- Encourage people to approach, not avoid, those who intimidate them or provoke judgments. Make congregational life a laboratory for learning new behaviors in the bigger world!

If our congregations embodied these seven component pieces, I believe that they would offer something vital and unique to our communities and to our world.

∼

Rev. Meg Riley is the director of the Washington, D.C. Office for Faith in Action, a department of the Unitarian Universalist Association.

Margin and Center

Rev. Dr. Tracey Robinson-Harris

At the core of our evolving Unitarian Universalist faith is our commitment to justice and to transforming structures of oppression and marginalization including those within our own community of faith.

In this paper I use this core commitment as a lens through which to view religious education. I also use it as the tool with which I shape goals for our future.

In June 1997, The Commission on Appraisal issued its report entitled *Interdependence*. The section of the report that addresses marginalized groups within our Association includes this:

> On the one hand, we place high value on religious education for children. On the other hand, how we think about religious educators . . . is sometimes inconsistent with how we think about religious education as a program that is central to faith development. Religious educators have a special identity that is rarely understood or affirmed as a central aspect of congregational life in our movement.

This is the heart of the matter. Religious education is clearly central to the health, growth, and vitality of our faith. We know this both statistically and anecdotally. But religious education occupies an institutional place on the margins. On this forming edge of the twenty-first century, we need to define new strategies for dealing with this paradox—for transforming congregations, transforming them/us from congregations with (or aspiring to have) good religious education programs toward congregations where educating is at the heart of all aspects of institutional life.

The goal is educating congregations. We need to get out of the "religious education as program" box and move toward broad institutional commitments to religious education as congregational ministry—a ministry of finding connections, forming identity, and transforming the world by the practice of our faith.

Neither the implicit strategy of developing quality programs nor the explicit one of focusing on "professionalizing" (or "ministerializing") the role of religious educator have proven sufficient to the task of bringing religious education in from the margins. While necessary, neither has been sufficient to address the paradoxical position of religious education in our congregations.

Charles Foster describes "religious education as program" in his book *Educating Congregations*. We have gotten to this place, he writes, because

> the inability of congregations to sustain an educational ministry for the individual learning of children, youth or adults has culminated in the subversion of most church education into learning activities designed to enrich student religious experience rather than to build up transformed and transformative communities of faith.
>
> Enrichment education seeks to create a positive experience for students . . . it moves closer to the dynamics of entertainment than to the transformation of life. . . . Its concern is to promote a momentary sense of well-being or self-esteem.

Charles Foster also points out that the religious educator, as program director, is responsible for a calendar of events and activities. Significant among the items on the calendar is the "church school program." The director is responsible for a variety of aspects of the program including selection of curricula (often with the involvement of a committee) to be used in classes usually sorted by age. The program's purpose is meeting the variety of needs and interests of individuals and/or small groups of learners as understood by the director and committee with whom he or she works. If the director and/or committee also attend to the needs and interests of adult learners, they may do so by offering a variety of "classes" and group experiences. Some of these offerings grow out of the interests and/or needs of (potential) leaders of the class or group. Among the primary concerns of those responsible for the program are recruiting volunteer teachers for all the classes, finding teacher-friendly and meaningful curricula and other program resources, managing the program well with appropriate training, policies, procedures, and ensuring appropriate behavior and safety of children and youth in church.

I know well, as do you, that attention to these concerns, and myriad other administrative details, is absolutely essential to a good quality program. In Unitarian Universalist religious education programs all over the continent, quality teaching and learning take place every week. And we also know the implicit lessons of marginalization embodied in this program model. Consider the children, and youth.

Children and youth figure this faith stuff out with help from others—peers and parents and teachers. We encourage them to come to their own conclusions and to explore, ask, imagine. More often than not, the time and space for that as part of religious community is in the context of the "program."

- How often do our children and youth leave the "adult" worship service part way through or not participate at all except when they are "performing"?

- Have you heard the disappointment of our youth when they say there is nothing for them after they age out of YRUU? Where there should be a bridge into the congregation in a new way, they find instead a cliff—the congregational equivalent of "write when you get work and visit us when you are home." What opportunities have there been for them to experience being valued members of the congregation except within their particular program "box"?

- Have you heard young adults in our congregations identify the boxes that keep them from full participation? Young adults have no money (so cost more than they give back), will be back when they're married with kids, only want to be with folks their own age.

- Have you been in coffee hour when children and youth are being ignored by most adults (except perhaps parents and teachers) or are having limited interactions with a few adults who are primarily doing limit setting with young people whose names they may not know?

- Is an occasional service project, week-long work camp, or a spontaneous or one-time response to support a cause or offer assistance practice enough to create habits of service or commitments to transform the conditions that called forth the response?

Boxes seem to beget more boxes. "The program" is the primary "container" (box) for participation of our children and youth; even at times young adults in the life of our congregations. Connected to this large program "container" is a whole assortment of related containers: children-in-worship-one-Sunday-a-month, Youth Sunday, RE Sunday, Young-Adults-Back-from-College-Sunday and more. The content in any one or all of these boxes may explicitly reflect commitments to inclusion. The containers themselves contradict us—separating, segregating, isolating.

I return to Foster's analysis for another sentence or two:

> To view education as a "program" bankrupts a congregation's efforts to . . . extend the life and mission of the church into the future. . . an identity and mission for the congregation's future is never identified. Programmatic enrichment education actually creates the conditions to intensify a sense of isolation rather than community.

The above questions are not intended as openers into a conversation about "fixing" or improving the program "box." They are intended to probe how a congregation understands its ministry of religious education, about how all of us, of all ages, find connection, form identity, and transform the world by the practice of our faith.

The other primary focus (in addition to quality programs) for our energy and effort in addressing the marginalization of religious education is the role of the religious educator. As the locus for "fixing the problems" of marginalization, we organized LREDA and support its ongoing work to address a variety of professional issues. We were successful in gaining official institutional recognition for the ministry of religious education. We created the Religious Education Landscape and its options. As valuable as each and all of these are, none of these strategies has led to broad, sustained, and deep institutional transformation.

In spite of LREDA, the ministry of religious education, and the Landscape program, religious educators still post e-mail after e-mail to the REACH list with questions about how to move off the margin. How can I negotiate for a more equitable salary? How can I encourage a reluctant congregation to be intergenerational? How can I get religious education needs on the table for the committee planning for the new building to consider? How do I get the parish minister to include children in worship regularly? What else can I do to get volunteers to say yes when I've reduced the time we ask them to commit to a month or a week per month?

The "status quo" structures of religious education in our congregations are supported by parallel structures in the UUA. We significantly support the quality program strategy (with resource and program development supported by leadership training such as REnaissance modules and curriculum leader trainings). The "professionalizing" strategy has also had support, though it has been limited. (Renaissance modules fit here too, along with financial support for continuing education and the few opportunities that we provide for recognition.) The "ministerializing" strategy has found itself victimized by administrative details and unresolved questions over the value and place of the ministry of religious education in our Association.

We know something of the cost of allowing this paradox to continue: short tenure and high turnover in religious education positions, congregations who take an "either kind will do" approach in a religious educator search, conflict between professional expectations and "juice and cookies" realities. We have, I think, been lucky that the cost of living in the paradox has been institutionally modest (though the cost to individuals and congregations is high) in this respect—quality religious education programs enrich many a congregation.

Clearly, life in this paradox is possible. We have gotten practiced at it and used to it. And it is a barrier to our congregations being all they can be. And it is not just.

We need to do a little DDT. We need to reconsider our diagnosis (D) and determine (D) new treatments (T), to borrow language from Bill Jones. We need to strategize. And we need to make changes—changes that can transform congregations toward educating congregations.

The diagnosis? Marginalization of religious education is built into the structures of our congregations. Nothing new here!

But when it comes to treatments, we need to be sure that they focus not on the programs of religious education nor on the role of the religious educator, but on the structures of the institutional life of our congregations.

We need to stop trying to "fix" the oppressed and change the structures of oppression.

I am not certain how this needs to happen. There some things I want to examine and change and try out. This is where the conversation needs to take us—into examining, changing, and trying.

What if we reinvent the Religious Education Covenanting process? What would it look like if the process addressed all levels of the institution—personnel, policy and practice, program, constituency, organizational structure, and mission and purpose—involving congregational leadership in institutional analysis and broad visioning? What if such a process were integral to every long-range and strategic planning process?

What if our training, education, and resource development also helped our congregations do a deep assessment intended to move them/us toward mission-centered religious education that focuses on the practices of faith and presence in the communities in which we live?

What if the UUA were to acknowledge that the structures at the continental level need transforming so that we can serve, support, and encourage those changes in congregations? What if we had an Office for the Education and Preparation of Religious Professionals? What if we had an office that provided settlement services for congregations seeking religious educators and religious educators in search? What if we increased support for continuing education with more visible guidance, more funding, and an expanded partnership between the UUA and LREDA?

What if the UUA was called to address its accountability and responsibility for the credentialing of professional religious leadership, including the religious educators who serve our congregations?

It is my prayer that we undertake this hard work. It is my prayer that we undertake it for the sake of our congregations and all those who have and will find/make religious community with us. And it is my prayer that we undertake this hard work because oppressions are interlocked and to work on one manifestation can build bridges to the larger work of anti-oppression.

At the core of our evolving Unitarian Universalist faith is our commitment to justice and to transforming structures of oppression and marginalization including those within our own community of faith. Audre Lorde calls us to that larger work with these words from *A Burst of Light:*

> Tomorrow belongs to those of us who conceive of it as belonging to everyone; who lend the best of ourselves to it, and with joy. It takes all of my selves, working together, to integrate what I learn . . . into my consciousness and work. It takes all of my selves working together to effectively focus attention and action. . . . Every one of these battles generates energies useful in the others.

∾

Rev. Dr. Tracey Robinson-Harris is the deputy director of the Department for Congregational, District, and Extension Services at the Unitarian Universalist Association.

Looking Back

REV. JEANNELLEN RYAN

What's at the core? That we agreed to disagree and still "walk together," mostly trusting in some intuitive way of our needs to do so and the goodness of the effort. What is at "the core of our evolving Unitarian Universalist faith" is something we spin answers to by how we live, all other claims to the contrary.

I must admit the phrase is not one I use in thinking of my personal religious orientation. As an agnostic, my perception is that my "faith" is steady and far less evolving than my understanding of it. Hopefully, in community, it is I who grow and evolve a deeper, broader realization of what it means to live as a Unitarian Universalist. If there is a core, then it must be our tradition, our history, our actual past and our deep desire to participate in the authentic forward projections of that resulting identity. But what exactly is it? Ahh—that is the stuff of which creative interchange is made. In reading through the papers and reflecting on my experience of the ministerial convocation in Hot Springs, it is clear that a simple and binding consensus did not emerge no matter how fine a process orientation occurred.

We have a history and an identity and a tradition, all of which are perceived as plural. We have formally stated, common Principles and Purposes that for some of us form the basis of our association with others. We have a promise that some feel is less fulfilled than others. We have an established faith with primary institutional reality inherited from the nineteenth-century origins of the Unitarian movement in Boston. We have a lesser subsumed thread from merger with the Universalist Church of America which occurred formally in 1961. Within this Association of individuals and congregations we have a vast array of poorly herded cats, their ideals, personal beliefs, orientations, hopes, and fears. The very question of "Who do we think we are?" often seems more likely to elicit the response, "Who are you to ask the question?" than a genuine answer.

We exist as an institution, and institutions once created tend to self-perpetuate themselves. I say this with the thought that if we did not exist, I question whether any newly stated "core" would have the compelling strength to bring together an evolving faith community committed to the existence we currently enjoy. Yet we are people who "are called upon to reject the easy answers and to struggle with the values and conflicts inherent in human life."

Nancy Ammerman, a professor in congregational studies, had a piece in *Christian Century* a couple of years back, reporting on research she had done on thriving churches. She was asked whether conservative congregations were doing better than liberal ones. She replied that her research showed those that used their own faith tradition to seek answers to the contemporary problems they were facing came out far stronger than those who looked elsewhere for their answers. And this was true no matter whether they were conservative, fundamentalist, or liberal.

Today it appears that Jeffersonian democracy is on the wane or is evolving into something unrecognizable. It's "show me the money" time in this competitive, materialistic age. Democracy is no longer at the core of our American culture, whether in politics, education, or the workplace. The capitalist workplace ethic of worker as commodity reigns supreme. Money talks and even churchgoers have been converted to consumers. In a world overrun with economic propaganda the self-determining aspect of democracy is lost. Family change, workplace change, economic change all cry out for a steady spiritual influence and nurture. The good news is that our tradition—experience based, open to ongoing revelation, process oriented—exists. And still, underlying all cultures, I believe, remains the need for religious expression in response to the gift of life. But is evolving faith at the core of most lifestyles today? No, participation is part of a lifestyle laundry list of structured activities for all ages. Life for the American middle class has become a series of overscheduled events. How are we to accommodate or adjust? In rereading *The Stonehouse Conversations* of twenty years ago, much remains true and valid. But the environment has changed. We have a call for new wine in new bottles. Still, even the Bible acknowledges that people really do prefer the old wine.

I tend to believe in the pendulum theory of history, that each age contains within it the seeds of its own destruction and each new form or format arises in response or reaction to what was missing or overdone in the era before it. Just as our origins with an emphasis on reason and nurture were a response to the Great Awakening and its excesses of thunderclap conversions of the fearful servants of the great Jehovah, so, too, do we seek to adjust our journey to an age of swift changes in technology, excess information, and the increasing cultural diversity that surrounds us.

In spite of ourselves we are seekers and we are not immune to the lure of pilgrims' progress and perfectibility. Having had our American Unitarian beginning grow out of a difference in content of preaching, we sometimes seem stuck in a notion of "salvation by proclamation" whereby if we just affirm the right formulations to/at one another we become sanctified as righteous and need not continue to work at changing our behavior. The pious intonation that worship is our only real center all too often collapses the sacrament of life itself to the light nourishment of the hymn sandwich. I stand with those to whom religious education, in its broadest sense, is a central act of our religious life together and I believe the needs of this time call for it to become "at the core" for Unitarian Universalists of all ages.

In *With Purpose and Principle: Essays About the Seven Principles of Unitarian Universalism*, Richard Gilbert recounts Eugene Picketts's response to Mother Theresa's quote on the meaning of life: "To become holy, and to go Heaven." Pickett's visionary Unitarian Universalist response was "to become whole and to create a heaven on earth." That's it.

What is my vision for goals for liberal religious education? My vision is that the goals should work, that they should be efficacious. I leave to others the specific formulations, for I believe we spend too much energy arguing the fine points and polishing goals than we do in implementing them effectively. It is as if a flawlessly refined articulation of intentionality was a substitute for the actual accomplishment of a goal.

What my vision for goals for liberal religious education is built around is my understanding of congregational polity. I expect that each congregation or educating group would periodically gather to review, refine, renew, determine, decide, and commit to its goals based on what our tradition has to offer the needs of that community at a given time.

Let me focus on one aspect that I feel I know something about and view as essential to a vision of goal accomplishment. Leadership is that critical element. One of my visions is that every UU congregation will have access to a qualified religious education professional, not on an every Sunday basis necessarily, but sufficiently to feel their program is "in care of" someone who can carry that role effectively for them and with them.

Association-wide, we have never fully embraced the notion of verifiable professionals qualified to carry the burden of ministry to children, youth, and families for every congregation. I state this as an observable fact, not an opinion. We offer a variety of explanations for this fact. We can't afford it. Our congregations are too small. Institutionally we remain too attached to nineteenth-century notions of woman as "natural nurturer," to 1950s' notions of available, young mothers who gladly turn to this work "to get out of the house" and to earn "pin money." The old ways have not been working well for two decades, and the situation is increasingly worse. The price we pay for generational change unattended is high. It may cost us our future. We do work within a cultural context and we must ask whether our formulations are supported by that context because the answer determines greatly what our strategies to achieve our goals must include.

If confidence in religious education leadership is insufficient, our goals and visions are invalidated. Institutional confidence in religious education leadership was so low and so poorly invested in that no living Unitarian Universalist religious educator was available and deemed worthy to occupy the Meadville/Lombard professorship when it was created. When the creation of district-level field staff in religious education (program consultants) was discussed with existing field staff in the early 1990s, it was reported that existing, generalist, field staff were concerned there were not enough capable religious educators to fill such positions and incompetents would be elevated beyond their ability. This notion is extremely significant and pervasive. We are all familiar with the phenomenon as it shows itself in many local congregations. The way the cycle goes, someone is seen as "filling in" because a "real" religious educator is unavailable. People apply themselves, learn their trade if they stay with it, begin to make advocacy or acknowledgment demands of one sort or another, and encounter the underlying assumptions that they are not entitled to the recognition or authority they may crave. Of course, ministers of religious education are subject to more subtle disparagement. Leadership without legitimate authority is handicapped leadership.

Interdependence, the 1997 published report of the Commission on Appraisal, identified "the need to reshape our understandings of lay and professional ministries, both to resolve current tensions and to meet new needs for religious leadership." I am not sure I truly know what the person who wrote that meant, but I take it to include valuing religious education leadership more appropriately. I applaud the report's acknowledgment that we as UUs are not free from the oppression of women, children, and others, even as middle-class white women, who form the bulk of recognized religious educators, participate in the other prejudices and oppressions in which our society is mired. A difficulty that we have is that the more visions and goals focus on oppression and marginalization the more we need to better understand our roles and stances. Specifically, members of an oppressed, marginalized group, such as religious educators, who are operating in a system that is unaware of its oppression may not be best suited to lead the transformative way.

If you read *Interdependence* carefully you may note that religious educators are themselves subtly marginalized in the section on marginalized groups. They are not identified in the list of marginalized groups at the start of the chapter, as are youth, ages fourteen to eighteen. The report lists "children and religious education" as a marginalized group. Is the religious educator understood to be somehow subsumed under the noun "religious education" so that no specific reference is needed? Or is this a bit like being included in the child-care budget line? Or is it part of the very fabric of marginalization that when advantages for "lay leadership" are cited religious educators are lumped with clergy? When clergy privilege is at issue religious educators are conveniently relegated to lay leadership. Most often religious educators are simply not mentioned at all and read themselves in much the way women once did when "man" was mentioned.

Further on, under headings of "Children and Religious Education," and "Congregational Polity and Religious Education," we find "the community of religious educators (MRE's and DRE's alike) emerge as a marginalized group" and the subsequent paragraphs go on to address the issue. Although, of course, we religious educators are thrilled to be mentioned at all in such a publication, it has a feeling of having been slid in the back door. Especially since, before the text goes on to address marginalization and theological identity in the next chapter, the section on children and religious education closes with a subsection entitled, "Affirmative Action—Yes or No?" and barely mentions religious educators as it focuses on the lesbigay community and people of color. Marginalized in its own section? Or are we to understand that it is simply that the perception of marginalization, when looked at in relation to other kinds of marginalization, turns out to be minor? I feel this is an especially good example because it represents the very best of intentions and effort. My point is that inadequate views of religious education leadership limit all that is possible, including progress on our goals for antiracism and healthy understandings of human sexuality.

When UU folks think of religious education, they think of children, they think of curriculum not leadership, and often not even adults, though we have for years stressed lifelong learning in our communities. My goal is a vision of clear acceptance and unambivalent valuing of religious education leadership with the understanding that, no, it is not "just for children"!

What are the vital components of our UU religious education? The vital components are leadership, community, experience, tradition, love, caring, kindness, inclusivity, and commitment. Myths, symbols, reason and democracy, nonsense, and culture are all grist for the mill. Modeling and spending time with each other are high on my list. Self, other, world, relatedness of world, self, other with emphasis on the phenomenon of alienation, separation, otherness in personal, interpersonal, institutional, and global forms.

Stories are a key element. Biography deserves special attention. We need an emphasis on narrative as the carrier of our abstract principles, as a way of telling individual and community stories. If we wish to succeed in using narrative modes we need to get better at interpreting our methodologies around narrative theology such that it is intellectually credible to adults. Just as the art and science of child care is underestimated, we must make sure intellectually oriented individuals do not dismiss them as just stories not "real" education.

In light of family time constraints, what specific process demands ought to be made? Which elements need to be preprocessed so that the key connections for transformation—awareness, deep intentionality, commitment to congruent behavior—have time to take place? There are times to use a cake mix and times to start from scratch with only the freshest ingredients. The days of all-day baking are gone and maybe we need to package up more "Curriculum Pop Tarts" if you will. Create instantly nourishing learn-bytes for kids on the go. It is hard to do that, but it may be necessary.

We know that children and youth have always benefitted from the attentions of caring adults who live their values. We know that perfect community may be beyond us, but that hospitable, accepting, nurturing human community is within our grasp. I think we should aim our materials more toward the small society (read village). Not so much to "help them out" or throw them a bone, but by focusing our attention on making small societies the laboratory for experiments to find these new ways we need for the future. We know change and needed innovation come not from the existing centers of things, but from the margins where there's not a lot to lose from trying something different. We need more honesty and integrity around financial provisions for resources. It takes a village, but the village needs a decent budget too.

Sometimes I think that instead of going for the new, we should renew more, like we are doing with *Church Across the Street* and *Haunting House,* intentionally creating more of a resonance with the past. Religious education needs greater scholarship behind it, more attention to theoretical analysis and philosophical underpinnings such that adults are grabbed and catch the passion and enthusiasm needed to be evangelists for Unitarian Universalism within our own multigenerational communities.

What are the appropriate realms of religious education if sex education is a major one? Others will no doubt address this more fully. With the view of UU adults as forming the base of the leadership pool for our religious education efforts, I question whether adult religious education has kept pace with children's religious education such that our expectations for learning and engagement for children are far too advanced relative to the two primary areas of antiracism and human sexuality, where if we have any doctrines, we have them here. A faith community that puts its children forward toward a progressive stance and yet permits its adults to dodge issues and has weak expectations for their spiritual growth and learning lacks integrity. Theologically, some UU adults seem as if they are primarily in unreconstructed reaction to previous faith orientations. Literacy areas for adults are "otherness," which might include all sex and gender issues; diversity and antiracism; democratic processes including congregational polity; and organizational accountability.

We must ask what are the *deadly* components and root them out however much we are used to them. In these times we need to address the "religion of the successful" charge and balance joy with appreciation of evil, sensitivity to suffering, and accountability around who we profess to be. A few years ago I had the privilege of participating in and providing lay leadership for religious education as a member of a congregation where "whites" were in the minority and socioeconomic factors were very different from the midsize suburban congregation that seems to be our basic stereotype. The "party on" spirit of many of our religious education programs was thin here where grounding, solidity, and predictability were more in order. I could see young people needed true substance and honest response. A carefree, colorblind world was far away and prayer for deliverance from evil a lot closer. Many of our publications did not transfer as well as our notions of ourselves as promoting "universalizing religion." I believe we are hard at work on these issues and need to keep seeing ourselves as others see us while we return again and again to those traditions that still fit, still work, and still convey meaning from generation to generation.

∼

Rev. Jeannellen Ryan retired from service as a UU minister in 1999, after serving UU congregations in various religious education capacities since 1972.

Doing the Work
of Becoming
Unitarian Universalists

KATHY M. SILVER

Raymond Nasemann and Elizabeth Strong asked the following question in their course, "Remember Universalism into Life": "Can you be a member of a Unitarian Universalist congregation and *not* be a Unitarian Universalist, and *not* know it?" That the answer to this question is often yes is the impetus for this paper.

As a half-time Director of Religious Education who is responsible for programming for 150 children and youth, I have not had much time in my work to lead, or even think about, adult religious education classes. Yet, as I searched for a topic for this conference, my thoughts returned again and again to the parents in my church. Each year on Religious Education Sunday, I tell these mothers and fathers that they are the primary religious educators for their children, and I urge them to think seriously about this responsibility. I have come to realize, however, that in our congregation, and in many others like it, we have not yet given our adults the inspiration and information that they need to fulfill this essential role.

To become a better DRE, I have taken extensive training to create an effective religious education program that basically provides one hour of classroom experience for each child each week, *if they attend.* I'm not minimizing what I do. I believe that it is important and blessed work to teach our children and youth. In contrast to me, the vast majority of parents, who spend hours each day with their children, receive very little training, if any, to teach religious values and answer questions about faith. In fact, they are often afraid or unsure of how to talk with their offspring about religious matters. These people, whom we designate as the primary religious educators of children, are often teaching by their silence that religion can, or should, only be discussed in church.

Most parents who join a Unitarian Universalist congregation say that they are seeking a religious education for their children. They are looking for moral and spiritual confirmation and reinforcement of their values. Many of them have never had a conversation about their personal beliefs with their children. Since they often feel confused by or alienated from their own religious backgrounds, they are apt to answer questions about God and religion by saying that different people believe different things, and then listing some of the beliefs of others. They feel unable or unwilling to share their own beliefs.

Many of the parents that I have taught in "Parents as Resident Theologians" and "Being a Unitarian Universalist Parent" don't realize that their children's questions are not those of disinterested observers. Rather, they are the questions of youngsters wanting to know exactly what their families believe, so that they know what they should believe. When the parents in a family each come from different religious backgrounds, they often find it problematic to share their own religious thoughts and beliefs, because they are concerned that they might upset or undermine their parenting partner.

In Jeanne Nieuwejaar's article "Fahs and MacLean: Fulfilling Channing's Challenge," Angus MacLean is quoted as saying that the home environment is "the most powerful center of religious education; the setting for most of the child's growth, most of his or her experiences, whether good or bad; the setting where love and trust are experienced and learned." In *Today's Children and Yesterday's Heritage*, Sophia Fahs insisted that what a person believes of himself is "like the main stem out of which the body of one's faith must grow. And what a person believes about himself depends on what he believes about his mother and his father, his brothers and his sisters. And what he believes about these persons in his intimate family influences what he believes about his neighbors and others in his larger world." As the child grows, these beliefs become linked to ideas about religion, humanity, politics, justice, society, and economics. The children of people who espouse liberal religious ideals often become liberal religious people. Does that make them Unitarian Universalists? I don't think so. In my mind, Unitarian Universalists are people who know something about our church's history, who understand who the early Unitarians and Universalists were, what they stood for, and how they suffered for their beliefs. Unitarian Universalists have some basic knowledge of our theology, our Principles, and our system of congregational polity, and they want to know more!

So the questions become, How do we help people with liberal religious leanings to become Unitarian Universalists? How do we help parents in our churches to go deeper into their own spiritual growth and development? How do we help them to integrate their religious backgrounds with their current beliefs so that their children can become more than nominal Unitarian Universalists? The simple answer is that we need to help people convert to Unitarian Universalism. Failing to do this, they will remain content with simply attending their local Unitarian Universalist church as a consumer of religious education for their children. This is not sufficient to motivate them to understand Unitarian Universalist theology, history, and traditions and our place in the larger religious culture. As a denomination and as individual congregations, we often struggle with our religious identity because we do not pay sufficient attention to the process of and the need for conversion to Unitarian Universalism.

I can't tell you how many times I have heard people in our congregation refer to themselves as Catholics or Presbyterians or Jews. I am always saddened to think that we have been unable to help them cultivate a Unitarian Universalist identity. A young man who has come to our church sporadically for several years still calls himself a Catholic. Only recently has he started attending services regularly on Sunday mornings. He told our minister that he really wants to become a Unitarian Universalist, and he now realizes that he has to work to make that happen. How many of our congregants ever come to the important realization that conversion requires conviction and commitment in order to develop a new Unitarian Universalist religious identity? The comfort of simply "being" in a liberal religious community is not an exercise in freedom of belief. It's a relief to feel *freedom from* our religion of origin, but we also need to feel *compelled toward* our new faith.

In his essay in *Salted with Fire,* Tony Larson stated that we should be recruiting our children for Unitarian Universalism. I believe that in the year 2000 we are doing much better at helping our children identify as Unitarian Universalists. In their religious education classrooms, our children and youth spend their Sundays doing the work of becoming Unitarian Universalists. They are learning the Unitarian Universalist Principles through every Unitarian Universalist curriculum that they study. They are learning about our history through the famous Unitarians and Universalists to whom they are introduced. They are beginning to understand congregational polity through classroom democracy. In religious education programs across the continent, our children and youth are developing a social and environmental conscience by working for various community service projects.

Most adults, on the other hand, are *not* able to spend time working regularly on their own religious development. They certainly don't appear to spend an hour every week discussing religious issues with their peers. That's not to say that attending a Sunday worship service does not promote religious growth. However, attending a worship service often has more to do with watching someone else bear witness than being directly engaged in that process personally. Adults, like children, need to explore their hearts and minds in conversation with others. They need to ask questions and voice opinions. They need to try out their ideas to see how others react, thus to benefit from the truths and insights offered in response. Worship can be a significant element in the process of conversion, but it, alone, is not sufficient.

Kirk Loadman-Copeland, in his paper "To Be Born Again," writes,

> Conversion in our tradition (correctly understood as a gradual and continuing process) historically involved entering into a covenant. The vertical dimension of this covenant connected the individual to a transcending, ulti-

mate reality, commitment, or value. Given our theological diversity, the terminus of the vertical dimension included God, Goddess, nature, the good, ultimate concern, reverence for life, life force, philosophic truth, and humanity. The horizontal dimension of convenant encompassed the gathered congregation (and defined a relationship with the larger society). These two axes play different roles in the transformation that occurs when a person moves in a new direction spiritually.

In the vertical dimension we turn *toward* that which is transcendent, while in the horizontal dimension we turn *with* the other members of the congregation. Conversion requires movement in a new direction, or a further step in the same direction. It requires a change in heart, mind, and soul that is direct and explicit. It requires the time to learn and the opportunity to grow.

It is the church's responsibility to itself, to its future, and to its congregants to provide avenues for lifespan religious education in which all members, adults and children alike, can *easily* participate. The key word here is *easily*. In our church, we offer many adult education courses on weeknights throughout the year, including one specifically for parents. Most of the people who attend these adult religious education courses are the folks whose children are grown and gone out of their houses. Sometimes they are unattached adults, both younger and older, looking for companions as well as information and spiritual nourishment. Very few parents of school-age children ever participate in these courses, even when babysitting is provided. I suspect that our families are just too busy to do one more thing on a weeknight, when homework has to be done, sports activities have to be attended, a meal has to be eaten, and a reasonable bedtime accomplished, all within a few short evening hours.

The time that these families devote to church is on Sunday mornings. So it seems to me that Sunday mornings are the natural and *easiest* time to expand our programming by offering courses and activities that will encourage individuals, couples, and especially families to delve deeper into the history, meanings, and values of Unitarian Universalism. It is by going deeper that we truly become Unitarian Universalists. I envision a Sunday morning experience that includes worship for adults and children, lifespan religious education classes, and a time for intergenerational activities such as singing, movement, arts and crafts, movie time, and lively discussions about interesting topics. I would like to see those adults who have benefitted from adult religious education courses share their knowledge and expertise by leading classes for others. Children with special talents and interests would be invited to plan programs in those areas for both adults and youngsters. I imagine families working together to develop worship services or to write prayers and meditations that could be used in their homes. I see children and their parents making posters about our Unitarian Universalist Principles and Purposes to take home and hang on their walls, as an ever-present reminder that they belong to a special church. Our homes could become filled with the artifacts of our faith so that strangers who entered would understand that we have a religion of profound value. Someday our parents might become knowledgeable enough and comfortable enough to tell their children that they should be welcoming to the new child who looks or acts differently, because our first Unitarian Universalist Principle teaches us that everyone is worthwhile and valuable, and worthy of our kindness.

Over the years, I have recruited hundreds of volunteer teachers for my classrooms. One of the comments that I hear from new people year after year is that teaching is a great way to learn about Unitarian Universalism. In our children's curricula, the story and Principles of our faith are presented in a way that is straightforward and easy to understand. These volunteers really seem to enjoy learning along with the children. They quickly learn that children can sometimes be our best teachers because they have such a keen sense of justice and equality. Children have not yet become adept at intellectualizing and rationalizing their feelings and their prejudices. Usually they know in their hearts what is right and fair. They are often willing to listen to that internal message and act on it. Learning about Unitarian Universalism by teaching religious education to our children is significant. I am forever grateful to the wonderful people who do it. *But, it is not enough.*

In our Association and in my congregation, we have honored the scientific, the intellectual, and the rational for so long that we sometimes lose sight of the fact that religion has a strong emotional component. When I teach my eighth grade "Coming of Age" students about Unitarian Universalist history, I tell them how proud they should be that King John Sigismund, as a teenager, was able to value religious freedom and issue the Edict of Torda. They feel John Murray's pain as he made his way to the new world alone, after his term in debtor's prison. They feel his ambivalence about preaching in Potter's meeting house. They can hardly believe that, through the centuries, our Unitarian and Universalist forebears have been branded as heretics, hounded into exile, and burned at the stake for their liberal beliefs. I want our children to know these stories. I want to impress them with the courage and heroism of our religious ancestors. I want them to experience an emotional connection to our faith history in addition to learning the facts. I believe that these same stories that move our youngsters can also help our adults to connect with our faith. Our history is rich with examples of people who lived their faith and even died for it; people who were faced with making choices that sometimes made them unpopular or even outcasts; people who made selfish decisions and then realized the error of their ways; people just like us, imperfect people, who tried to lead good lives and make the world a better place for everyone. Our adults, as well as our children, need to know these stories. They should feel pride in the history of our tradition and know *what we believe,* not simply what we don't believe.

We need to make it easier for our people to be in community and to share stories of what it means to become a Unitarian Universalist. Adding programming on Sundays, when the majority of our congregants are already at church, is the ideal way to do this work in my church and probably in many others. It may mean more work for the professional staff and additional volunteers to coordinate the classes, activities, and programs I envision. It will offer opportunities to many more of our people to find ways to share their gifts of knowledge and leadership with others. Most importantly, it will give the parents and other adults in our congregations a chance to go deeper into Unitarian Universalism, to share their stories, and to learn more about themselves and about the other members of our church communities.

In an interview in *Liberal Religious Education*, Thomas Groome asks, "Who's going to keep alive this tradition . . . of being open to the universal? That story, that Unitarian Universalist story somehow must get told, renewed, and passed on! That Unitarian Universalist vision must get imparted, or else you [meaning we] will die." As we mature through the stages of faith development, as we experience the process of becoming Unitarian Universalists, as we become more spiritually grounded in our own religious beliefs, we also grow in our ability to be in community with others, to listen keenly, to honor our differences, and to be open to the universal in our churches *and* in our families.

~

Kathy M. Silver is the emerita director of religious education at the Unitarian Universalist Church of the South Hills in Pittsburgh, Pennsylvania, and the director of religious education at the Universalist Unitarian Church of Farmington in Farmington Hills, Michigan.

Taking Our
Children Seriously

REV. GARY E. SMITH

A story Dennis Benson and Stan Stewart tell in their book *The Mystery of the Child* about an encounter between a young child and an old man probably comes as close as anything to what I would want to say about Unitarian Universalist religious education:

> An old man is sitting in a hospital emergency room and tears are rolling down his cheeks. His shoulders rise and fall as he sobs with his head in his hands. When his grief can bring no more sobs, he begins to moan like a foghorn wailing in the night. People begin to shift around on the hard uncomfortable chairs. In their embarrassment over the man's suffering, people don't know what to do. The pain is too close.
>
> Then a small child squirms loose from her mother's arms and runs around the room. The tired woman does very little to restrain her. This active child begins to play with the ashtray, the water fountain, the magazines. Ashes, water, and torn pages follow in her wake.
>
> The twenty or so people in the room discover that it is easier to focus on this curious child than to deal with the sobbing old man. Then the little girl finally stops in front of the suffering adult. Her face becomes very serious and intent. She moves forward carefully and looks deeply as tears roll down the face of this grief-stricken person. The

waiting room becomes very quiet. All eyes are on this encounter between adult and child.

What will the child do? She toddles over to his knees. Her hand reaches out to his face, and she wipes the tears from his cheeks. 'All right, all right, all right,' she says gently. The man opens his eyes. The shape of his mouth changes slowly. He looks at her as the littlest one in the room continues to roughly wipe his face. He gently catches her hand in his wrinkled fingers and kisses it.

This raises the question: As much as any catechism, aren't we teaching our children how to be in right relationship?

I may have been invited to participate in this consultation because I am the current president of the Unitarian Universalist Ministers Association. I am also one of the ministers of the First Parish in Concord, Massachusetts, one of our largest congregations. And I am the father of two children who moved through our Unitarian Universalist religious education programs in three different UU congregations. ("Yes, you ARE going to church today!")

And so, from the smallest circle first, I am the father of two now-grown children. Perhaps the most telling moment in their Unitarian Universalist religious education came when their maternal grandparents died within a year of each other. My children were then four and six. My wife's family was devoutly Roman Catholic. During the Irish wake for the grandmother who died first, my children played with their Catholic cousins. When we rode home one of those nights in the car, these are the questions that came from the back seat of the car, came from the darkness: "Daddy, is there a heaven? Is heaven up? What happened to Grandma? Will she be buried in the ground? What's a soul? Will I go to heaven?"

Will you understand if I say that this is when I introduced Bobbi Nelson's "Parent as Resident Theologian" to our church's adult religious education program? My own spiritual odyssey had taken me from a ministry in the United Church of Christ to a ministry in Unitarian Universalism, but, in my case, the Ministerial Fellowship Committee had neglected to ask me these important back-seat theological questions. I was unprepared and I realized the parents in my congregation were unprepared as well. We come-outers had relinquished a creed, but we had not yet begun to build the foundation of a belief. Our children are often concrete and quite literal. We Unitarian Universalist adults end up vague and quite slippery.

Ask my children what they remember of their childhood church [and I did], and they remember a breakfast every Wednesday morning in a local restaurant for some of the retired folks in my congregation, just breakfast and conversation. I brought my children to this breakfast from the earliest age. They sat on laps. They had their pancakes cut up for them. Someone would slip them an extra slice of bacon. They were loved, and they showed the same love in return.

The circle widens. I am one of the ministers of the First Parish in Concord, Massachusetts. When I arrived there in 1988, there was a "children's church" in the chapel each week a half-hour before the adult service. Children came to the "big church" for the first fifteen minutes or so on Christmas and Easter. We began having our children come with their parents every other week, then every week. In a book I've loaned and cannot find, a professor at Emory University writes about two metaphors of church health and life. How is money talked about, he asks, and are the children hidden away? At First Parish, our children are not hidden. They are present. (And we talk about money.)

Here in Concord over the years, I have been blessed with working with three outstanding DREs: Jan Devor, Ginny Steele as an interim, and Diane Rollert. We have been strong teams. Diane and I collaborate weekly. Mostly, she is the storyteller in worship, and it is tied to the music, to the prayer, to the sermon. We have more than 350 children registered now, in two sessions. There are two children's choirs. The children recite the chalice lighting "by heart."

We celebrate many of the holidays of the world's religions. Come on the first Sunday in November and watch the children come up in single file to light a candle for one who has died. Come in the spring and watch our children solemnly bathe the baby Buddha. We commissioned our children's choir to be worship leaders, gave them stoles to wear, and told the adults that it was not necessary to clap and take pictures each time. At the outbreak of the Gulf War years ago, I invited all the children up into the pulpit with me. I told them how sad I was that adults could not stop fighting, and I asked them to be near me as we sang the first hymn, "America, the Beautiful," the America and the world, I said, that we wanted for them.

On the tenth anniversary of my settlement in Concord, the children surprised me with a gift and then three children came to the microphone to tell all the others what my ministry meant to them. I cannot imagine when I will receive a greater tribute. When CBS and "The Public Eye" descended on Concord and our *About Your Sexuality* program, we held several parish meetings. The most memorable was held in our sanctuary and was well attended. More than twenty high-schoolers, graduates of the *AYS* program, came forward to the microphone that night, and their spokesperson delivered an impassioned and eloquent defense of *AYS*. Then they thanked the adults for treating them like adults and for telling them the truth, the whole truth, nothing but the truth, about sex and their own sexuality.

As the minister of one of the larger churches in our Association, I can tell you that we are grateful for the Religious Education Department's effort to continually generate new curriculum. In our four terms in Concord throughout the year with each and every grade represented, we struggle to make the building blocks of learning come together. We have written some of our own material, and we have reached out to other congregations of our size for their own material. We need this cross-fertilization, and we will need more of it.

Finally, the concentric circles are now growing larger. I am currently the president of the Unitarian Universalist Ministers Association. I have tried to mark my presidency with a renewed commitment to reaching out to the various constituencies of the wider Association and network more effectively. Cynthia Breen joined our UUMA Executive meeting in San Antonio in January 1999 to introduce us to the *Our Whole Lives* curriculum, so that we could encourage our colleagues to collaborate with their own religious educators in *OWL*'s important introduction.

Pat Ellenwood, the current president of the Liberal Religious Education Directors Association, and I have been in regular contact, recently writing a joint letter to our constituencies, published in each of our journals, asking for mentoring that goes both ways in our professions, disdaining the turf battles that too often tear at the fabric of the congregations we both serve. I was proud to bring greetings, on behalf of the UUMA, to LREDA in the fall of 1999 at their fiftieth anniversary celebration, and I look forward to congratulating the Ministers of Religious Education this June on the occasion of the twentieth anniversary of that particular designation.

The UUMA Exec in the winter and spring of 2000 has worked in collaboration with the Ministerial Fellowship Committee and the Department of Ministry to bring a proposal to our ministerial colleagues on the equalization of the three tracks of ministry: parish, religious education, and community. The proposal calls for all candidates for the Unitarian Universalist ministry to enter preliminary fellowship with the same training and expectations: more educational training and theory for all tracks, more community organizing and public witness for all tracks, more training in preaching and administration for all tracks. Then, in the renewal for final fellowship, a candidate will move toward a specialty in one track.

We of the UUMA are committed to working with LREDA, with the MRE Focus Group, and with the Department of Religious Education at the UUA in the development of new curricula. The UUMA is prepared to take a place at the table in the identification of what our congregations might need in the new century and in identifying those congregations and ministers who might be helpful in that process.

All this is prologue to my two passions for Unitarian Universalist religious education for the next century: one is task and the other is relationship. The task, I believe, is the identification of a corpus of material we would like our children to know, to own in their beings, by the time they have come of age in our programs, be it at the age of thirteen or seventeen, somewhere short of when we send them out with our blessings into the wider world. We are trying to do this in Concord. What are the pieces of scripture we expect our children to know—from the Torah; from the Christian Bible; from Islam, Buddhism, and Hinduism; and from Earth-based spirituality? What are the essential stories that we would expect a "graduate" of our Unitarian Universalist religious education program to know?

What pieces of our own Unitarian Universalist history do we expect our children to know? What names should they recognize? What about the history of our own local congregation? What about the way we are organized? Who is the president of the UUA anyway? What are our Unitarian Universalist Purposes and Principles, and how, if at all, do they apply in their young lives? We may be strong in our tolerance for other faiths. We may tip our hats to all the holidays. We may chant and walk the labyrinth and visit all of the faiths around the corner, but I believe we must have a much stronger commitment to what I will call a Unitarian Universalist literacy.

We need some focus. We're all over the place. If our faith draws from many sources, do our children know what these sources are and can they identify what is essential about each of them? Do we have to believe in the prayer of Jesus in order to be able to say it? Do we have to believe in a punishing God in order to know what happened in the Garden of Eden? Do we have to surrender to Allah in order to know the five pillars of Islam? Have we encouraged our children to learn at least one form of a spiritual discipline?

We do not have a catechism, but we do have a history. We are not rootless. We do not teach our children that any behavior is OK. We have an ethic. We have morals. What underpins them? How did we come to this point? Who taught us these things? What is the poetry? When our children come up against it, and they will, where should they turn? What have been our gifts to them? At least part of this answer needs to be concrete. We as Unitarian Universalists did not arise out of nothingness. People made sacrifices. People told stories. Our history has been written. We are charged with passing this on to the next generation. That is the task.

But we also dare not lose sight of the relationship, and this brings me back to the story of the encounter between a young child and an old man. Unitarian Universalist religious education in the next century must be about relationship as well. I believe we are in a unique position to recognize the ministry of our children. We may say that our children have "come of age," but we do not use language like "confirmation." We do not say that our children must be at a certain age before they can be our ministers. We do not say that our children must have a collection of answers, that they must toe the party line, before they can have a place at the table.

I believe Unitarian Universalism religious education is about mutual respect. When our children sing, as they did this winter in Concord, a song entitled "Shalom," with American sign language, I felt my soul transported to wherever that place is we call holy. When I dedicate a child, and that child looks so deeply into my eyes as I say every word, I am left wondering who has been dedicated. When one of our teenagers is called upon to tell the younger children why participating in Boston's City Year has made such a difference in his life, I know these younger children would follow him anywhere. When one of our older members some years ago was suffering with a facial cancer and pushing almost everyone away with her anger, and a child ran to her in the coffee hour and gave her a hug, I know that this child gave this woman a ministerial presence I could never have offered. I saw it on the woman's face.

In our Unitarian Universalist congregations, as in other religious communities, are we not offering one of the last places of intergenerational contact in our culture? As our nuclear families drift apart, here is the chance for grandparents and grandchildren and for extended families to come together in new ways. Here is a chance to live out the Principle that we learn as much from *who* teaches us as we do from *what* we are taught. When we create the kind of community where our children feel loved and welcomed and safe, this is the imprint we leave for that later year, after the inevitable rebellion has taken place, when they may return with their own children. This is respect for children. This is what it means to take children seriously. This is Unitarian Universalist religious education in the next century.

～

Rev. Gary E. Smith is the senior minister at First Parish in Concord, Massachusetts.

Our Seven Principles

LAURA WILKERSON SPENCER

 ∼

The world of the twenty-first century demands a great deal from its citizens. The fast pace of change and the bombardment of information requires us to be adaptable, creative, innovative thinkers, and lifelong learners. The world today is one of greater interconnectedness. What we do, the choices we make today, may have an effect on the other side of the world tomorrow. The effect of continued oppression based on race, socioeconomic status, gender, sexual orientation, ableness, ethnicity, or nationality on both white and nonwhite individuals, coupled with the realities of living in a multicultural America, require us to actively work for equity in human relations. As our communities become more and more diverse, we must be able to live, work, and play with those around us. For all of us to live a better life, we need to be able to prioritize the good of all over what may be best for us personally.

Developing a community that can survive and succeed in the twenty-first century is a daunting undertaking. It will take cooperation from schools, families, churches, and community organizations. The family must be the strong center or core of this process. The church must provide support and programs to help its members in the challenging jobs of personal growth, raising children, and helping everyone become ready for the twenty-first century.

What does this mean for Unitarian Universalist religious education? What do we, as an Association, need to provide?

The vision of religious education must shift. This vision must become an understanding that religious education is composed of an interplay of all the forms of ministry that exist in the church. We must begin to realize that not only does the church *have* an education program but it *is* an education program. The shift must be from seeing individuals as teachers to seeing the whole community as a teacher; from seeing the participants as the children to seeing the whole community as learners; from seeing the purpose of learning as history and lore to engaging in ministry in the midst of the world. It is therefore difficult to separate religious education from the life of the church as a whole. Religious education must be an integral part of every aspect of congregational life. A partnership between religious education and other programming is essential. Therefore, what I see as important for religious education I also see as important for the entire church.

Within our seven Principles we have the foundation for all we need to do. These Principles hold the keys to the survival of the individual as well as of the world as a whole. They offer a guideline as to what our churches and religious education programs need to become, to how to see ourselves and relate to others. Most congregations probably have the Principles printed on church brochures or posted on the walls. We talk about them and affirm their importance. Do we, however, really make them come alive? Are they the core of our church programming and a part of our daily lives? Do they guide the church in its operations?

I think we need to take a hard look at our religious education programs, policies, and practices, and indeed the church as a whole, and make sure each of them is aligned with our seven Principles. Our hiring and employment policies, our governance, activities, and programs should all adhere to these Principles. Everything we do should be aligned with and correspond to the seven Principles.

There are three areas where I see particular need for attention. These I feel will be key to our moving forward as a strong and meaningful force in the twenty-first century.

First, if we really "affirm and promote the inherent worth and dignity of all people," we must seriously address issues of diversity in our congregations. It is one thing to *say* we welcome diversity and quite another to *be* welcoming. As long as we continue to see ourselves and be comfortable with seeing ourselves as a religious movement appealing mainly to people who are middle and upper class, highly educated, professional, and mostly white, we remain part of the problem of the oppression in our society. What is our role and obligation as a liberal religious church in addressing the lingering and difficult problems of racism, classism, and other forms of oppression? Can we become a place where we create bridges between these differences, allowing understanding, appreciation, and bonds to be created? What can and should we do as congregations to fight these beliefs and biases in our children and in ourselves? Do we have an obligation to help fully embody our first Principle—to affirm and promote the inherent worth and dignity of all people?

I believe we do. With divisions between us widening in today's hierarchical society, the dangers are real. We cannot continue to simply shake our heads at the problem. We cannot point our fingers at others and pretend it's their problem, while believing we do not play a role as well. We must take an active role in promoting understanding, respect, and tolerance. I believe we *must* move toward creating churches that are understood as spaces in which a new sense of humanity is affirmed and experienced, and in which liberated ways of thinking and dwelling are explored.

What does this mean? How do we go about this momentous task? It means we must become very intentional about creating diverse congregations. This is probably the most difficult and yet the most important step. This step will require us to take a hard look at who we are as congregations and as an association, much the way we have with the Welcoming Congregation around issues of sexual orientation. In what ways might we be preventing greater diversity, particularly in respects to socioeconomic status? Who occupies leadership positions? How are decisions made? How do we talk about money? The Unitarian Universalist Association has been engaging in this process. Programs are available to aid individual congregations as well. The process must continue and congregations should be strongly encouraged to accept the challenge. The Liberal Religious Educators' Association (LREDA) grants, given only to congregations who (among other things) are working on anti-oppression, are an example of how the Association can emphasize how important this work is.

Our religious education programs need to provide and promote anti-oppressive education at all levels of church life. Regular and ongoing anti-oppression training for the board of trustees, for church staff, for teachers, and on down to the children should be a part of our programs. We all need to explore our own fears and prejudices as we work together to develop and create a better understanding of what it means to be a truly diverse, liberal religion. We will then be affirming and promoting "justice, equity, and compassion in human relations."

As our diversity increases, we become a united community, working together, worshipping together, learning together, and sharing our stories of family, tradition, joys, and sorrows. We become people *coming together in community* in significant and meaningful ways with those we perceive as different so that we can discover our distorted perceptions and find instead the common thread of being human. It means defying the code of silence that so often surrounds cross-cultural conversations. We will then be promoting the "acceptance of one another and encouragement of spiritual growth in our congregations."

Creating such a community will not be easy. It will mean making changes that may be difficult and painful to many. It means confronting our beliefs and ourselves. True growth is rarely simple or without discomfort. Without change, we can never challenge ourselves to become better.

We must ask ourselves, What do we want to be able to say about our congregations and their impact on the larger community? What do we want to hand down to our children? How do we want to live? Do we really have a goal of "world community, with peace, liberty, and justice for all"? If so, then it must begin with us.

Our curricula need to take an inclusive approach to diversity. Unitarian Universalist history should include our African-American, Latino, and Asian histories as an integral part and not just as a separate chapter. It should include our failures and stumbles as well as our successes. We need to encourage curriculum development by minority participants in a wide range of subjects, not just "diversity" projects. We need to have many different perspectives included at all levels of religious education programming and development to insure that we stay on track. This diversity can only add richness and beauty to our Unitarian Universalist mosaic.

In *Uprooting Racism: How White People Can Work for Racial Justice*, Paul Kivel includes a long list of questions and actions for becoming anti-racist. Our churches and religious education programs need to ask these questions. As you will see, Kivel's thoughtful list is also a call to action.

- Is it multicultural? Who is involved? Who is excluded?
- Is it democratic? Who holds power and how are decisions made?
- Is it anti-racist? Is racism talked about and dealt with effectively within the group?
- Who needs to be brought into the group? How would we need to change to truly be open to their participation?
- How could we be more democratic?
- How would this change affect how we operate?
- What forms of racism need to be dealt with?
- Who can you talk with about these challenges?
- Who might be allies in changing the dynamics of the group?
- What is one thing you will do to begin this process?
- What fears or concerns do you have about raising these issues?
- What will you and the group lose if you don't raise them?

The second area for our religious education programs to focus on is creating community that nurtures members in their individual spiritual growth and development. We should aim to create a place rooted in love that moves us toward the healing of division, toward overcoming brokenness, and toward achieving wholeness.

Many of us find ourselves in environments where, for much of the time, we are segregated by age. We have little time to spend with generations older or younger. Many of us are also separated from our extended families. We mature in an environment that offers little to guide us or to celebrate and embrace our passages through the stages and transitions of life.

Churches and religious education programs offer a unique environment and opportunity to create a place where people of all ages, beliefs, and perspectives can come together in a space that transcends cultural and societal boundaries in an open, caring, cross-generational community. We need to assist our members in finding connections within the congregation that will create two-way paths for nurturance. Only then can we become a truly sacred space with a collection of individuals centering around and joined by the experience of finding deeper meaning in our lives.

We have become the de facto extended family for many people. We can fulfill this role through the use of support groups, establishing or encouraging women's circles, men's groups, singles groups, young adult groups, and family activities. Religious education programs can also provide opportunities for informal social activities that allow friendships to grow. We need ample time to form connections to age mates as well as those older and younger. Relationships with individuals with similar values and religious perspectives can play an important role in our lives.

As our church members, young and old, pass through stages of development and life transitions, the church community can play an important role. Programs that celebrate births, coming of age, marriages and commitment, retirements, and other transitions combined with mentorships, support groups, and classes can make these transitions easier and more meaningful. When we have strong connections to those of all ages we have a rich resource of information, support, and understanding.

Life also brings many unplanned events, such as divorce, death, abuse, illness, and other difficult and challenging experiences. When we are part of a loving and supportive community, we discover others who have also experienced similar problems in their lives. Programs that foster communication and connections where individuals can get advice, or simply find an understanding, listening ear, are important for those who are in the midst of difficult times as well as those who have emerged on the other side.

To be able to address all these issues seriously, we must then focus on a third area, religious education leadership. The scope of religious education for the twenty-first century encompasses all aspects of church programming. To seriously address these issues will require religious educators to become involved in the worship service, the children's Sunday school program, adult education, community programs, and church leadership and administration. Churches must realize the important role religious education and religious educators play in their congregations. Religious education staff must be seen as professionals in religion. Churches must hire well-qualified individuals who can address these areas with vision and insight. Continuing education and networking are vital for religious educators to keep growing and developing with their congregations. Churches must support religious educators in their growth and education by paying for and encouraging participation in professional development and networking opportunities.

Churches must have realistic expectations of the scope of the job and the hours required to do it. They must be willing to strive for fair compensation and benefits for religious education professionals. Our programs cannot grow and develop to meet the changing needs of our congregations if our religious professionals leave their positions after three or four years. Burnout and feeling overwhelmed, undervalued, and unsupported cause high turnover rates in many of our congregations.

If we are to have successful links between religious education and congregational life, ministers and religious educators must work collaboratively and create genuine collegial relationships. Regular staff meetings to discuss plans for worship, educational offerings, and community events are crucial. Ministers must receive significant training in the philosophies of religious education. Without their understanding the importance and scope of religious education, growth is difficult. Ministerial presence and participation in religious education committees ensures that vital links travel in both directions.

Religious educators must be included in the leadership activities of the church. Attendance at board meetings, executive committee meetings, and other gatherings where leadership decisions are made should be expected. Many decisions that have direct and indirect impact on religious education programming and on children and families are made at this level. Religious educators must have an opportunity to express the needs of the program and be sure that these needs are included and considered in all facets of the decision-making process.

Creating a religious education program for the twenty-first century requires us to rethink our definition of religious education. This process must be led by strong religious professionals and must involve the participation of church leaders as well as other congregants. We have an incredibly large and complicated job ahead of us. It will require us to make hard decisions, to make changes that will make some uncomfortable, and to stretch and grow into a new vision of what it means to be a Unitarian Universalist. It is of crucial importance that we take these steps toward creating the life-transforming experiences that will support our journey into the new century.

~

Laura Wilkerson Spencer is the director of religious education at First Unitarian Universalist Church of Ann Arbor, Michigan.

Sunday School Is Dead—
Long Live Sunday School

REV. GREG STEWART

"Without a vision the people perish" (Proverbs 29:18). The same thing could be said of liberal religious education. In fact, that is exactly what I am saying. This is no doomsday prediction from some mentally unstable prophet. (Your diagnosis may differ and I will fight for your right to defend it.) Rather, it is based on my own experience and convictions along with those who, throughout history, have been calling for commonsense reforms regarding the way we "do church." The educational ministry of the church is one of the institution's pillars and has traditionally been the place where innovation most easily and significantly occurs. It is the launching pad from which vision is catapulted into reality.

Do not try and tell me that a congregation's worship life is its soul and the sanctuary is its laboratory for experiment and change. Go ahead, mess with worship's content or, blasphemy of blasphemies (in liberal churches, at least), its form, and watch various factions prepare for battle. My guess is that the hymn "Onward Christian Soldiers" was inspired not by the desire to conquer infidels but to curb civil disobedience within the ranks. Traditions, whether high church or low, reign supreme in most of our holiest of holy places. "Marching as to war. . . ." It is a wonder some of our choirs don't march in military formation during processionals.

Go ahead. Make changes in the canon of the order of service. Stagger church and Sunday school schedules so that children worship with adults regularly and then adults and children all attend religious education classes simultaneously. Take two offerings because an insufficient dollar amount was collected during the first one. Robes for the choir or clergy? Organ versus piano. Forget to light the chalice. Add or subtract a time for joys and concerns. Eliminate or introduce opportunities for the participation of the laity. Hell, change the font used in the printed order of service. Then listen to the uproar in decibels that encourage a howling chorus of the neighborhood's dogs.

In fact, the sanctuary is the last place to introduce relevant change to tired religion. I, for one, am glad for that. When worship practices do change their authenticity ought to be based on the community's shared conclusions of rigorous theological inquiry which has been and should always be the domain of the educational ministry of the Church. I will not bother listing reasons for why the Church's music, social justice, and administrative ministries make poor change agents. Suffice it to say I have yet to meet a board of trustees that could accurately be described as "cutting edge." "Cutting," perhaps. "Edgy," no doubt. But innovative? Not on your life.

The curriculum of place has had more influence on my perceptions of both Unitarian Universalism and religious education than any other factor. My first job as a DRE took place in a decidedly urban environment at a church that did not care one whit that their new DRE was not a Unitarian Universalist. (I was a born-again Baptist whose spiritual journey had led me to candidacy for ministry in the more liberal and liberating United Church of Christ.) I plead guilty to gross naiveté and no little ignorance. Why would this largely humanist congregation put their faith in a man who consistently referred to Christian education during the interview process? (Not to worry, they were quick to correct me.) Why advertise in the city's underground newspaper? Why not hire from within? You know, tap an already burned out religious education committee member, offer an embarrassing meager salary, call it a quarter-time position, and then assume from the time of hire that everyone knew that quarter-time actually meant eighty hours a week.

In reality, it may have been a dearth of prospective candidates that sent these seekers into uncharted or at least irregular territories. And please hear me on this: the church had an excellent program already in place provided by a DRE who was held in high esteem by congregants and colleagues alike. So it may also have been that insiders were intimidated to fill those professional shoes. My guess is that both of these factors figured into my initial hiring. My subsequent experience also suggests the search committee was aware that the curriculum-based, classroom-centered, age-divided format had taken the religious education program as far as it could go.

And grow. "Just add love [to the curriculum] and stir," to quote the church's teacher recruitment brochure, which was as inaccurate as it was emotionally liable. Story circles, flannel boards, arts and crafts projects, and a transplanted public school ambiance no longer communicated what it meant to be a religious liberal near the end of the millennium. Curricula that lifted up a multicultural world were nullified by the lily-white coffee hour that followed. And never mind the built-in bias of other curricula that assumed all learners where white and middle class or that a classroom of five learners constituted a viable learning environment. Come on, the dark recesses of the church's musty basement were no place for anyone of any age to learn much of anything. I remember one six-year-old proclaiming of Sunday school, "This is just like regular [public] school, except we have more lights at my other school, and it is warmer, too." Remember that we were being dissed by a pupil from the Chicago public school system! Clearly, it was time to breathe new life into dry bones (Ezekiel 37:1–14).

The time was right to change or die.

As what I now understand as the curriculum of place, the faith community in which I was introduced to the vocation of religious educator was, arguably, the single most significant contributor to the approaches to religious growth and learning I now advocate for the twenty-first century. As a congregation, Unitarian Universalist or otherwise, the church where I first served as a DRE was atypical and, therefore, ripe for an educator who would necessarily take religious education outside the Sunday school box. I had no choice. I had no idea what I was doing. Like many new DREs I had great ambition and no experience.

And, to top it off, I somehow got a hold of the wrong reading list. You know, Renaissance writers, then the venerable John Dewey, and later Maria Harris, bell hooks, and so on. Not knowing any better, I took them seriously. I did what they said to do, but localized it to meet the needs of my specific community of learners. And that is when the trouble started. That is also when a fresh infusion of the vibrant, relevant spirit of God breathed new life into a worn-out format. With the blessing and support of the church's Children's Religious Education Committee, we put lived experience before the dissemination of information, took Sunday school out of the church's basement and into the city's streets, eliminated age divisions, used curricula as a resource rather than a recipe, intentionally invited (and transported) non-UU children to Sunday school from area shelter and group homes—yes, we became both missionaries and evangelists—and we confused social action with religious education. We called this approach "Way Cool Sunday School."

On the penultimate point I still plead confusion. I would have our religious education leaders and learners—adults and children alike—spend ten weeks working in a food pantry, retirement home, or public housing project. Afterwards, take a week or two to reflect on how those experiences affirmed or challenged their religious principles, rather than reverse that process. (The more typical lesson plan: Study hunger or gerontology for weeks on end in a sterile, isolated classroom and then embellish it with a day-long field trip.) Do, then reflect. This is what we did in Chicago.

I would first have our learners conduct their weekly worship on public transportation (picking up new converts on the way!); fill hundreds of trash bags with litter from public parks and nature centers; make and distribute hundreds of bag lunches for homeless men, women, and children; paint colorful murals amidst gray tenements; and investigate and protest a professional baseball team's choice of mascot at the ballpark. Don't forget to invite the staff and kids from the area group homes! Then, if there is any time left, we might choose to define our faith by those actions. (Forget written curriculum; actions speak louder than words.) This is what we did in Cleveland.

Let us get our learners out planting trees and gardens on the campuses of our nation's beleaguered public schools—and use church funds to finance it. Let us assemble and deliver Halloween bags full of candy and handwritten messages of hope to children and families with HIV/AIDS. Let us not confine Sunday school to Sunday and limit attendees to the children of pledging units. (This, to me, is blasphemy. No one can call himself or herself a Unitarian Universalist and also insist that all children in Sunday school have parents, paying or nonpaying, on the premises. Are we here to give life or avoid lawsuits?) Instead let us offer Saturday Sunday School and make sure that we intentionally invite and evangelize the wider community on both days. We may not need a larger Sunday school but there is a whole wide world out there that needs the gospel of Unitarian Universalism! So let's start a youth drop-in center for gay, lesbian, bisexual, transgender, and questioning youth whose own houses of worship condemn them for the way God made them. Yes, let's engage in a little constructive sheep stealing. This is literally a matter of life and death, for both the oppressed and the institutions and programs that serve them. This is what we are doing in Pasadena.

But Will It Play in Peoria?

One of the temptations religious educators face is the idolatry of formula. That is, since an experiential, hands-on, intergenerational, community-based program worked in, say, Chicago, then it has got to work everywhere else. Just transplant it and proceed as usual. Or maybe it is just a matter of laziness. I will take this program and make it fit because it is easier to do so than to approach new challenges with the same degree of creativity that I had as a new and enthusiastic DRE. My pegs are round; it is the learners and leaders who are the squares.

Of course, in many ways the latter groups are square when it comes to what to them constitutes viable educational ministry. Mostly, this is no fault of their own. If they have succumbed to the tyranny of curricula, if they have been fed a steady diet of circle time, story time, and arts and crafts, all crowned by the spiritual high afforded by snack time, then why in the world should they risk it all and make more work for everybody in the process? They probably should not, so long as they are getting good results. You know, results such as learners knowing who they are and Whose they are; knowing how to articulate the tenets of their liberal religious faith and then applying them to their daily decision making; actively putting hands and feet on our cerebral Principles and Purposes; experiencing total involvement in all aspects of church life and not being relegated to some form of glorified child care; investing as much of their time, talent, and treasure in their spiritual lives as they do in their careers, 401Ks, and mutual funds; developing pride in and being contagious about Unitarian Universalism; and seeing that who they are and what they believe is quite literally a matter of life and death in the twenty-first century.

I have given considerable space to the innovative program called Way Cool Sunday School that evolved at the Second Unitarian Church of Chicago. When I became MRE at the much larger, more conservative, highly traditional, upper-middle-class, and very successful First Unitarian Church of Cleveland (actually located in the affluent, racially diverse suburb of Shaker Heights) I almost always encountered resistance—initially, at least—to change. Why should they change? With an enrollment of over 350 learners in their youth religious education program and a thriving adult counterpart, what needs to be fixed? On the surface, nothing. But outward appearances belied cracks in a long-overlooked foundation. And this time both the church leadership and the religious education committees knew it.

The move to a more experiential, intergenerational, and community-based approach to religious growth and learning for children and adults at the First Unitarian Church of Cleveland was both gradual and limited compared to my first experience as a DRE. In Cleveland we always maintained an age-specific, classroom-based, curriculum-focused program that took place concurrently with the eleven o'clock (read, "main") Sunday worship hour. In other words, we offered what most congregations would consider a "traditional" religious education program, one that consistently drew a large enrollment. An intergenerational Way Cool Sunday School program similar to the one at my first congregation was offered during the earlier, nine o'clock worship hour. This was also the religious education session to which children and youth from area group homes (read: "outsiders" or "not our kids") were strongly encouraged to attend. Even with the influx of these "newcomers," the program attracted at most eighty additional learners and leaders. These numbers gradually began to decline as it became clear that such a program required both more structure in a suburban setting and a greater degree of commitment on the part of learners, leaders, and the institution. Unlike their low-income, urban counterparts in Chicago where the church's programs encountered little competition and, therefore, fewer time constraints, First Unitarian's more affluent learners and leaders were less comfortable with spontaneity—an essential element of the Way Cool format. The format also benefits from an open-ended time frame which busy suburbanites found difficult to work around. So in effect, the Cleveland leaders of Way Cool attempted "to plan" spontaneity to make sure their kids were not late for soccer practice, polo lessons, play practice, and the Green Peace rally all scheduled later in the day.

Nevertheless, even as the experiential program at nine o'clock called for more structure and commitment, at the same time we witnessed a greater increase in experiential applications to the more traditional program at eleven o'clock. Other benefits were also realized. For example, there were more frequent and experiential intergenerational worship services. Moreover, assumptions about who should be in the sanctuary (adults) and who should be in the religious education wing (children and youth) nonintergenerational Sunday on became blurred and no longer enforced. Thankfully, traditional age-related divisions in virtually all aspects of church life—from board and committee membership to social activism and worship—began to outlive their usefulness (assuming, of course, they were ever useful). If the church's newsletter is any indication, experiential learning models and intergenerational formats continue to influence positively the way they "do church" at the First Unitarian Church of Cleveland.

A Viable Plan for the Twenty-First Century

The program at Pasadena combines, in my opinion, the best of the Way Cool programs in Chicago and Cleveland, though neither by design nor desire. Rather than offering one experiential program each Sunday (Chicago) or two distinct programs—one traditional and one experiential—at two different sessions (Cleveland), a monthly rotation of learning formats is utilized in Pasadena that incorporates experiential, behavioral, cognitive, and traditional ways of knowing. In this way virtually all learners and leaders can connect with Unitarian Universalism in a way that is life-giving. It also provides more opportunities for a greater number of congregants to be a part of and, therefore, advocates for the educational ministry of the church. In this format, many areas of church life take their rightful place in religious education programming, as do the adherents of those areas.

So if worship is your passion, then the first Sunday of every month is designed for you. Each first Sunday of the month is a Community Worship Sunday at Neighborhood Church in Pasadena. (We intentionally avoid the term "intergenerational worship" because too many of our congregants equate that with "children's worship." Instead, "community worship" accurately describes both our intentions and their results.) On Community Worship Sundays there is no Sunday school, at least in the traditional sense. Frequently that means we all worship together in the sanctuary (usually, but not always, in our own sanctuary; we've been known to visit neighboring faiths). Our rather "high church" approach to worship at Neighborhood precludes the nauseating possibility of dumbing down our worship to relate to the least mature (chronologically or otherwise) among us. Most often adult worship is modeled even as youthful presence and participation enhances it. This necessarily includes participation in the pulpit by children and youth.

Alternately, on other first Sundays of the month, we offer the aforementioned sanctuary worship and Way Cool Worship simultaneously at different locations on our church campus. Way Cool Worship is described as "upbeat, contemporary, decidedly UU worship, not for the faint of heart." We actively recruit facilitators from the church's music and worship committees. In both places, content is similar but the format often varies. On those Sundays when two opportunities to worship are provided there are no age requirements or restrictions in either the sanctuary or Way Cool worship settings. It is simply and only a matter of choice and preference. It comes as little surprise that Way Cool Worship usually draws a younger crowd than does its sanctuary counterpart. But some of the times of greatest transformation have taken place when risk takers at either end of the age spectrum take a worshipful walk on the wild side. More and more this is becoming the rule rather than the exception. When we add a third worship service to Sunday mornings next fall we have few preconceived notions of what it will be like. And that, I believe, will be one of the keys to its success.

The second and third Sundays of each month are Classroom Sundays. This is where intimate connections among children and adults are formed purposefully. We recruit adult leaders from among parents, nonparents, singles, and seniors. On these Sundays religious education classes are age-specific, either classroom- or community-based, both experiential and reflective in nature and informed by a Principle-based, social justice curriculum that was (and is still being) developed specifically for this rotational religious exploration format. The continuity of being together twice a month in small group settings results in the kind of community building that is necessary to sustain and enliven the multigenerational gatherings that characterize the formats of the first, fourth, and occasional fifth Sundays of each month. Prior to each session of Classroom Sundays learners and leaders engage together in a brief time of worship and celebration. These Sundays are about as close as we get to what most folks think of when they think of Sunday school.

The fourth Sunday of every month is designated an Outreach Sunday. We recruit leaders primarily from among the church's social activists. Again, there are no Sunday school "classes." Instead we take the entire Sunday school out of the church and into the community or bring a substantial part of the community into the church. We purposely mix it up to receive from and give to groups we are not likely to otherwise encounter in our personal, professional, and spiritual lives. Reciprocation is the key. Our whole lives are far more enriched by the gifts given to us by our partners in these outreach endeavors than are our partners' lives via our meager offerings. We often have money to burn and lives full of stress to prove it. We come to our outreach work financially blessed but emotionally and spiritually needy. Our outreach partners, on the other hand, are often (but not always) deprived financially but are emotionally and spiritually overflowing. As we work together side by side, gifts are exchanged and friendships are formed. Our work in the world is preceded by a brief time of worship and celebration.

Our Outreach Sundays have put to rest the notion that we need to talk about the "isms" *ad nauseum* and raise awareness of the shortcomings they create. Our churches and Sunday schools will not be integrated until our lives are integrated. It is the dinner table, not the worship table or the diversity committee table, where "isms" can be eliminated once and for all. The journey toward wholeness begins at home, not at church, and it will be reflected in our churches and Sunday schools when we start bringing our friends to church. Hard work and hospitality, not workshops and curricula, are what are necessary to realize the beloved community. Our Outreach Sundays are designed to make us "doers of the word and not just hearers," for "faith without works is dead" (James 1:22, 2:17). Or, to coin a phrase, it is deeds, not creeds.

Fifth Sundays of the month are Arts Sundays at Neighborhood Church. Again, after a brief time of worship that declares we are proud to be Unitarian Universalists, all ages gather together and are joined by artists and artisans, actors and musicians, potters and playwrights to explore our Unitarian Universalist Principles through the fine and applied arts. (Again, to clarify: There are no age-specific classes on Arts Sundays.) These facilitators are recruited from both within and beyond our church community. At one time in the history of organized religion, the arts were central to the expression of faith. In the twenty-first century we don't need to rely solely on verbal skills to practice a rational religion. Our Arts Sundays ensure that our learners and leaders systematically engage all five senses in the exploration of their liberal religious faith.

So, Kill All Curricula?

If Way Cool Sunday School is idolatrous about anything it is curricula. In its design, preparation, and implementation, more time is spent on curricula than any other component of the program. In fact, what binds this multifaceted approach to religious exploration (the term we prefer to religious education) is its foundational curricula. What underlies each rotational component of Way Cool Sunday School—worship, classroom, outreach, and arts—is a common content: our Unitarian Universalist Principles and Purposes. Let me be clear: We use curricula every Sunday, presented in differing formats—worship, classroom, outreach, and arts. We tackle one, or at most two, Principles per year. We start at age two and complete the cycle at age eleven. The Principle(s) becomes the guiding force, the theme, the raison d'être for all of our worship, classroom, outreach, and arts experiences.

Only after our learners have been grounded firmly in their own Unitarian Universalist faith do we intensely explore the faiths of others, with learners ages twelve to twenty. This doesn't mean younger religious explorers ignore altogether the multifaith world around us. We compare and contrast our beliefs with the beliefs of others with a missionary's zeal and a scholar's skepticism. But we find the hodgepodge, smorgasbord approach of much of the available Unitarian Universalist curricula to be counterproductive to our quest to make our particular faith known, both to us and to others. I am tired of hearing liberal religious learners and leaders lament how they know all about what everyone else believes but virtually nothing about what Unitarian Universalists believe.

We don't find the curricula themselves to be the culprits, assuming they are localized and adapted both for and by the learners and leaders who intend to use them. Nor are we criticizing the authors or their content. Indeed, we use curricula on a weekly basis precisely because they are the products of both salvific passion and sound research. Our challenge has been to order these materials in a way that encourages personal and social transformation because of the specificity of our beliefs and values, and not because we are all things to all people. We are persuaded that Unitarian Universalism offers unique beliefs that we can cling to and rely on and that can sustain us during life's mountaintop and valley experiences. Furthermore, we believe that liberal religion in the twenty-first century resonates with the oppressed and the marginalized far more than it does with well-educated, upper-middle-class, white male New Englanders. (Not exclusively, only more so.) If our learners can spend ten years exploring seven Principles and, as a result, become new creations (2 Corinthians 5:17), then this has been time well spent. We may not cover as much material as other programs do, but our learners will retain and be able to viably apply more of what they have learned.

Instead of using curriculum packets, we have assembled (and are still assembling) lesson plans—from both UUA and non-UUA curricular resources—that best explore our seven UU Principles. Call it a "greatest hits" version of Principles-based lesson plans. We purposely delete things like lesson timelines, sample projects, and diagrams, anything that may keep our leaders from using their own imaginations to make the lessons their own. The curriculum is thus a resource, and not a recipe, for what takes places in the classroom, the worship center or sanctuary, the community, or the arts studio. It offers the facilitator guidelines, not God-ordained, Gestapo-like dictums that must be followed to avoid failure. It also allows for those times when someone or something other than the adult leader takes the lead (perhaps the learners, the curriculum itself, or God).

The Vision, the Village, and the Verdict

I do not offer these twenty-first century alternatives to so-called traditional models for Sunday school to call attention to myself. None of the ideas are mine; all have been "borrowed" from someone else. Moreover, none of these ambitious programs could work without the support and cooperation of learners and leaders, parents and congregants who want more for their children than just a place to put them during Sunday services. It takes fully 25 percent of our congregation to be actively involved in children's religious education alone to make experiential religious exploration happen at Neighborhood Church. Add to that percentage those involved in an adult religious exploration program that is also largely experiential and you'll see why I reject the notion that worship is the primary port of entry into the life of the church as well as its most substantive anchor.

Either the entire congregation owns the educational ministry of the church or it is simply a euphemism for babysitting. I offer these alternatives to avoid the latter and to promote more ways (though not necessarily better ways) to live a more fully human life. When educational ministry thrives it creates a world in which "there is neither Jew nor Greek, slave nor free, male nor female" (Galatians 3:28). Imagine life without the divisions of race, class, or sex. By faith, together, we can educate and advocate for a world without walls.

Take this a step further. Imagine the possibilities for new church planting if these fledging institutions were first conceived of as weekly experiential, community-based, justice-bent Sunday schools instead of occasional worshipping communities. Establish a vibrant religious exploration program in the neighborhood first and then, maybe five years later, grow a worshipping church from the deep roots of educational ministry. What would it mean to "do church" and "be the church" if we saw ourselves primarily has community centers for education rather than houses of prayer, pews, and pledging units? The Koran says, "One act of social justice is worth seventy years of prayer." Of course, it is a lot easier to pray and pay than it is to build the beloved community.

This brings me to one of my biggest concerns: We adults, especially (but not solely) parents, must take greater responsibility for the spiritual lives of all our children in the twenty-first century. Forget the over-used "village" metaphor. I think it has been used to sidestep the individual responsibility that is inherent in educating children religiously. First and foremost, it takes a villager to raise children who grow up with principles. A twenty-four-hour-a-day, seven-days-a-week villager, not an hour-and-a-half, written curriculum-dependent village once a week on Sundays. So I frequently ask learners and their leaders: Are you a villager? You are if you take time to read to each other at home and introduce each other to stories that embody our faith's tenets. You are if you light a chalice at home and spend time in prayer and meditation as a family. You are if good deeds outweigh gossip when it comes to your neighbors. You are if social action days are more important than Blockbuster nights. You are if Sundays are different from other days. You certainly are if you spend a portion of your Sunday morning in a religious exploration classroom or activity. Forget the village. Become a villager to all the children of our church and community.

For some educators (and their boards of trustees) numbers are the primary identifier of success. If I were to measure our success by body count alone I would throw more than a few parties. At Chicago's Second Unitarian Church we went from 50 to 150 learners over the three-year time period during which we developed the pilot program for Way Cool Sunday School. We added more than 150 learners to the youth religious education program in the first year of Way Cool Sunday School at the First Unitarian Church of Cleveland. The attendance increased by 30 percent in the first year of the Way Cool format at Neighborhood Church of Pasadena. In both Cleveland and Pasadena, we were/are the largest Sunday school in their respective districts.

While it is true that numbers will keep our Sunday schools from dying, they are not the only or final antidotes to the heart failure many of our religious education programs are experiencing. Other kinds of growth also provide the saving grace that will keep the Grim Reaper at bay. When we took Sunday school out of the traditional "box" and created Way Cool Sunday School we experienced other kinds of growth that to me, at least, are far more life giving. In each case, at each church, we experienced growth in terms of diversity in all of its facets, programmatic growth with all of its headaches and opportunities, and most importantly, spiritual growth. In this last instance, no number accurately puts a value on what this has meant to our liberal religious communities and larger movement. Not unlike the followers of Moses in the Hebrew Bible, we have realized that God "set before [us] today life and death, the blessing and the curse. Therefore choose life, that

you and your children may live" (Deuteronomy 30:19). Or, as we like to put it, "Sunday school is dead. Long live Sunday school."
The joy continues.

∼

Rev. Greg Stewart is the minister of religious education at Neighborhood Church in Pasadena, California.

To Teach
an Abiding Faith

Rev. Dr. Elizabeth M. Strong

Growing up in a small, rural Universalist church I came to know and personally understand that at the center of my religious faith was a powerful belief in the inherent goodness and worth of all life. I believed in a god who loved me and all of creation. That belief, and Universalist teaching, grounded how I lived in the world and gave me an ability to trust that world as a safe and affirming place to exist. It empowered me to act as a capable human being who could be in relationship with other human beings who were also inherently good. It enabled me to be in relationship with what I now believe is a creative and creating force in the universe. As we Unitarian Universalists enter the twenty-first century this belief, as now stated, in the inherent dignity and worth of every person can sustain us in the face of an increasingly conservative and technological world.

For me, a belief in the inherent dignity and worth of every human being is at the core of our evolving Unitarian Universalist faith. It is a doctrine of human nature that affirms the ability of each individual to be in relationship with the holy. It is a doctrine of human nature that affirms the humanness of our existence. To accept this belief, and to affirm and promote it in our daily lives as a religious people, enables Unitarian Universalists to follow the call to justice, equity, and compassion in human relations and to respond to the call of the holy in our understanding of the sacred. Whether we adhere to the theological heritage of Universalism and believe that a loving god bestows this inherent worth and dignity, or to the theological heritage of Unitarianism and believe that a worthy humanity inspires a just and loving god, we come to the core belief that there is an inherently worthwhile humankind. This understanding of human nature must remain vital and central to our programs of religious education in the twenty-first century.

Alongside this core, and in many aspects just as central, is the ensuing free and disciplined search for truth and meaning in human life. Unitarian Universalists have always been seekers for more insight into the truth as we know it. The orthodoxy of the day is never as enticing or significant to us as the heresy of tomorrow. We are seekers and we are capable of the search. Encouragement of our children's ability to search must remain at the center of our religious education efforts.

In our congregations we are called to act upon these core components of our faith. Through worship, education, social action, and pastoral caring for one another, we live out our faith. The actions we take embody our faith in life and in each other, thereby increasing our dignity and worth in the world around us. It becomes our task to hand on this faith to our children so the future might benefit from our existence.

As we move into the twenty-first century we are faced with an ever-expanding globalization at all levels. Religious institutions are becoming mega churches with membership in the tens of thousands. The technological depersonalization of our lives and the homogenization of information dispersed to the general population will only increase. The struggle to affirm individual worth and dignity and each individual's search for meaning and new truths will become more and more difficult for those of us committed to uniqueness, inquiry, and ingenuity.

But new truth is always there to find, and each individual will always be of worth. This realization shapes the vision for goals in our liberal religious education.

We can ground our visions, goals, and content of Unitarian Universalist religious education for all ages in this core of Unitarian Universalist faith. Our faith, history, and tradition have been formed in the Protestant movement and from it we have emerged into a global understanding of religion. If we are to remain a unique expression of a global Protestantism, or if we choose to move further into the global expression of religion and away from the Protestant tradition, we must be well grounded in our history within that tradition. Our pluralism will surely keep our feet in both worlds for some time to come, and the tension will be with us however we move. Our programs of religious education can provide a centering place within this movement.

Our current curricula have begun to provide this centering, but more is needed. I envision our goals of religious education as we enter the twenty-first century to emerge from the core of our Unitarian Universalist faith, expressed as freedom, reason, and tolerance from our Unitarian roots and faith, hope, and love from our Universalist roots. Our goal will become one that will beckon us into future exploration of new truths and sources of meaning grounded in the themes of our heritage.

Unitarian Universalism has emerged from a Judeo-Christian paradigm that is considered by some to be in a postmillennial reframing. The twenty-first century bids us into an age of quantum physics and space exploration of the solar system and beyond. We need not only roots and wings, but earthly grounding and space consciousness. These new demands on our knowledge of who we are as a people and where our future lies call us to be more fully grounded in a faith that has a profound commitment to environmental ethics. At the same time our faith must challenge us to respond to an ever-advancing movement out into the universe. The concept of grounding is not as relevant as the possibility of things alien to our current paradigm.

What can we bring forward and what must we leave behind? Is there anything from our Unitarian Universalism we can leave behind as the outdated past, and is there anything from our faith we can bring forward into the unknown future? Keeping in mind who we are as a religious people in the dawning twenty-first century, what might these things be?

The ages of science and religion are becoming increasingly parallel as we imagine the expanse of the universe and ponder a creation beyond our current abilities to comprehend. We respond with awe and uncertainty, as did our ancestors in ages past. As we look toward the life we know on this planet, we discover there is still miracle and wonder within the seed in the cup on the windowsill of the kindergarten class. Somewhere in between is the ground on which we stand to look out at the stars and respond to faith in the life we know and the life we have yet to know, and possibly cannot know.

What will our God look like now that we know there is such a vast universe that is part of creation? What will our belief in human nature look like now that we are exploring the idea that we most likely are not be the only creatures in the universe? What will our understanding of truth look like now that we have been told there may be parallel universes and parallel timelines floating about in which all possible realities are viable? What will be the role of religion as we wend our way through the twenty-first century?

Our programs of religious education need a grounding in our current worldview and religious tradition. As we step out into uncertain times it is necessary to have solid places on which to rely and to rest while we make sense of what is new. Our children, youth, and adults need an understanding of what they know as true if they are to have the critical thinking abilities to discern the truth of the future.

The goals for our programs of religious education will need to provide our children, youth, and adults with the history, philosophy, theology, and tradition of Unitarianism, Universalism, Unitarian Universalism as well as the broad liberal religious tradition in which our denomination moves. The presentation of this will need to be centered in critical thinking about how changing truth through expanding discoveries will affect the validity of what is now held as sacred faith. Science and religion will need to be rewoven into a coherent and vibrant design embracing both the technological and natural aspects of our world and lives to create the ability to continue to move into the future as a religious people.

Unitarian Universalism has always moved into the future and responded to new truths. As an example, at Saint Lawrence University in the late 1800s and early 1900s, the Reverend Dr. Orello Cone, professor of biblical theology, brought science and religion together with the theories of Charles Darwin and *The Higher Biblical Criticism* to create for Universalists a new worldview in which reason and faith could continue to evolve with integrity in faith and rational spheres. We must do the same once again as we give our people the tools to weave quantum physics and religion, technology and human caring, community and globalization into a meaningful worldview.

We are faced with some practical and methodological questions as we face the twenty-first century. Shall we incorporate more technology into our curricula? Shall we incorporate more experiences with living things into our curricula? Shall we center our curricula in our Unitarian Universalist traditions and beliefs? Shall we focus our curricula on interpersonal relationships in a Beloved Community within our congregations and communities? Shall we link our curricula to our Judeo-Christian taproot in specific ways unlike our links to other religious roots? Shall we create an interstellar map into the future using the map of our past? If so, how?

We are also faced with more philosophical questions. Ours has been a movement of ideas, actions, events, and theologians with powerful heresies. How shall we tell our story to our children, youth, and adults? How shall we remember Unitarian Universalism into the kind of life that will be relevant into the twenty-first century?

Themes of our Principles that have been central to our movement through the centuries need to be brought to life in our curricula. Through stories, drama, biographies, music, art, and timelines, these themes must come to life in the technological, quantum physics age.

Who are we? We are a people who cherish freedom of faith. We are a people who exercise the awesome responsibility of free will. We are a people who hold a faith in the transformative power of love. We are a people who emerged from the Judeo-Christian tradition and are grounded in that tradition as the tap root of the many root theologies, philosophies, and movements that have formed our living tradition. We are a people who reflect the great ideas of the ages passed through the freedom of faith.

Why are we Unitarian Universalists here? We are here to empower the free spirit of our heritage and to stand against humanity's technological homogenization and depersonalization in the current age. We are here to keep a religious quest for new truths ever before the communities in which we live as the face of fundamentalism reaches backward to rely on old truths based on old paradigms. We are here to remember to empower the inherent dignity and worth of every person. We are here to work for justice, peace, equality, and equity in the world. We are here to build communities of liberal religious faith. We are here to be Unitarian Universalists and to let the world know who we are and why we are.

If we are to foster a trust in the world and the universe that will enable our children, youth, and adults to be in relationship with each other and with the world(s) around us, then we must have at the core of our religious education an explicit affirmation of a faith in life and in the inherent dignity and worth of all creation. We must have a "reverence for life," to quote Albert Schweitzer.

We must understand the events that have brought us to this point in history and that inform us of who we are as a religious people, and why we exist now. In *Educating Congregations* Charles R. Foster reminds us that an educating community must be able to maintain its heritage into the present, or renew its identity or vocation for changing circumstances. But if, like clay on the potter's wheel, our heritage is ever to be reshaped to relevance, we must know what the original vessel looked like, we must know how to shape a new one, and we must know why we want a different shape. Foster states,

> All discussions of faith have some relationship to certain events of the past. Our relationship to these communal events has an educative character.
>
> We begin to identify with them. We take on their character. We discover in them sources to commitments distinguishing us from people who identify with the values, perspectives, and norms of other events. We discover ourselves in a community of people identified with that

event. We begin to see the world through the perspective of the community originating in and shaped by that event. ... These events not only tell us who we are, but also to whom we belong. They provide us with clues about how we are to relate to others and to participate in the world around us.

Congregational life is shaped around the ways it remembers certain events.

In Volume I of *A History of Unitarianism,* Earl Morse Wilbur reminds us that the distinguishing and communal events for Unitarians are those historical markers that shaped our theology and our heritage and formed our traditions.

Our curricula for the twenty-first century need to link us to this past and remember us into new life as a powerful legacy to the principles of freedom, reason, and tolerance from our Unitarian tradition. In Volume I of his work *Universalism in America,* Richard Eddy links us to the powerful legacy of the principles of faith, hope, and love from our Universalist tradition.

From the second century in Alexandria, Egypt, and the Alexandrian School with Origen came the teachings of a universal salvation and free will in humankind. In the fourth century at the Council of Nicea came Arius's espoused theology of God as one. In the fifth century came the teachings of Pelagius that humankind has free will. These principles of human thought and faith formed a movement that entwines strong, common, and continuous threads to tell us who we are as Unitarian Universalists today and show us where we have come from.

On down through history we came without a name until the sixteenth and seventeenth centuries. We first see the name *Unitarian* in Transylvania and Poland in the 1500s. We first see the name *Universalist,* signifying the idea of a loving God who bestows universal salvation, in the 1600s in England and in the writing of Universalist preacher Paul Siegvolk in *The Everlasting Gospel.*

Events of the fifteenth-century Renaissance and the sixteenth-century Reformation further defined and strengthened the links of our religious journeys, espousing the principles of freedom, faith, reason, hope, tolerance, and love. It is these events that shape our identity and link us to our past and inform our present understanding of who we are as Unitarian Universalists. It is this linkage that we must raise up in educating our future generations as we move into the twenty-first century.

The substantive forms of such a religious education program need to be relevant to each age and stage of our human development, while also challenging each one to "reach for the stars." Science and religion, nature and humanity, art and music all need to be part of the lessons of life we present. The format of our curricula must foster interaction among the participants to counter the depersonalization of the larger society. Extracurricular activities that deepen relationships and enrich content are crucial to successful faith communities.

As vital components of Unitarian Universalist religious education I propose the use of the guided discovery method of teaching and learning, in which the teacher presents information and the students discover the answers or responses from the experiences they bring to the learning environment. This method provides our teachers and children with a form of education that empowers both to exercise their free, disciplined, and responsible search for truth and meaning in an environment that encourages critical thinking and personal growth.

The use of multidisciplinary, multimodal, and multimedia resources allows the participants the freedom to utilize all styles of learning and intelligence. Those who have learning difficulties will find an approach somewhere each Sunday that they can connect with and access.

All the developmental stages present in the participants will need to be recognized and valued in the religious education experience each week. The content must connect with the personal experiences of each person and carry the lesson to the depth of worship.

Extracurricular experiences that enrich the development of relationships will foster the creation of community among our children, youth, and adults. The nourishment of participation in the full life of the congregation and the empowerment to weave social action into each lesson will enhance the commitment to the congregational community and the community at large. Our congregations can become educating communities that work for transformation and for the transmission of our heritage and history, our faith and traditions, to our children and youth. Utilizing these methods we can better achieve the goals of grounding our children, youth, and adults in our Unitarian Universalist history, heritage, and tradition around the principles of freedom, faith, reason, hope, tolerance, and love. We can help our children and youth to develop critical-thinking skills as they engage in the free and disciplined search for truth and meaning. Through child advocacy groups that work to include children, youth, and adults of all abilities, we can create a place where we feel that we have a home, a place where we all belong.

Social action needs to be an integral part of each lesson so that our families will be grounded in our tradition of working to bring about a world with peace, liberty, and justice for all.

In closing, I offer this meditation:

How shall we know which way to go? Our lives offer conflicting and competing choices and opportunities, and we turn to the values and beliefs that will ground us as we make our way into the future. May our religious tradition and faith be the core out of which we respond.

Who am I? Why am I here? What is the purpose of my life? Can I make any difference at all? We cast our questions out into the universe, not expecting an answer, yet hoping something will guide us. And so we gather in our communities of faith and worship to seek answers that will enable us to meet each day with hope and courage.

In our congregations we strive to create a purpose and a meaning for our living. Here we strive to make a difference in the world by working for the well-being of our religious community. Each commitment, each concerned effort, brings us satisfaction and affirmation.

We need one another for the celebration. We need our community for companionship on the journey. We gather each Sunday to be with one another, and that can be enough when the questions flung out into the universe go unanswered.

∿

Rev. Dr. Elizabeth M. Strong is the minister of religious education at the May Memorial Unitarian Universalist Society in Syracuse, New York.

Child's Play

REV. DR. JOHN W. TOLLEY

As I sat at the desk in my office overlooking Fifty-Seventh Street on the south side of Chicago contemplating the writing of this paper, I was stunned to find myself where I was. And this was a year after my arrival at Meadville/Lombard, our Unitarian Universalist theological school affiliated with the University of Chicago. I had been charged, along with six other faculty and administrators, to guide the educational preparation of one-sixth of the people entering our UU ministry. The call to such a place and the trust the entire Association places in us few professor types are humbling. That alone caused me to stop and ponder the responsibility of being invited to comment on my concerns and passions for Unitarian Universalist religious education for the twenty-first century. But my stunned state also stemmed from the fact that it was I, John of the hopscotch educational experience and suspiciously diverse employment background, who was called and invited.

I had determined that my training as an artist, my profession in church work, and my call to education would never find a home. At least one aspect of myself would need to be severed or sidelined to avocational pursuits. But the call came, first as a director of religious education, then as an associate minister, and now as an educational administrator and professor. In each of these subsequent opportunities, the call came precisely because I was an artist working in religious education. Something was moving within our religious association that was valuing the role of the arts in our congregational lives more so than had been true in the recent past. A respect for how art addresses mystery and the expression of new church members for more emphasis on the spirituality inherent in our faith communities have led our leadership to understand "art" as a powerful tool toward effective religious education and expression. Now I understand that the need was there, and I was simply fortunate to bump into it at the right time!

While at first glance the dynamics of art education and religious education may appear dissimilar, an appreciation for their parallels and convergence is growing. The confluence of these two streams of thought is our evolving understanding of the vital role that reflection, integration, and ingestion of educational experience play in the maturing of the individual mind and body. In *Christian Religious Education,* Thomas Groome has resurrected the Greek term *praxis* to describe this phenomenon:

> Let it [the term *praxis*] be understood as "reflective action," that is a practice that is informed by theoretical reflection, or conversely, a theoretical reflection that is informed by practice. . . . The term "praxis" attempts to keep theory and practice together as dual and mutually enriching moments of the same intentional human activity.

Art educator and author Eric Booth describes the state of human consciousness as a "yearning for more," the unnamed spirit that pushes us to know more, to feel we understand, to be connected to the world outside our isolation, to yearn for a feeling of control of the complexity of stimuli that bombard our senses daily. Such yearning leads us toward realization of our potential, our *entelechy*—another Greek term!—which Booth defines in *The Everyday Work of Art* as "to have the goal; to embody perfection; the full realization of one's inherent potential":

> Realizing our own entelechy, yearning our way toward it, takes work: the work of art. There is no human practice that takes us more directly toward our entelechy. Many other practices are good—religion, intellectual study, meditation, career success—but none is more encompassing, powerful, or flexibly responsive to individual need; none is more effective or more beautiful than the work of art.

When Booth writes about the "work of art," he insists "work" be understood as a verb. The dynamic is not only the abstract appreciation of another's endeavors; it is the doing of the work of art. "There is something about the 'doing' of the arts that communicates their importance, that incontrovertibly answers 'the question.' [How are the arts really useful?] When people dig into the work of art, they no longer have to ask about its value because they know."

My experience in the theater, in the classroom, and even in Sunday morning worship is that the "reflective action"—praxis—required in the work (verb again!) of art draws us closer to the "full realization of our inherent potential" than any other form of pedagogy. Whether we are working alone at the canvas or piano, or in a group of others in dramatic improvisation, art demands that we bring the experience of our lives to the moment, discern how to use that experience in the working of the art, offer our interpretation of color or sound or movement, and then step away to consider the effect. This stimulus-action-reflection cycle is necessary to integrate the experience so soundly that it will influence the next action we take, and the next and the next. The ways in which we typically act, both in my experience and my observation, leave out the reflection. Consequently, we move from stimulus to action and back to stimulus and the next action. Our lives become a series of goals to achieve instead of a process of maturation, enrichment, and enlightenment. Religious education in the twenty-first century must come to a better understanding of education and life as a process, an action-reflection process. If we do not, the wisdom of where we have been as a people of faith and the clarity of a future defined by our Principles and Purposes will elude us. One important way back to an integrated approach to inherent fulfillment, of both us as individuals and us as a religious community, is through art.

Fifty years ago Sophia Fahs wrote, "We would make self-understanding an important and continuous goal in religious development to the end that the child's emotional autonomy may be developed." Julia Cameron, contemporary poet, playwright, and teacher, describes the work of art as child's play in her book *The Artist's Way:* "Far from being a brain-numbed soldier, our artist is actually our child within, our inner playmate. . . . What other people may view as [the artist's] discipline is actually a play date we make with our own inner child." Coming to trust the guidance of this inner source, this child within, sometimes means a painful release of culturally defined milestones of success. Goals attained without reflection are not education. Cameron continues, "In short, we are learning to give up idolatry—the worshipful dependency on any person, place or thing. Instead, we place our dependency on the source itself." If we trust the voice of that child within, we can come to a self-understanding and state of autonomy that meet the imperative articulated by Fahs decades age. That same trust can push us into a future where our individual talents and perspectives become the stuff out of which we build a personal identity and, from there, a religious community. We are not culturally defined; we are self-defined and we can perceive that definition most clearly in our work in the arts. As Henry Nelson Weiman wrote in *Weiman's Philosophy of Art*,

> Only art can awaken all the powers of perception in depth, scope and clarity, so that what is given to perception takes on religious significance. . . . Only art can offer a presentation in such form as to stimulate and facilitate the human capacity for perception which is comprehensive, clear and true.

To order our conception of how art can serve our educational purpose eliminates the artificial boundaries between child and adult education. The source of our yearning to meet our potential is the inner child seeking order, understanding, and connection. The inner child is our guide whether we are five or ninety-five.

What I am suggesting for Unitarian Universalist religious education for the twenty-first century is nothing less than a countercultural revolution. Our educational goals must first free themselves of the expectations of society and focus on the individual needs, dreams, and constructs of each one of us. Education itself must embrace the idea of process, a lifelong honing of experience into meaning. The frightening aspect of such an approach is that while we can gain insights from the observation of history and our community, each of us must filter the experience through our own construct. We must make sense of this day-to-day journey called life for ourselves. No one else can do it for us. The joyful aspect of the same is that "no one can do it for us" and if we allow our inner child to be our guide, the creativity, innovation, diversity, and originality of the results will build communities far more in touch with the human potential. A new arts-centered pedagogy will require us to rethink our sacred Protestant work ethic. Rather than success being weighed on how many tasks are completed, the reflection time of praxis will demand a release of some tasks for the integration of others. The "priestly listening" that Maria Harris claims is necessary to cultivate receptivity to the immanent source of nurture and creativity will demand time. To relinquish our dependence on scientific method and give each child, and our child within, the opportunity to contemplate mystery through intuition, action, and creation will be swimming against the currents of measurable achievement, intelligence quotients, and the summation of the human's worth on the attainment of high test scores and model personality profiles. I will not be satisfied until every evening on the newscasts of major television networks as much time will be dedicated to coverage of the arts as there is today coverage of sports!

By human nature, everybody is an artist, whether or not the person understands himself/herself to be "talented." Our innate urge to reach beyond the physical body to find meaning and connection is the source of symbol, creativity, aesthetics, and religion. "Rituals, myths, symbols and gestures rising from the collective unconscious of a people are the means employed by all peoples in communicating with or communicating about objects of ultimate concern," according to artist and scholar Patricia Griest. The process of reorienting our ideas about ourselves as artists is a recovery process. Recovering the image-making of the child, the fantasy beneath and beyond language, is to rediscover the innate means each of us has to communicate with or about those things we hold most dear. Julia Cameron cautions us to be slow to judge what we produce as we reclaim our rightful identity as artists. The tendency in a results-obsessive culture is for us to view our creations in the light of masterworks of famous artists, living or dead. When we come to understand all education as process and not perfection or product, we begin to give ourselves permission to move slowly. Cameron challenges us to remember "that in order to recover as an artist, you must be willing to be a bad artist. Give yourself permission to be a beginner. By being willing to be a bad artist [in terms of product], you have a chance to 'be' [process] an artist, and perhaps over time, a very good one."

I know the truth of these assertions because as a drama director and teacher of educational theater over the years, I have witnessed lives transformed through the visual, kinesthetic, and auditory engagement in the creative process. Some of this transformation has been simple, some profound. In the compilation of raw data from a long-range plan that was produced for the church-community theater I directed for sixteen years, a distillation of written comments included this simple affirmation of the power of engagement in the arts:

> I only wish I could describe the difference this theatre has made in my life. I lived [in this city] for two years before I first came to the theater; I was lonely and depressed and scared to death. I showed up on a dare to myself. [Now] my friends have all noticed how I've blossomed, in fact, most of my friends are people whom I've met through the theatre, or through someone who knew someone, etc. My faith in God and in people has been confirmed and has changed me forever.

More recently, in the context of the Arts and Aesthetics in Ministry class I teach at Meadville/Lombard, some more profound transcendent moments have occurred. While working with a class in the visual arts and movement, my colleague Patricia Griest and I used photographs of George Segal's sculpture, "The Holocaust," and poems written by children in Nazi concentration camps to illustrate through movement, image, and poetry the power of art to connect the present to lives and situations in the past. Having worked with body sculpting earlier in the week, I positioned class members in the formation of the Segal sculpture. We asked the students to remain in that position while we drummed various rhythms over a period of five to seven minutes. Following the sculpting activity, we invited the students to witness slides of the sculpture while we read the poetry of the children. Only at the end of the activity did we identify the title of the sculpture and the authors of the poems. Within the class of a dozen or so students there was a holocaust survivor whose mother had carried her in pregnancy while she labored in a concentration camp. There was also the daughter of a Nazi soldier. The two women, who had known each other prior to the activity, now knew each other in new ways, shared tears of remorse and forgiveness, and saw in the face of the other the reflection of herself. They proclaimed the freedom they experienced through the art, having spoken hidden truths and discovered community beyond their silence.

More recently, in the context of a worship service during Meadville/Lombard's Modified Residency Program, a student shared the story of the murder of six of her family members by another family member. The ethic of her surviving family would not let them discuss the tragedy in a world where "everything was God's will." For years she suffered in the silence of those she loved until engagement in an art course released her suppressed anger, disillusionment, and fear. In the process of making paper—the rending of the cloth, the tearing of the whole, and the reconstruction of a different, more textured and beautiful whole—the power of that horrible memory released its hold on her. From the paper she made a book of memory with the pictures and names of her relatives who, in truth, had vanished from the family's collective biography. She found healing in the process of "doing the art," and in sharing her story, she gave her classmates emotional permission to explore the depths of their lives' experiences as the foundation and fodder of effective ministry.

Each of these examples, and many others that could be named, required a childlike risk to engage in fantasy, a fiction that exposed truth. They required reflection and a "priestly listening" to inner voices and outer proclamations. Each of these people was led to participation in an aesthetic endeavor because of a soul's yearning to come to some kind of understanding of loneliness, family disgrace, or personal tragedy. And only by passing through the experience of making art did each of these good people reach a sense of entelechy, the realization of her/his full human potential, free from cultural definitions and rooted in individual, emotional autonomy.

What are the two or three messages I would encourage the community of Unitarian Universalist religious educators to consider in these dawning years of a new century? To answer that in part I would return to the quote from Weiman:

> Only art can awaken all the powers of perception in depth, scope and clarity, so that what is given to perception takes on religious significance. . . . Only art can offer a presentation in such form as to stimulate and facilitate the human capacity for perception which is comprehensive, clear and true.

We Unitarian Universalists have wasted a valuable tool in the arts for decades, perhaps because of our Protestant iconoclasm, or perhaps because of our dependence on the rational mind, which is the heritage of our Enlightenment ancestors. But just as the year 2000 finds us looking toward holistic approaches to health care and the aesthetics of the styles of several generations past, we must have the courage to revisit the intuitive knowledge we carry in our genes through engagement in and with the arts. The very act of creating in image, movement, song, and speech is co-creation with a universe that yearns for our participation for its very survival. When we realize our own entelechy by participating in our chosen art form and gain the skills to release that power in those we teach, we create a faith community whose process is understood as its worth and whose reflection makes the whole educational endeavor effectual, rewarding, and transformative. Such praxis requires our time; but such use of time realizes our full human potential. It is elementary. It's child's play in the most sacred sense of *play*. It is one way—a very important way—back to our roots which feed our branches. Let the play begin!

∼

Rev. Dr. John W. Tolley is the associate dean of modified residency and an assistant professor of arts of ministry at Meadville/Lombard Theological School.

Outcome-based Religious Education

REV. DR. TOM YONDORF

The old religious problem was how to overcome a genetic and cultural endowment that makes us grasping as well as fearful and violent. The question was, given our nature, could we cultivate the habits required to live together in harmony, and could we expand the blessings of acceptance to ever-larger groups, from family and clan, to tribe, to nation, to humanity?

We thought we could solve the problem. By recognizing one another as children of God. By creating democratic institutions. By recognizing one another as being of inherent worth and dignity. By creating and sharing vast wealth. By teaching the children well.

The New Problem

Life for many is no longer as nasty, brutish, and short as it used to be. We have learned to shape the world to feed, clothe, transport, heal, and amuse ourselves. We have learned to live together in sufficient harmony to number six billion. Kudos! Take a bow!

However, our failure to control our impulses to acquire, dominate, and make ourselves comfortable now results in the destruction of the other species with which we share the planet and an onslaught against the ecosystems on which we and those species depend for existence. Our failure to ease our fears of one another has resulted in the invention of thousands of bombs each packed with the power of a holocaust. Thirty years ago the wealthiest, most democratic nation on the planet rained napalm and high explosives on the innocent of a Third World nation on the other side of the globe. Last year a man tied another human to the back of his pickup truck and dragged him to death. As I write this, we are once more at war.

Capitalism

As the century ends, many of us celebrate the downfall of totalitarian communist regimes. Good riddance to horrendous tyranny and to corrupt and inefficient economic systems. But the list of values that we have neglected or destroyed in our celebration and defense of capitalism is long and harrowing.

Capitalism harnesses our self-interest and competitive nature to create brilliant systems of production and distribution. As a result, many of us enjoy tremendous wealth, more freedom than in controlled economies, and the relative peace that occurs when people trade with, rather than throw things at, one another.

On the other hand, capitalism has contributed to a mounting disaster for other values: rain forests, ozone molecules, other mammals and birds, income and wealth equality, job security, and political and economic experimentation.

Thus far, neither the communistic principle of sharing "from each according to his ability, to each according to his need," nor that of the "free hand" of the competitive market has solved the problem.

Democracy

Democracy evolved as a means of requiting our desire for freedom; as a means of checking our impulses to dominate others; as a means of freeing human genius to pursue every art and science; as a means to respect the worth, dignity, and spiritual endowment of every person; and as a means of tapping the presumably saner wisdom of a people as a whole as opposed to the partial perspective of one or a few.

To flourish, a democracy needs to be nourished from below by systems of education, by civic and moral training, and by habits of commitment that help us to cooperate with one another.

In our day, these foundations for democracy have eroded. We have hallowed individualism and the pursuit of self-interest. Now we suffer pangs of anxiety as other bonds of association and cooperation—family, neighborhood, school, political party—have been laid low.

The corruption of democracy has been boosted by our reliance upon dollar voting as the mechanism for decision making. It is not that the pursuit of wealth is terrible. It isn't that advertising in and of itself is bad. It isn't that wealthy people might occasionally be able to make good decisions for the rest of the people. The dilemma is that this market ethos crowds out the competition—alternative value systems.

Other value systems that might help us to solve the problem are overwhelmed. Less materialistic systems of association and value, including those that nourish democratic habits, ride at the back of the bus.

Faith

In the name of God, and the highest of which we can conceive, we call on one another to act with humility, moderation, and love. But then the human character sets to work upon these inspirations. Our intimations of affection and nobility and spiritual depth must run the gauntlet of our limitations—the two-edged sword of our genius not only for the good and the true and the beautiful, but also to act out our anxiety our lust and our ambition.

The result is that all too often the religious institutions meant to nurture humility, moderation, and love are either marginalized or reduced to yet one more tool to make ourselves feel comfortable and justified as we are swept along by the consumptive culture. The faithful burn fossil fuels and pour pesticide on their lawns, the faithful take care to step over the homeless on their way to work and vacation, the faithful watch the time vacuum that we call TV and cluck at the ills of the world. The faithful have a hard time living up to their ideals.

Which is to say that religions also participate in the problem. Such precious drops of religious faith as we are able to gather are inadequate to stem the fires of our nature and our nurture.

Civil Religion

In liberal democratic societies the civil religions have foundered as well. Those civil prophets who wrote the Declaration of Independence, the Bill of Rights, and the Gettysburg Address had a vision that the human project under freedom could be a noble one. But those mystic chords of memory that must be sounded to keep the faith alive, how can they be heard above the engines of comfort and competition, the slow drip of a billion advertisements, the tilling of the planet without Sabbath?

We have not yet found the faith and the institutions and the habits that will solve the problems. We continue to wreak havoc on the planet.

What is to be done?

Diligence

Unitarian Universalism is not the solution to our problem. However, it may have something to contribute. And with that in mind, it would be helpful if we pursued our faith with more diligence.

UUs are superb at recognizing hypocrisy, unreason, injustice, and overweening authoritarianism. We are quick to adopt a better Principle or Purpose as well as a richer source of inspiration. But the genius of Unitarian Universalism has its price. The price we pay for this high doctrinal ground is a lack of sweatshop focus, day-to-day discipline, and spiritual practice. We are like the long-range planners who sit at the edge of the bed, endlessly telling our partners how great it is going to be. When we end racism. When we end classism. When we put a stop to sexism. When we stop our robotic consumption.

God forbid that we ever stop speaking of love and justice. But to speak of love is not to love.

Flunking

I attended UU churches and religious education classes regularly through junior high school and sporadically as a young adult. Years later, when I told Langdon Gilkey, professor of theology at the University of Chicago, that I was considering going into the UU ministry, he responded with delight. He talked about a number of people in the UU tradition in whose footsteps it would be wonderful to travel. I didn't know whom he was talking about.

I think I should have flunked something.

Flowers Everywhere

One theory of UU religious education curricula is what we call blossom theory. We help each child to realize his/her full potential. At each stage. Morally, psychologically, communally, biologically, spiritually. Some parts nitrogen, some parts potassium. And then, voila: fully human.

Fallen Petals

Then something terrible happens. When our kids become young adults they leave the UU church, usually forever. We know this, but we tend to shrug it off, like news from Botswana.

Enculturation

When I was in theological school the word in religious education was *enculturation*. What does that mean? It means that one purpose of our programs is to help our kids to "experience the UU way of being in the world." One soaks up religious liberalism unconsciously, rather like a sponge.

Then you become a young adult and leave the church, usually forever. Is this good?

With a few exceptions, our children desert the cause. Our "graduates" do not join the alumni association. They don't contribute to the big capital campaigns. In terms of the pragmatic theory of meaning (pay attention to what I do, not what I say,) they do not love this institution. The church is not high on their list of priorities.

Some say, well, since they are good people, our children out there in the world, then that is OK. I say, since the decisive forms of goodness are institutional, this is a disaster. We are like the churches in Europe after World War I—full of the symbols and rituals, but lacking an entire generation of young men.

Which generations are we missing? The ones who have already been "enculturated" by an initial lifetime of Unitarian Universalism. Our grown children, ages eighteen to death. Why is the harrowing of our children a disaster? It means that to survive we have to focus on attracting the next generation of come-outers from other faiths to fill and fund our churches. We tend to mirror the short-term myopia of businesses focused on quarterly profit. We become fiduciaries of a heritage rich in concepts and buildings and bank accounts and advertising, but much too grateful for the holidays and holy days we have off to try something radical or risky. We are chickens.

Most of the lifelong UUs I've worked with in our churches are terrific institutionalists. I just came back from lunch with one. When he was a young man he went to Selma, Alabama, to support embattled Civil Rights demonstrators. These days he takes good care of our church. Men and women like him could help us to deepen our faith as an alternative to what the culture has to offer. Take some of the come-outer buzz off of things. But they are few and far between.

We are not serious about addressing the problem. Unless of course we are convinced that the freedom-from-UU-religion option that our children choose in droves is a core accomplishment.

Outcome-based Education

A word about America and her problems educating children. We want our children to learn how to read and count and write so that they can be informed and get jobs and vote. The problem is that at the end of school lots of kids have not learned well. They can't do word problems. They don't know the names of the countries to our north and south. They can't read a newspaper. They don't know which came first, the Declaration of Independence or the Gettysburg Address. When they get a job, many have to go back to school to learn the basics.

Some reformers support outcome- and performance-based education. The measure of the success of the education is not whether or not the student has been in class or whether or not the teacher has addressed the topic. The measure of the success of the education is whether or not at the end of the day the student has mastered tasks, can do the work. Can you read? Can you geometrize? Can you spell tomaeto? Let's hear you play that piano.

Outcome-based Religious Education

UU religious education in the next century should be outcome-based. Our teaching should be to the test. No, not all multiple-choice tests. On a regular basis we should also ask: Show me your portfolio of accomplished human being.

Other Religions

Some of the UUs I know have attended a bar or bat mitzvah. They come back tremendously impressed. Those Jews! When I was in Utah I went to a memorial service for a parent of our church organist. He and his siblings spoke with eloquence. Those Latter Day Saints!

Some of my distant relatives are members of a large and growing born-again denomination. With terrific community support they do an amazing job of raising their children. Those Christians!

Time

I overheard this comment between UU religious educators: "We can't teach much in fifty-two minutes on Sundays forty weeks a year. So we expose them to the UU way of doing things." Enculturation!

Deculturation

Our children are also exposed to something like ten thousand advertisements for food a year, of which the majority reflect the best efforts of leading minds to convince them to obtain fast food, soda pop, and candy. Thoughtful critics say that the job of parents in our day is not simply to introduce children to the culture, but to protect them from the culture. Therefore, what is needed is not adequately defined by the word *enculturation*. We also need *deculturation*.

Getting to Carnegie Hall

When I began Zen Buddhist practice, each sitting was composed of a number of twenty-minute intervals separated by the ringing of a bell (beautiful bell!) signifying that it was time to rearrange our limbs and trunks. Last time I went it was thirty minutes between bells. Those Zen Buddhists. They were upping the ante!

When I began Zen Buddhist practice, I went on three-day retreats. That is a lot of time spent being present, emptying and becoming full, saving the world! Now, in the Zen newsletter, they advertise things like "thirty days of awareness" and "sixty days of awareness." You commit and you find help to practice mindfulness throughout your night and day.

Now that's enculturation. It is also an effort to inject the religion into the culture. If our religion is good, then this is what we want to do too.

Three days of Unitarian Universalism? Sixty days of Unitarian Universalism? What would that be?

Content

Growing up I came to associate three things with our churches: social activism, critical intellectual religion, and singing in the choir. As a young adult, I returned to our faith looking for friends and community, and later, when my father died, for healing. In recent years, I have come to appreciate the profound power of a mild spirituality. I find that the rational intellectual faith of my beloved parents and their generation is made stronger by an embracing of a larger poetry, softer eyes, fuller quiet, and a deeper sense of communion.

At every stage I have met in our movement people whom I admire tremendously. Good people. Marvelous ideals. Good causes. Fine curricula. Then and now. But our children leave our faith. And the Problem endures.

Outcomes for UU Religious Education

These are good outcomes of UU lifespan religious education:

- We live simply on the earth.
- We treat one another with dignity and respect.
- We lead mildly spiritual lives.
- We participate in the institutions of freedom.
- We tell others the story of the earth and of our own evolution, using diverse arts to make persuasively clear why the preceding accomplishments, with the associated ideas, skills, and habits, are essential.

Implementation

To pursue these five outcomes, skills and discipline are needed. So that when it is necessary to abstain we can abstain. So that when it is necessary to give we can give well. When it is necessary to quiet we can quiet. When it is necessary to participate in self-government, we can behave as citizens. So that when it is necessary to proselytize our vision and faith, we can speak persuasively.

Whatever we teach, it must be to the test. To performance. Thus, not only will our children pick up a vaguely defined "UU way of being in the world" but also precise ideas, skills, and above all, habits. Adults and children alike, we must be afforded the dignity of having something to flunk.

Therefore let us bathe in the speaking and practice of these outcomes. Let our curriculum development be devoted to these outcomes. Our preaching. Our counseling. Our protests. Our applause. Our meditations and dances and songs and poetry and painting. Our money. Our work. Our bequests and tombstones. Our dress and lyrics. But above all, lest we get caught up in the lesser and the means rather than the higher and the ends, let us hold one another accountable for the extent to which we realize the five outcomes.

Objections

Critical readers will see many flaws in this analysis. Not all religious education programs are in trouble. Outcome-based education is not a panacea. I am too hard on "come-outers." My view of human nature is simplistic. It sounds utopian. We already have Purposes and Principles. Where is the funding going to come from? Will it pass the Board of Trustees? UUs aren't supposed to proselytize, are they? There are other desirable outcomes. Some of your outcomes are of questionable value. It's too simplistic. It's much too hard. . . .

To which I would say, you are right. Now, shall we start with living simply on the earth?

∽

Rev. Dr. Tom Yondorf was the minister at Allen Avenue Unitarian Universalist Church in Portland, Maine, from 1987 to 1994, and at Unitarian Universalist Church West in Brookfield, Wisconsin, from 1994 to 2000.

Recommended Readings

Adams, James Luther. *An Examined Faith: Social Contexts and Religious Commitment.* Boston: Beacon Press, 1991.

Alexander, Scott W., ed. *Salted with Fire: UU Strategies for Sharing Faith and Growing Congregations.* Boston: Skinner House Books, 1994.

Beach, George Kimmich, ed. *The Essential James Luther Adams: Selected Essays and Addresses.* Boston: Skinner House Books, 1998.

Boys, Mary C. *Educating in Faith.* Franklin, Wis.: Sheed and Ward, 1989.

Cameron, Julia. *The Artist's Way: A Spiritual Path to Higher Creativity.* New York: Jeremy P. Tarcher, 1992.

Church of the Larger Fellowship. *Religious Education at Home: A Handbook for Parents.* Boston: Church of the Larger Fellowship, 1998.

Daloz, Laurent A. et al. *Common Fire: Leading Lives of Commitment in a Complex World.* Boston: Beacon Press, 1997.

Edelman, Marian Wright. *The Measure of Our Success: A Letter to My Children and Yours.* Boston: Beacon Press, 1999.

Eisler, Riane and Nel Noddings. *Tomorrow's Children: A Blueprint for Partnership Education in the 21st Century.* Boulder, Colo.: Westview Press, 2000.

Fields, Ann et al. *Starting from Scratch: How to Begin Your Own RE Program for Children and Youth.* rev. ed. Boston: UUA, 2002.

Fitzpatrick, Jean Grasso. *Something More: Nurturing Your Child's Spiritual Growth.* New York: Penguin Books, 1992.

Foster, Charles R. *Educating Congregations: The Future of Christian Education.* Nashville, Tenn.: Abingdon Press, 1994.

Freire, Paulo. *Pedagogy of the Oppressed.* Translated by Myra B. Ramos. 1974. Reprint, New York: Continuum Publishing Group, 1993.

Gadotti, Moacir. *Reading Paulo Freire: His Life and Work.* Translated by John Milton. Albany: State University of New York Press, 1994.

Gardner, Howard. *The Unschooled Mind: How Children Think and How Schools Should Teach.* 1991. Reprint, New York: Basic Books, 1993.

Gilbert, Richard S. *Building Your Own Theology.* 2nd ed. Boston: Unitarian Universalist Association, 2000.

Groome, Thomas H. *Sharing Faith: A Comprehensive Approach to Religious Education and Pastoral Ministry.* San Francisco, Calif.: HarperSan Francisco, 1991.

Harlow, M. Susan. "Sophia Lyon Fahs: Religious Modernist and Progressive Educator." In *Faith of Our Foremothers: Women Changing Religious Education,* edited by Barbara Ann Keely. Louisville, Ky.: Westminster/John Knox Press, 1997.

Harris, Maria and Craig Dykstra. *Fashion Me a People: Curriculum in the Church.* Louisville, Ky.: Westminster/John Knox Press, 1989.

hooks, bell. *Teaching to Transgress: Education as the Practice of Freedom.* New York: Routledge, 1994.

Kegan, Robert. *In Over Our Heads: the Mental Demands of Modern Life.* Cambridge, Mass.: Harvard University Press, 1994.

Kivel, Paul. *Uprooting Racism: How White People Can Work for Racial Justice.* Gabriola Island, B.C.: New Society Publishers, 1995.

Lepore, Jill. *The Name of War: King Philip's War and the Origins of American Identity.* New York: Vintage Books, 1998.

Meadville-Lombard Winter Institute. "Congregation as Theological School." Milwaukee, February 18–21, 1999.

McLaren, Peter and Peter Leonard, eds. *Paulo Freiere: A Critical Encounter.* New York: Routledge, 1993.

Mendelsohn, Jack. *Being Liberal in an Illiberal Age: Why I Am a Unitarian Universalist.* Boston: Skinner House Books, 1995.

Miller, William R. and Kathleen A. Jackson. *Practical Psychology for Pastors.* Upper Saddle River, NJ: Prentice Hall, 1985.

Moore, Mary Elizabeth Mullino. *Teaching from the Heart: Theology and Educational Method.* Harrisburg, Pa.: Trinity Press International, 1998.

Moran, Gabriel. *Religious Education as a Second Language.* Birmingham, Ala.: Religious Education Press, 1994.

Morrison-Reed, Mark. *Black Pioneers in a White Denomination.* 3rd ed. Boston: Skinner House Books, 1994.

Muir, Fredric John. *A Reason for Hope: Liberation Theology Confronts a Liberal Faith.* Fred Muir, 1994.

Nelson, Roberta and Christopher. *The Parent Trilogy: Three Programs for UU Parents and Other Adults.* Boston: Unitarian Universalist Association, 1998.

Nieuwejaar, Jeanne Harrison. *The Gift of Faith: Tending the Spiritual Lives of Children.* 2nd ed. Boston: Skinner House Books, 2002.

Palmer, Parker J. *The Courage to Teach: Exploring the Inner Landscape of a Teacher's Life.* San Francisco, Calif.: Jossey-Bass, 1997.

Pazmino, Robert W. *Basics of Teaching for Christians: Preparation, Instruction, and Evaluation.* Grand Rapids, Mich.: Baker Books, 1998.

Pipher, Mary. *The Shelter of Each Other: Rebuilding Our Families.* New York: G. P. Putnam's Sons, 1996.

Rasor, "The Self in Contemporary Liberal Religion: A Constructive Critique," *Journal of Liberal Religion* 1(1): October 1999.

Rubin, Lisa et al. "The Report and Findings of the 1997 Youth Programs Review Committee to the UUA Board of Trustees and the Youth Council of YRUU." Boston: Unitarian Universalist Association, 1997. Available at uua.org/yruu/resources/15yr/15yr.htm

Shor, Ira and Paulo Freire. *A Pedagogy for Liberation: Dialogues on Transforming Education.* Westport, Conn.: Bergin & Garvey, 1987.

Tatum, Beverly Daniel. *Why Are All the Black Kids Sitting Together in the Cafeteria? And Other Conversations About Race.* Rev. ed. New York: HarperCollins, 1999.

UUA Commission on Appraisal. *Interdependence: Renewing Congregational Polity.* Boston: Unitarian Universalist Association, 1997.

West, Cornel. *Race Matters*. Boston: Beacon Press, 1993.

West, Cornel. *Prophesy Deliverance!* Philadelphia: Westminster, 1982.

Westerhoff, John H. III. *Will Our Children Have Faith?* rev. ed. Harrisburg, Pa.: Morehouse Publishing, 2000.

Whitehead, Alfred North. *Modes of Thought*. 1956. Reprint, New York: Free Press, 1985.

---------. *The Aims of Education and Other Essays*. 1929. Reprint, New York: Free Press, 1985.